Because He Loves Me

By

Richard Van Regenmorter

P&R Publishing Company

ISBN: 0-9702364-0-9

Library of Congress Control Number: 00-135380

Printed in the United States by:
Morris Publishing
3212 East Highway 30
Kearney, NE 68847
1-800-650-7888

Acknowledgements

I would like to express my sincere thanks to all those who helped in the various phases of this project:

To Rev. Arnold Punt, for planting the seed of encouragement, and stressing the importance of recording our past experiences for the present and future generations.

To Rev. Dick Evers, who after reading the manuscript encouraged me to publish it for distribution.

To Walter Kerfoot, who spent countless hours, helping me put the manuscript in a readable form and then taking some of his vacation time to finish editing the last section.

To Phyllis, my wife, who spent hours typing, rereading, and correcting the manuscript. I will never be able to thank her enough for the forty-six years she stood by me through many exciting but difficult times. She understood the stress that I was under and why I had those awful nightmares. During those years, she spent many nights gently waking me up from nightmares and patiently helping me find realism.

I thank God daily, that he led me with his providential hand when I had all but given up. The Holy Spirit would reveal the right passage of scripture to help strengthen my faith and keep me going. I am ever grateful that Christian parents raised me. I am also grateful that I survived the war to be able to enjoy our five children and eleven grandchildren. Each one is a special gift from God.

CONTENTS

Foreword

Buffed And Polished But Not Crushed

The lyrics of an African folk song say, "When an older person dies, it is as if a library has burned down." It is true. There's a richness and heritage in each person's life that will be lost if it isn't passed on to the next generation.

This book is not about personal achievements or acts of heroism, but it is a book that describes the wonderful providence of God at work in the life of one individual. At the time these incidents occurred it was not always apparent to the author how or why God's hand was leading and guiding and on what course it would take him. Then in later years, through counseling, it became very clear that each step of the way, God led this individual through these experiences.

This book is written to enable the readers to take an account of the events that they have experienced in their lifetime and hopefully also see God's divine guidance through those circumstances. The primary purpose of this book is to guide the reader into a closer walk with God.

It is the author's hope that the reader will be guided to examine carefully and prayerfully their own personal experiences and incidents in life, and hopefully see God's hand in budding the seeds of your personality.

For the reader to grasp the full impact of the life of the author, it is necessary to insert the chapters of the writer's childhood and growing up in Sioux County, Iowa. This book describes a little about the background of his parents, who, no doubt, were so influential in guiding the author's life. It then becomes apparent that things they observed in their developing years from their parents or other role models have influenced the life of the author, and presumably everyone who reads this book. It is then important that the readers of this book also consider what type of influence they are having on those who are observing them, namely their children and grandchildren.

The second part of this book relates what the author experienced as a soldier on the front line in Korea, as he describes what it was like being a machine gunner while under massive enemy attack. Also, here are vivid expressions of what it was like to patrol into the enemy territory and experience being ambushed by the enemy under impossible odds.

In part, this book is written that succeeding generations will know the great sacrifices and devotion the Korean War veterans endured. This effort helped put the free world on the road to victory in the Cold War. Blocking of the Communist invasion of Korea was an important contribution to all free people everywhere.

The Korean War received very little publicity at the time it was fought. This book may help the readers realize that from 1950-1953, there were 1.5 million Americans in who fought in Korea. The following figures come from the *VFW magazine June/July 2000 from the 14 major combat units that fought in Korea. These figures do not include the casualties of the units who were in support of the ground troops. The complete figures are listed in chapter 10. From this account, 32,192 Americans died in Korea, 102,494 were wounded, 389 were POW's and 8,168 are missing and have not been found as we commemorate the war fought 50 years ago.

The physical and emotional pain that these combat veterans endure as they experience flash backs and nightmares, is something that cannot be measured. For some of them it will only end when they breathe their last breath.

Most importantly, the author firmly believes that stopping this communist threat would not have been possible without the providential help of our God. This is the God whom our forefathers wisely inscribed on our coins, "In God We Trust"

The third area of this book describes the post traumatic stress that the author lives with as a result of his war experiences, especially that of taking human life and also witnessing the lives of his comrades taken in battle. The author experienced the loss of friends and comrades without being able to deal with the grieving process because of the demands of battle.

It is the author's wish that this book will help someone who is going through the grieving process, and the behavioral changes that take place because of a trauma. Perhaps recognizing it will help the reader to seek help to understand the emotional effect of PTS (Post Traumatic Stress), a complicated condition that includes experiencing a guilt complex because you were a survivor.

The author would often grope with the question, "Why God, did you spare me when so many of my comrades gave their lives?" The author will describe what effect PTS (Post Traumatic Stress) has had on him every hour, both while asleep and awake. It is the author's desire that the readers who have experienced trauma in their lives whether in the military, an accident, injury or death of a person whom they love, would seek and receive Christian professional help. This help is necessary to try to gain mental normalcy and to prevent your reactions to the trauma from robbing you of ever feeling any inward peace.

The author

Chapter 1

Freedom Isn't Free

Have you considered the price that our ancestors paid to fulfill their dream for their children to live in a land in which they would have all the basic freedoms that we carelessly take for granted today? Have you ever wondered what it was like to have lived in Europe in the era 1650-1890s with all the glowing reports of the newly discovered land of America? I can just hear them discuss it with each other about this place of religious freedom and the vastness of this new land. As these reports came back to Europe from America, many young men had dreams of leaving their homeland to start a new venture in this land of opportunity. A large number of men who were married and had young children decided to join those who left for America before.

Such was also the case of my mother's grandparents. Her mother was born to one such adventurous young man from the Netherlands who chose to take his young family to America. The ship that took them over was very crowded and many of the passengers became very ill. It seems as though the fresh water storage tank turned black with bacteria. The catastrophic result of that situation was disaster, most passengers became very ill and most of the children as well as weaker adults were soon critically ill. My mother's family, especially the children, was very sick and resulted in their having to bury two of their children at sea.

Consider how hard it must have been first to watch your children die, and then to slide them into the ocean for burial. Then, in a letter that my great grandmother sent to her sister in the Netherlands, she wrote about her experiences coming across. She stated that because she was pregnant, an uncle was caring for another child that was very sick. She told about how she got separated from the child and three days later discovered that the child, the uncle was caring for, had already been buried.

Her comment to her sister was, "This country will never be big enough to cover the pain that we suffered on the trip to this new land." It is hard for me to begin to understand their pain or what it would be like to bury your children at sea, and then to have the third child who was so ill to be separated from it's mother at the time it was dying.

I recently took a tour of the Statue of Liberty and also of Ellis Island, where all the immigrants were processed as they entered this country. It was during that narrated tour, which included interviews with those who went through the process, that I understood how they could get separated. As immigrants came in, they dropped their baggage on a pile and the men and women were separated. They walked upstairs where doctors observed their climb and did a minute long physical to check for breathing problems and physical defects. Then they waited for their name to be called for processing. After processing they were sent out to a train depot for transportation to their destination. The husbands and wives many times would remain separated until they arrived at their new location.

My maternal grandfather had two brothers who came across together. When they came through emigration their names were spelled differently, one officer spelled it Bos and the other Bosch. The families never changed it, so we always had two different names in the same family. It seems hard to realize unless you have been in a location where no one speaks your language. Then you find out how difficult it really is to communicate even on the simplest terms.

My father's relatives came across on the ship the *Hugo Grotenhuis* that was most likely named after the attorney general of Holland. In 1609 he wrote a document entitled, *Free Sea,* which stated that no nation could claim right to the open seas.

My father's grandparents settled in Michigan in the town of Holland. My grandfather was a factory worker, and was killed tragically as he was walking across the train tracks. He was distracted by a switch engine and failed to see a flyer coming down the second set of tracks and was killed instantly. When he died, he left a widow with four children. At that time a widow had no benefits from either the government or the place where her husband worked, so they had no choice but to take the children out of school and put them to work. My father was in the fourth grade in school when this happened and he was removed from school to work herding cows to earn family milk.

My father often spoke about how they would be hungry but dare not go to the soup kitchens that were open for families of laid off workers. My grandmother was too proud to have her

11

children eating at a soup kitchen, so if the children ever tried to get food there they would be spanked for it.

In the winter months my father made baskets for a pickle company and also worked in a furniture factory. He really disliked working in the factory and hated the abuse that the boys suffered at the hands of older factory workers who thought it was smart to treat children like dirt. I would not print some of the gross things my father told me about how all newcomers were treated when they started in the factory.

Along with such conditions, as well as the fact that now his mother remarried, they had three families living in one household. This household consisted of my father's family and his stepfather's three children, his two brothers and two sisters, and the two children that his mother and his step dad had together. Their family had 10 children living in one small home.

This led my father to beg his mother to let him go to an agriculture area of the country. He saw adds for workers in Galveston, Texas. After promising his mother he would support her, he rode the rails in boxcars until he arrived at Galveston, Texas.

He found himself on the streets of Galveston with no money, so he went to a hotel lobby where he found some fellows who said they would give him lodging and have a job for him the next day. As it turned out, he discovered that they were preparing for a bank robbery the next day. During the night he sneaked out of the window and started running down a country road. A person driving a buggy asked him if he would like a ride. After talking with the man he discovered the man was interested in hiring a person to help him cultivate the corn.

The climate in Galveston, Texas was very hot and humid especially while driving a single mule on a plow, like a cultivator, in the tall cornfields. In the tall corn there was no breeze to help you cool off. So he wrote a letter back to Michigan complaining about the awful climate.

Dad's sister was dating a seminary student from Western Theological Seminary at Holland, Michigan who at that time had a summer preaching job at a church in the Midwest. When he found out that my father did not like the heat, he wrote to him. "I am in a place which is like the Bible's description of *The Promised Land*, flowing with milk and honey. The soil is so good that you can't plow too deep that you run out of black soil."

With that type of encouragement Dad rode the rails to Hospers, Iowa and found a job at a cattle feeder whose farm was located west of the town of Sioux Center. His job at the cattle-feeding farm was to bring in two loads of hay and two loads of corn bundles per day. This had to be accomplished whether rain or shine, and even if it was a snowstorm, all the cattle needed that much feed daily. This job was not a 40-hour workweek as you might have guessed.

At the third farm where he worked was the place where Dad fell in love with the farmer's daughter, who he married. He then started farming on his own using the experience he gained on the three previous farm locations.

My parents didn't start out with any modern conveniences in their first farm home. They came from parents who had to struggle to feed their families.

13

All of us learned very early in life many valuable lessons for our future existence. The first was that no matter what happens we can trust God to walk along side of us to carry us through. The second lesson we learned was to work hard and long hours, and the third thing we learned repeatedly was that money doesn't grow on trees and every dollar that we earned needed to be stretched to the limit if we wished to survive. We also learned early if some one is in need, share with them what you have, either in finances, food or work, and help in whatever way you could. Much of what we learned from our parents was that no matter what happens in life, it is important to remember to place our dependence on God and hold on to Christian values.

The time in which my ancestors lived was one that was influenced by losses, pain, and hardships. This taught them to have a complete dependence on God. The values that they gained through experience in life, they shared and taught to their children. Along with teaching us those basic values they also emphasized the importance of building our lives having a character that no would ever need to doubt that our word was as good as gold. They knew that having instilled Christian values into their children they would be able to stand the test of time. These values would be greater than anything that they could give in a tangible way to their children.

The question that I ask is this, "What values did I learn from my parents and what am I handing down to my children and to their descendants? Will this, and future generations, accept our values without dissecting them until our values become meaningless? Only time will tell what will remain of those values. Will you, the reader of this book, decide to accept the values of the past? That will only be determined as future generations observe and reflect on how you responded to your circumstances in life.

CHAPTER 2

What a SURPRISE, ANOTHER BOY

I was born in the late twenties, and when I opened my eyes there were four brothers and one sister gazing down at me in my crib. In a way I am glad I was unaware of the fact that I was born the last child in a family of six children. Including my parents we were at the table with the eight of us. In those early years on the farm it was considered a blessing to have a large family of boys because then the father would have lots of help to do the work. My father farmed 360 acres of land in a time when all the work had to be done with horses and horse drawn equipment so another hand to help on the farm was welcome, even though they were entering into the great depression.

Being the youngest of eight sitting around the table, also meant I had to be fast if I was going to get my share of the food. No one dared to put anything on his or her plate until after the prayer of blessing was asked. When Father would say, *"Amen,"* it was a flying of the forks to try and get to the plate first, especially when we had chicken for dinner. The chicken drumsticks were a prized catch. We had to be fast or we would never get a drumstick; we would always end up with the back or a wing or neck.

When we butchered a hog or cow we all liked the taste of cow tongue. Mother would very carefully divide the pieces among us and put them on our plates. If we ever stole a piece of meat off a brother's or sister's plate, believe me, that would be the last time we stole food from our brothers or sister. We never had to fight for our share when Mother served beef or pork liver for dinner, there always was plenty left.

I remember my parents were overwhelmed and often said, "How will we ever pay back the money that we borrowed?" The reason they were in debt was because they bought eighty acres of land during inflated prices and now were faced with a huge debt. Even though they had this debt they always provided us with food. Our food always consisted of the basic farm products that my parents produced, either on the farm or in the garden. We never had food that was prepared commercially other than flour, sugar, and coffee.

Butchering Day

The process of butchering a hog or a cow would today be considered an unsanitary and an uncivilized method of slaughtering livestock. When I was young, this was always accomplished in the fall or winter. It had to be done then because the out door temperature would have to be cool enough to have killed the flies and cold enough to chill the carcasses to keep the meat cold. The animal, either hog or cow, would be led to the alley of the corncrib and then a big brother would either shoot the cow in the forehead or hit him with a sixteen-pound sledgehammer on the head. At any rate it usually took one hit to drop the cow. Then Dad would quickly cut the artery in the neck to get the cow to bleed. After hearing the rifle shot or the sledgehammer I would hold my hands over my ears, run outside, and then risk taking a peek through the cracks of the building. Then my older brothers would attach the feet to a tackle block hooked to a ceiling beam, hoist the carcass up in the air for the easy skinning and eviscerating the carcass.

The next morning Dad and Mom would get up very early to cut up the meat into smaller portions for processing and canning the meat. They also ground meat in a hand cranked meat grinder, which was no easy job. My folks always made meatballs, cooked them, and placed them in 20-gallon crocks. Dad would also rub smoke salt into the long side of pork and hang it up to dry to make his own bacon. The butchering processing day was the day you soon learned to keep away from your parents because it was messy and they were tired from working around the clock. Dad and Mom would salvage everything that they possibly could from the animal that they butchered.

The day after butchering we knew that we would have ox tail, pig's feet, liver, heart, and tongue on the menu. The lard was rendered out on the old cook stove in the wash shed that was attached to the house.

The reason Dad and Mom processed in that room was to keep our house somewhat livable, and the kids away from a greasy mess. Mother didn't take too kindly to any one tracking through the spilled lard and then walking through the house. Believe me you only did that once. Even though our floors were wooden floors with grooves and the kitchen table area was covered with half worn linoleum, Mother always kept the floors clean and waxed. When the weather was bad we could walk into her kitchen to warm up while wearing boots only if we stayed on her rug.

After the lard was rendered out, the grease would be poured over the meatballs in the 20-gallon crock. That would seal the meatballs and keep them from spoiling and drying out. The big crock of meatballs was put into the cellar.

Those Great Dutch Foods Were Tasty.

A Dutch food we often had was made from the cracklings that remained after rendering out the lard. They were saved for the Dutch breakfast feast called, *Balken-brij*. This food was made by boiling a quart of the cracklings in a gallon of water with salt, pepper, allspice and cloves. We then added one third each of buckwheat flour, wheat flour and graham or white flour. We kept adding this flour mixture to the boiled spiced cracklings until it was so thick that a strong man could not stir any longer. Then it was put in a cake pan to cool and in the morning it was sliced thin, fried in a pan until crisp and served with maple syrup. That recipe was used repeatedly during the depression. We all liked it and my mother saw fit to ration it out according to our age and work we had to do that day. That recipe, my wife and I carried into the next generation since we both were accustomed to that breakfast food in our homes. I have noticed that in the next generation there isn't the universal acceptance of this food for their diet.

When Mother churned butter, she used five gallons of cream at a time. After carefully taking out the butter she would save the buttermilk. Then the next day she would boil the buttermilk with barley and had a pudding that the Dutch called

Buttermilk Pop. It tasted somewhat sour but we were permitted to add syrup or brown sugar to it.

That way my parents very carefully avoided wasting anything, and conserved to the point that they had very little waste. This left a strong impact on my life, and that is why it is hard for me to understand and condone the waste that I see in this generation. Dad often jokingly said, "The only thing we don't keep when we butcher a hog is the squeal." When you understand how we lived, it will better help you understand why this generation expresses themselves strongly on issues pertaining to wasting food.

Our generation also doesn't understand a generation that needs to have so many choices of food and are so dissatisfied with what they have. Our parents never fixed separate dishes for their children and only dished out the amount they thought we would eat. If we didn't finish our food it meant no snack of Mother's delicious home baked goodies at coffee break. Our household, when I was a child, was one of order and ritual; we knew every day what food we would have. The menu was designed by the type of work my mother was doing.

Wash Day Ritual

Monday was always washday. That was a ritual that started at 4 o'clock in the morning. Dad would first light the cook stove in the washroom. The source of fuel was corncobs. Then he would go outside to pump from the cistern several cans of water and put the water in the large washtubs on the old cook stove. Then he would cut up several bars of homemade soap made from lye and lard and put those flakes of soap in the tub of hot water.

Dad always managed to squeeze enough space on the back of the stove to put a coffee percolator somewhere near the fire as he always needed his early morning coffee.

Then Dad would uncover Mom's old gas driven Maytag washing machine, mix some oil in gas and pour it into the one cylinder engine. Many people in those years started their homes on fire by filling the washing machine motor with gas while the engine was still hot. Other homes would explode into fire when the gas vapors would reach the burning cook stoves.

Dad had purchased for Mother a gas heated clothes iron. This was done to help Mother keep the house cooler in the summer months, since she then would no longer have to heat the flat irons, that were chunks of smooth steel placed upon the hot kitchen cook stove. These new gas irons were very dangerous and many of them caused fires either by spilled gas or pumping too much air into them causing the tank to explode.

I will not forget as I grew up that I always had a fear of that washroom. This fear of that room was because as a toddler I stepped in a very large pot of boiling hot potato water that Mother always saved to make homemade potato bread. She had just drained the potatoes as she was preparing dinner for the oats threshing crew of about 16 men. I was holding on to her dress to look out the window and as she turned I fell into the extremely hot water. When Mother took off my knee-high stockings; the skin came off with the stockings. I suffered with that a long time. Daily I would scream, "No, not again," as they

21

dressed me and carried me off to the doctor to change the bandages.

Mom never complained about her gas-powered washing machine. For her it was really living compared to what she had in her home in earlier years. When she was a young girl they washed with the washboard and later progressed to the washing machine, which was driven by a large collie dog running on a treadmill to power the machine. She often said the dog always knew when Monday morning would come. He would hide so he didn't have to go on the treadmill. One thing my dad was very careful not to do, he never dared to leave the farm on washday. This was because if Mom's washing machine motor stopped and he wasn't there to get it running he would experience the cold shoulder from her at best for the rest of that day. The worst thing that could happen to her was if the wash machine failed to work it would ruin her whole weekly schedule.

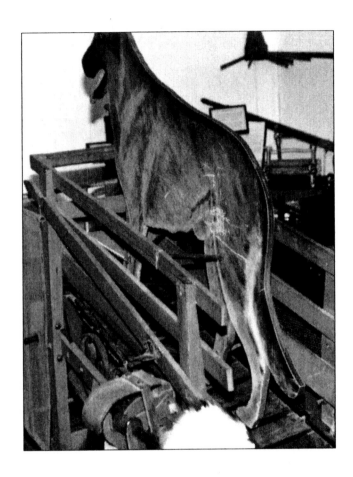

Dog-Powered Treadmill

This is a replica of the dog-powered washing machine that my mother used when she was a little girl.

Each Monday was washday. They always had to hunt for the dog, because he would try to hide on washdays.

Mother's whole week was guided by getting the wash aside on Monday. She would iron the clothes and churn butter on Tuesday. The mending of the clothing, darning (mending) socks and sewing new clothes took place on Wednesday. Thursday was set aside for baking bread in the morning. Every other week she went faithfully to Ladies Missionary Society for Bible study in the afternoon. There they did fancy work while they listened to the topic being discussed. Friday was the house clean up day as well as helping Dad with any outdoor activity that needed more hands.

Saturday was the day for cleaning, refueling and putting in new wicks and mantels on our gas lamps, washing and putting Bon-Ami on all the house windows. The Bon-Ami came in a bar, went on wet, and dried into a powder; then we buffed it off. While doing the lamps mother would go over all the kids' questions and answers for our Saturday catechism lessons.

Remember the Sabbath Day to Keep It Holy

My parents made sure that our whole family was prepared for Sunday.

We had to know our Sunday school memory verse by Saturday night. The hay to feed the cows on Sunday, had to be thrown down from the haymow on Saturday. Water had to be carried into the house for our Sunday's use and our Saturday night baths.

Sometimes if Mom would be behind with her Saturday's work, I would have to go in the house to peel Sunday's potatoes, and help dress out a chicken that Dad brought in from the chicken coop.

All the Sunday meals were prepared as much as possible on Saturday. My parents saw to it that everything that could be done in advance for the Sabbath day was always finished before we went to bed.

Some of the Games We Played

In every way my parents strictly observed Sundays. With our many restrictions, we had a much larger list of don'ts then the list of things that we might do.

One of the things we were not to do was to play ball on Sunday, but with a little luck we could bend the rule enough to play catch or *Annie-Annie-over*.   This game was played something like this: we would throw the ball over the roof of the building and if it went over we would call out, "Annie-Annie-Over." Then the team on the other side of the building had to catch the ball, quickly run around the building and catch the player from the side that threw the ball, before they got to the goal which was a safe place decided on before the game was started. If we were throwing the ball over the roof and it didn't roll over the other side properly, it was called a "Pigtail."

Playing cards in which we would bid and guess how many points we were going to get was forbidden on Sundays because they were called "D*evil cards*." But we could at times get away with playing the game of *"Pig."* In this game called *"Pig"* we passed the cards around until we got a book of four of the same cards and then we would quietly take a spoon off the table. There always was one spoon less than the number of players. If we didn't get a spoon we were then called a *Pig*. If you had 3 *pigs* you became a *Hog* and no one could talk to you. If we talked to a hog, we then became the *Hog* and had to sit out the next game.

But my older brothers could play cards during the week after all the work was finished in the morning or after evening chores. My brothers played a lot of cards with our cousin when he was working in our neighborhood. Our cousin would come over either on bicycle or by riding horse. To say those card games always were ended on a friendly basis would be far from the truth. I remember that Dad had to step in between the brothers because of the fighting over a simple game that had become so intense that if Dad hadn't stepped in between there would have been shedding of blood.

There were times we would violate the Sunday card rule if my parents had visitors with children our age who were permitted to play cards. We would quietly find the cards and sneak playing those devil cards. We would also have to be careful to pay attention when mother would come in the kitchen to make lunch. We would listen for Mother to say, "Well, I will set coffee on." We knew that was our signal to get rid of the cards before she got to the kitchen door. If we got caught we would say, "We weren't playing cards, they were showing us a new card trick." Looking back I don't think she believed that any more than she would believe if we said that man would some day walk on the moon.

We could play carom and Dad had bought a carom board that we used a lot when we were young. On one side we could play with four people shooting carom rings into pockets somewhat like pool is played today. The other side of the board had a checkerboard where Mom loved to play with us. She played either *keep away, or give away.* Mother was very good at it and if you ever beat her you were really getting good.

In the summer months we played outdoor games a lot and when the folks went visiting to large families we were guaranteed a night of high adventure. One of those nights we were visiting along a well-traveled gravel road. We got a wild idea to make our own adventure. We found a big old sack and filled it very full of packed straw, tied a long rope on the sack of straw and put it on the center of the road. We would wait, hiding in the field, and when we would see a car come close we would pull the string. This would cause the driver who was attempting to miss the sack find that we had pulled it right under the front wheel of the car. It went okay for a couple of cars. Then a person came along who hit the sack with his car very hard.

He jammed on his brakes and was backing up. So we started running for the tall cornfield but we had to cross a couple blocks of alfalfa to get safely to the cornfield. All the while this person was cursing and running after us. The more he cursed the faster we ran, dragging the younger kids through the alfalfa. When the victim of our prank knew he couldn't out run us he drove to the farm that we were visiting and reported to our dads what we had done.

Now how do you dare go back to the house? The little kids had green alfalfa stains on their clothing and we were too scared to go to the house. We stayed outside until my folks went

27

home hoping for them to cool off. It worked. We got a stern lecture about behaving ourselves and about our causing danger to the driver. We were soon in our beds, but later we many times chuckled over how fast we ran through that alfalfa field that night.

The Epidemic Of Scarlet Fever

Our lives weren't all fun and games. I remember when we came home from school and told our folks that one of the families was quarantined to their home because the children in the home had contacted *Scarlet Fever*. Mom said, "You know, Pete, I bet the whole school has been exposed. We better watch the kids close so we catch it in time, this is a bad one." Mom was reflecting on the fact that two children from the community had already died of Scarlet Fever.

Mom's fears were soon realized. One morning I woke up with a rash so Dad wisely kept the three oldest brothers outside and later brought them to a neighbor where they boarded them so they wouldn't be quarantined into our house. Dad told Mom to call the doctor and when he came to the house he said, "He has the bad kind, I can tell it by the rash. Get the boy in bed and nobody comes into the house or leaves the house for 30 days." So the doctor put a large sign on the door that said, "QUARANTINED." My older brothers did the chores, the shopping and brought the mail and food to the end of the sidewalk.

I remember I spent one night with such high fever that I was only permitted to have a teaspoon of water every 15

28

minutes. They said I was delirious for a day and night. I do remember having fever blisters and toward the end of the quarantine the rash itched so much Mom made me wear corn husker gloves to keep me from scratching the sores open.

After I healed, the whole house had to be fumigated. I was wrapped up in clothing and blankets on the side walk waiting for the house to air out. Then the doctor took down the sign and my brothers were able to come home again.

For a long time we were living with the effects of the dark cloud of economic depression that was so severe that it would take a lifetime of hard work to recover.

Bankruptcy for my father was out of the question; he had farmland he had bought for far too much that he had to pay back a 1st, 2nd, and 3rd mortgage. My father would say, "I borrowed this money from these individuals, and if it takes a life time of hard work, so be it. I plan to pay back everybody with interest." My father lived long enough to not only pay back all his debts but he left enough money to take care of Mother in her later years.

When she died there were enough funds left for her burial expense and a small inheritance for each of the children. The principle that my Father taught was to be honest and always keep all your promises, not only in word but also by example. I have often been reminded of my father when I read the Psalms.

"The steps of a good man are ordered by the Lord: and he delighteth in his way. Though he fall, he shall not be utterly cast down: for the Lord upholdeth him with his hand. I have been young,

29

and now am old; yet have I not seen the righteous forsaken, nor his seed begging bread. He is merciful and lendeth; and his seed is blessed."

Psalm 37:23-26 (KJV)

When I read that passage I am reminded of my father over and over again. How much impact he had on the lives of his children! He may not always have really seen it, but deep down in his heart I believe he knew how much influence and impact he had.

Chapter 3

Years of the Great Depression

When I look back I now realize what was it like to grow up in a large family when everything around us was falling apart. My father and mother were loaded with debt that their banker said they could never begin to repay. In fact Dad's banker recommended to him to declare bankruptcy but for my father to do that was completely out of the question. Dad always said, "If I am man enough to make promises to pay a debt, I will be man enough to work until my debt is repaid." In spite of all odds they tried to carry on day by day and face each obstacle one at a time.

I ask myself, "How would this generation who are entering into the next century and a new millennium, that were raised with all our conveniences, cope with the type of conditions that our parents struggled with during the years of the *Depression?* If our children had to live during the *Depression* and the conditions of that time, our children and grandchildren would say, "That must have been a real b*ummer.*" Did we call it a b*ummer* because we didn't realize how poor we were? No, when we compared ourselves to our other farm families and friends, it didn't matter because we were all in the same boat, so we didn't realize how rough it really was. In fact we learned values that can never be learned in a time of prosperity

The Dreaded Cob Detail

I recollect the one job we all hated the most, but we all had to join in, at least until we were old enough to do the big man's chores.

We would come home from school and Mom would say, "Hurry kids change your clothes and have your lunch. We got to pick up the cobs."

Like it or not, Mother would march us to the hog yard and we had to pick up the cobs that the hogs had already chewed the corn off. These cobs always were co-mingled with manure. If we were lucky we could find old gloves in the glove box that had most of the fingers left in them. We would each have an empty wooden peach basket to fill up. We had to pick up the cobs and be so careful not to put our hands into the hog manure. When we had our basket filled, Mother would carry it to the yard where they were laid out to dry some more. When she came back she would praise us for doing a good job and spur us on to keep picking up those dirty cobs.

Then there was always the nosey pig that would come quietly sneaking up to us when our back was turned. The pig would give us a playful nip or poke and cause us to scare so much we would land with our hands and knees in the hog manure. We never dared swear out loud but we sure did under our breath. The devious hog would always get a cob tossed at him and I believe those hogs thought it was a big joke.

We had an uncle and aunt who were even poorer than we were. Our uncle was working on farms for a $1.00 per day when work was available plus sometimes some farm produce. Dad, with his big heart, would let him come with his trailer and scoop up cobs that we had picked up and were laying on our yard to dry. We would be so angry and say, "Dad why can't they get them out of the hog yard like we have to?" Dad would reply, "They live in town with no place to dry those wet cobs and after all, he works very hard to feed his family, that is something you kids can do to help them."

That was another lesson Dad taught us early in life, to be generous to those who need help. The conditions that prolonged the suffering in the Midwest were economic, but were also accompanied with severe elements of nature.

THE DUST STORM

I was only a small boy but I remember that day somewhere in the early 1930s, and even though I was very young I remember the day like it was yesterday. In fact I was so young that I was hanging on to my mother's dress for security. I was so afraid of not only what was happening but I could see fear on the face of everyone in the family.

The day was warm and my dad and older brothers were taking advantage of the nice weather and were hauling manure from around the old straw stack pile. They had hauled several loads of manure to the field already and just had a load full on our old steel wheeled horse drawn manure spreader. Dad came into the house to check if the lunch was ready for the boys

33

while my oldest brother was taking the load to the field about one half mile from home.

Then in the sky appeared a reddish cloud, which looked more like a bank, across the whole horizon, and as he was talking to Mother the sky turned dark. It was a strange dark color, but mixed with red. They were looking at the sky wondering what was about to happen when the wind started to blow with hurricane like force. My other brothers ran into the barn for refuge from the wind, and clouds of dust started blowing across the yard like drifts of snow in the winter.

Dad said, "I have to get the boys in the house, the old barn isn't a safe place to be." So he left the shelter of the house to go in the direction of the barn. He turned back and called to Mom, "Get all the kids in the cellar." The dust was blowing so heavily as we watched Dad disappear into the clouds of dust. He had no more than 10 to 15 feet of visibility. As Mother hustled us down into the small cellar she was ringing her hands and chewing on her factory teeth. Whenever that happened we knew she was either very afraid or very angry with us but now we knew she was very concerned. Mother knew that heavy wind in such a severe dust storm could cut your face as if you were standing in front of a sand blast.

Mother knew her oldest son, who was out in the field with the horses, had no protection from the storm, and it was doubtful he could make it home. In a wind or snowstorm, usually the horses would just stand with their backs to the wind. The house back door slammed open and Dad went to get the boys out of the barn. They put their coats over their heads to keep the dust from cutting up their face. They made it by

34

walking blindly towards the house. Dad called down the basement, "I got to find Jake, he is in the field and hasn't come back yet." Mom said, "Don't go out again, it's too bad, you won't make it." Dad said, "Jake is out there and I am going." and he left.

It didn't take long but to us it seemed like eternity until Dad said, "Jake made it home. The horses kept right on walking into the storm even though Jake couldn't even see the road; the spreader box protected him. We'll hurry and try to get the horses in the barn, it isn't right to tie them up outside." Dad dashed out to help Jake unhook the horses and when they got into the house their faces were red like someone had rubbed sandpaper on them. How thankful to God my parents were to have their children inside huddled together in the cellar waiting for the storm to pass.

This storm was an extension of the major dust bowl that took place in the area of the Oklahoma/Texas Panhandle and adjacent parts of Colorado, New Mexico and Kansas. This was caused by a severe drought between 1934-1937 with some records of South Dakota showing that in April, which is usually known for being a rainy month, Mitchell SD. had less than 1/3 of an inch of rain for the entire month. It was accompanied with unusually hot weather. In 1934 for six days the temperature exceeded 100 degrees and on May 8 it reached 109 degrees and in the town of Sisseton, SD, on May 30, the temperature hit an all time record of 113 degrees.

The one and only time I remember communicating with my grandmother was when she was visiting Iowa from her home in Michigan. In July of that year the temperature was around

103-105 degrees every day of the week she was in Iowa. She repeatedly said to my father, "Pete, Pete, what are you doing in this country, it is too hot for man and beast."

Following the Drought Came the Grasshoppers

The 1930s will be known as the years of disaster after disaster. It was hard to grow crops with the heat and drought and that made it harder to pay land mortgage and property taxes. So property after property went back to the banks in foreclosure. Many farm families were forced off the land by bank foreclosures.

The drought also made conditions right for the reproduction of billions of grasshoppers. Our oats had come up with a good stand. That made Dad happy because we needed the oats to feed our horses. One morning Dad said, "Mom, the grasshoppers are eating everything in their way." My Father learned from the *County Extension Office* that if he mixed a certain poisonous material with saw dust and added a flavor-enhanced ingredient he could maybe control the grasshoppers.

The poison was designed to stay active for only a few hours. After the sun came up it became inactive. I remember Dad starting at 4 o'clock every morning with the wagon mounted seeder, spreading this mixture to reduce the grasshopper population and to try to keep them from finishing off all the oats and corn crop.

The Year of our Total Loss

We were all taught at an early age the value of working hard and in every job we always had to do our best. We were not only taught that, we witnessed it every day when we observed our father and mother work.

The way my dad took care of the land was also easy to observe; he liked the country and farming. We practiced crop rotation and always seeded in any waterway with clover to keep the water from washing away any soil. All our fields were walked to take out every weed that the cultivator missed. He also cared for his livestock in the same way.

In the early 1920s *Farm Atlas,* Dad was listed as a breeder of white leghorn chickens. It was early fall and the crops all looked promising. Dad had 500 good-looking pullets soon to be ready to house in the chicken house. It was exceptionally hot and humid during the day. When Dad came in from milking the cows he said, "Ma, it is sure to work up a storm tonight, it is so hot, and still as mouse."

As I remember it, we woke up because we heard what we thought was a loud noise of a train coming with occasional flashes of light streaking across the sky. When Dad got out of bed to check the weather, suddenly a fierce wind came behind the storm with a loud noise like a thousand hammers all coming down at once hitting on our roof. Then we could hear the sound of glass breaking and hailstones came bouncing into our room, stones larger than golf balls, driven by a heavy wind.

It didn't take long and we heard Mother scream our names, trying to be heard above the roar of the stones beating down into the house. " Pete we got to get the kids downstairs and into the cellar." There was a north window near the stair door and we couldn't get down without being hit with flying stones so Dad, still in his night shirt, took the wooden ironing board and with his body behind it pushed it against the broken window. With his holding the ironing board to protect us from the hailstones we then could make it down to the cellar.

The storm pounded for a good thirty to forty minutes and as soon as it ended Dad took my oldest brother and they went to survey the damage. When they came back they said that almost all the chickens were lying under the trees dead. They roosted in the trees because it was too hot in the brooder houses.

The crops were all gone, and the cattle were badly injured. A lot of the fences were out because an old straw stack washed away taking the fences with it. Mother had been busy trying to clean up the glass and water. She was quietly crying and occasionally wiping away a tear. Deep inside she knew what they would have to go through, no crop, no eggs and the rent soon was due. The egg money bought the groceries and what little clothing we bought. The question was now, how would they manage?

Early in the morning before anyone was out of bed, Dad had taken inventory of what was needed for windows, roof shingles and siding. Dad jumped in the car that was still okay because it was inside the garage, and took off to town before the stores were even open. He bought the supplies that were needed to bring the farm in working shape again.

When he got home he called the landlord and told him of all the loss, and when the landlord arrived, he was shocked. He said, "You know Pete, that nice crop wasn't yours in the first place. It was the Lord's and he decided He would harvest it."

They were talking and with one leg on the hog fence he turned to my Dad and said, "How are you going to feed these pigs? How many do you have here?" Dad said, "About two hundred." "Well, I tell you what, load them up and sell them. We will take the hogs for the rent and you keep the milk check for your family."

That day we helped Dad fix house windows. My brothers dug a big hole with our scraper, went around with wagon and pitchforks and picked up over 300 pullets and buried them.

What lessons did the five sons learn that day? First of all that everything belongs to the Lord and it's okay if he wants to take it away; it never was ours. When everything looks hopeless and impossible you are only beaten if you let it beat you. Dad rose up early, assessed the situation and went about to correct it.

We learned when trouble strikes, get up and go to work to improve your situation. I only hope that my children have learned that from my life as well.

How Did We Survive?

Our family, as most families did in those days, rose above the situation. Those who had the best education did not have any advantage over the uneducated persons. The measure of success was how much ingenuity that you had.

My mother was able to make warm clothing for the children. We all went to school with hand me downs or with overalls made over by taking Dad's worn out overalls and cutting off the good material to make the school jeans for us with them. The same was true of the girl's clothing. The mothers made dresses from flowered feed sacks. We would get the protein and minerals for the chickens in flowered feed sacks. The women would go along with the men to town and look for the feed sacks that all had the same colored print. They chose the colored sacks so they would have enough to make the dress and many times they would make matching bloomers.

Some times the bloomers were made from some far out material and when the girls would arrive at school the naughty boys would poke fun of the girls' far out colored bloomers.

I remember a little rhyming song, which was sung by the boys sitting on the grass, where the girls were swinging in the school swings that went around like a merry-go-round. The verse went something like this. " I see London, I see France, I see Jane's (or whoever was on the swing) underpants." Then we would tease the girl who had the weirdest bloomers on. This would go on until the teacher caught on and forbade us from sitting near the swings when the girls were on them. Then secretly the boys would make a game out of who could discover the weirdest color bloomer. They would use hand signals or pass notes announcing their find to the other boys.

What Did I Miss as a Child Because We Were Poor?

I am getting ahead of myself. The pre school years for me had a lot of unanswered questions.

Why were there so many pictures of my older brothers and none of my childhood?

Why did everybody forget my birthday?

I don't remember what year it was but I know it was before attending school. I was feeling so sad because it was my birthday without anyone in the family remembering it. My folks never made a big deal of birthdays but Mom usually made an angel food cake and her tasty cream puffs. The two always went together. She used the egg yolks for the cream puffs and the whites for the angel food cake. Mother would ring the party line phone and would invite relatives over.

I remember that day hiding behind the house crying and being angry thinking nobody cared about me. I found Dad's pump oil can with used oil in it and I began squirting oil into the holes of the yellow jacket bees that lived in the ground and then watched them try to get away. I know now that it was my way of taking out my frustrations on those poor bees.

What Was School Like?

Returning to school meant that we would have a couple of painful weeks trying to get into shoes and then trying to keep our feet in shoes for a whole day at school. All summer we walked barefoot. Our feet would swell up and it was torture to get used to wearing shoes again.

Our education system left a lot to be desired by today's standards. To understand the farm boys you need to know more about the rural school system back in 1930s through the 1940s. We went to a one-room schoolhouse with a total of 26 students at one time. The teacher had to teach all the subjects and had all eight grades in the same room.

The teacher had to each morning start the fire in the furnace by scooping the cobs into the furnace and after it was burning well, she would add coal so the fire would keep the school warm until noon hour. The furnace had only one large register in the floor where we could stand and often in the mornings we would push and shove to stand as close as we could to warm ourselves before we had to go to those cold seats.

The teacher was also in charge of keeping the school clean and scooping the snow off the platform and steps. Our teacher was good at giving responsibilities; she would assign some to clean the blackboards, some to scoop snow, some to sweep up the school and then we all had to rotate turns.

But the worst job was hauling water that had to be hauled for one quarter of a mile and in the winter it meant carrying 4 gallons of water, which was a day's supply. We generally had two persons assigned to it at a time but it was a cold chore and often we got wet doing it.

Our classes started with the 1st grade and they would go up to what was called, *The Recitation Bench* where we would recite answers to the problems that the teacher assigned to us the day before. This would go on for all eight grades until all the subjects were covered. You must also consider that most of the teachers could start teaching right after high school with just a few weeks of summer school. Any subject that the teacher was incapable of communicating meant that the students also did not get a full well rounded education.

Fox and Geese

We enjoyed some of the games we could play after fresh snow fell the night before. We made tracks into a large circle with spokes like a wagon wheel. Then we would appoint someone to be "It." That person would have to catch the others before they get in the center hub but we might never walk out side of those tracks that were made earlier. If we made it to the center hub without being touched we were home free. If there was fresh snow on the ground we always insisted that no one walk in it until we had stamped out our fox and geese game.

The Memories of the Schoolhouse Toilet

We should not forget the ever-present outdoor toilet all country schools had. The famous boys' and girls' toilets were always equipped with last years *Sears* or *Wards* catalogue. The catalogue sheets were torn out one by one to be recycled and used for toilet paper. The boys always kept the pages of the women's dainty under wear to be the last pages used in the boy's toilet, so they would have those pictures to observe longer. I often wonder if the girls left the boys underwear pages for the last to be used. I guess we will never know because I was never brave enough to check. On our toilet walls we had written in prose form a five-minute course on sex education.

Boys Will Be Boys

Even at our farm home, all we had for our bathroom was the outdoor toilet and with that we created our own brand of fun. We devised games and pranks that were some times bordering on the mean and naughty side. One of our favorite things to do was to play tricks that were focused on our famous outhouse. The toilet was a dreaded place to go to, because it was never heated in the winter and it was freezing cold especially if there were snow on the seat. In the summer months because of the lack of ventilation, it not only was hot, but you had to enter with a clothespin on your nose.

These *Outhouses*, as we affectionately called them, were equipped with an adult size hole and a child size hole. Our city born relatives who would come to our farm would receive an education that they would not soon forget. I remember we couldn't wait until they would have to go to the toilet. We would dash outside to carry out our evil plan. We would wait until they would be seated comfortably, then they would have a surprise of their life. Unknown to them we had previously drilled a hole in the rear of the toilet just below the seat. We listened for them to be seated, and then we would take a small smooth wire from below and poke them in their seat. It never failed; we would hear a pair of feet hit the floor very hard. That was our signal to run as fast as we could to save our lives. We would hide behind the chicken coop and if need be, we would run into the cornfield beyond the grove of trees.

Some of comments by our victim after being stuck and finding out that we kids did it weren't fit to be put in print. Most of our victims were unsuspecting.

The hardest part was not to laugh in anticipation of what would happen. When the person assigned to do the poking with the wire hit their target, we knew we had to run fast or get caught.

My Dad was one who liked to do jokes, but we didn't dare tell him how we dealt with his visitors.

Our best victim was Dad's brother Bill from Michigan who got caught in our prank. He screamed, **"Sewer rats!"** and went running out the door, pants down and complained to Dad about getting bit in the behind by sewer rats. We couldn't hide our joy of getting our Uncle Bill. When he found out what happened, we had to be on our guard through the remainder of their visit expecting pay back every time. From that time Uncle Bill was forced by his wife to escort her to the toilet and he then would patrol the outside when she was inside because of her total fear of what these country kids would think up next.

Another one of the games we played was, *Kick-the-Can*. One person would be *"It"* and the rest would have to hide. Then when *"It"* would look for the persons hiding others would try to sneak out of hiding and kick the can. If they got the can kicked before the person who was searching, you were *"It"* again" Then if you got caught, you or another person would be chosen to seek while everybody would hide.

There was no electricity, no TV and we didn't get radio until I was eleven years old, so all our games were home made games that we would either invent or adapt for someone we visited. We always liked visiting kids where they had big families because we learned new games. At times the things we learned were not always with the approval of our or their parents.

45

Aunt Fannies "Model T"

One of my mother's sisters was a very pious woman and my dad would debate with her for hours about religion. She had a habit, when cornered, and didn't know what to say, she would roll her false teeth in her mouth. We kids, behind her back, would shamefully poke fun of her, by pretending to shove our teeth forward and roll them. This was a habit she continually had when she was excited.

She was quite good at hanging wallpaper with my mom. Dad did the entire fitting, cutting and pasting while Mom and Aunt Fanny would hang it on the wall. It was usually amusement enough to watch them hang wallpaper during which time Dad continued to argue with her. We were soon kicked out of the house so they could make better time hanging their paper.

After supper, while they were still wall papering, a neighbor boy came along and my older brothers thought it would be great sport to take Aunt Fanny's old Model T Ford for a ride down the road. The plan was to push the Model T Ford away from the house, around the corncrib, down the hill, around the grove and out the back driveway. This we could pull off and not make any noise close by the house.

My sister Wynn drove it. She bravely got behind the wheel and turned to all us kids behind the car and said, "Now push as hard and fast as you can." Well, we gave *Old Tin Lizzy*, as the car was affectionately called, a mighty shove and pushed it with all our might down the hill.

Meanwhile Wynn was trying to start it and to her fright, *Old Tin Lizzy* was coasting so fast she didn't dare turn the corner in the grove for fear of tipping it over. So T*in Lizzy* hit the tree with a mighty bang and the front end of the Model T Ford, climbed right up the tree and stood proudly on its rear wheels. We all ran to see how the front end looked.

One headlight was pointing sadly towards the ground, the other one had the glass cracked and the front bumper was in a sad looking bow. Did we ever panic! Who would volunteer to tell Aunt Fanny? No volunteers! So into a quick family conference and we decided it would be far better for our seats if we patched up the bumper and lights and pushed *Lizzy up* the hill, parked it by the house, and hoped Aunt Fanny would not see the lumps and bumps and broken lights.

We were hoping maybe she would be so ticked off at my Dad's debating her about her church, she wouldn't see the damage. We were fortunate it was little bit dark when she went home, and we had pulled off what we thought was a perfect crime. Later in life that neighbor boy went into the ministry and in his retiring years became our minister to the elderly. The first time he was in the pulpit I couldn't help but remember the night of Aunt Fanny's Model T and the mighty push we gave it.

Adventures of Snow and Snowstorms

One of my earliest recollections of snowstorms was when I was 6 years old. We lived at the base of the seven-mile creek that went twisting and turning through our pasture and crossed the section one mile west of our house. When the pasture had a big layer of snow and the northwest wind kicked up, our farmyard was the first stopping place for the snow and the drifts would pile higher and higher on the center of the main yard.

This story took place before there was any way of warning anybody of a coming storm and we had to rely on what the elderly people were predicting by the signs they saw in the color of the setting or rising sun. Some of the kids in school were predicting storms by how Grandmother's rheumatism was acting up. Others would watch the cattle hustling about, or the way birds were acting, or if they all sat in a row with their tails to the wind, on telephone lines.

Well, Dad didn't like the way the sky was building up and it looked like we could get a lot of snow. It was beginning to snow and it was falling quite fast with a lot of white fluff on the ground.

He came into the house and told Mom to get the soapstone hot and the horse blanket ready because he was going to hitch a team of horses to the sleigh and get my older brothers and sister from school. Mom quickly put more cobs in the kitchen stove, opened the oven door and put the soapstone inside to get it ready to take in the sleigh. This stone was a foot square, flat, with a handle on it so you could carry it around. It was used to put your feet on to keep them warm while you were all nestled under the horse blanket. Unless of course you were a big boy, you stayed up front with Dad until you were out of sight of school, then you too would try to shove yourself under the blanket.

We knew that Mom was worried about the weather too because she cleaned the kerosene lantern, lit it, and sent it along too. So I knew Mom was worried, because as heavy as the sky was, it was going to be dark before they got home. It was nearly two miles to school and it took 45 minutes when the conditions were good to make that 4-mile trip. When they got to school, visibility was very bad and with everything being white, it was hard to find the road.

Dad came in and said, "Quick Ma, feed the boys lunch and get them out to the milk barn. I am going to feed the pigs and put new a sack in front of the door to keep the cold and snow out of the hog house." We always had from 15 to 25 cows that had to be milked by hand. We had no electricity so everything had to be done with the light of a lantern.

The wind was already blowing snow through the sill of the door and also was fizzing in through the cracks in the wood siding. Nobody wanted to milk the cows in the back shed part of the barn because that part was even a lot colder and we occasionally saw a rat or two there.

At that time, after the cows were milked, the milk had to all be carried to our lean-to on the house where the cream separator was. We had to take turns turning the handle to separate the cream from the skim milk. I can still hear that old separator bowl hum as it started to gain speed. I remember one time as I was cranking it up fast; the bowl flew apart with tins flying everywhere.

Now Dad and my older brothers had to go back through those snowdrifts with the skim milk to feed the little calves and bring the rest of it to the pigs. I always liked teaching newborn calves to drink. I enjoyed sneaking my finger out of their mouth once I had their head in the milk bucket and they would drink without any help.

In the house meanwhile, Mom was frying out bacon, making a big stack of pancakes, and she had the stove so hot the water in the stove reservoir was steaming. The reservoir was a built in container at the end of the cook-stove. When the stove was on, the water stayed very warm. We all liked washing in warm water after being out in the freezing cold. So Dad and the boys would get a basin of water and get washed up in the back porch.

When Dad came inside the house he was covered from head to toe with snow. He said, " Mom, do you have enough water?" She shook the five-gallon water can. "It's just about full, but we need some cobs for the stove and also bring some pieces of wood so we can keep the stove going longer when we go to bed." That was one thing about Dad; he always wanted to have everything ready in case of an emergency.

You would never believe how fast those pancakes disappeared once Mom put them on the table. Then we knew what the next comment would be from Dad, "Go easy on the syrup boys, it's expensive, that gallon has to last at least a month." After we finished off our last pancake Mom would get out the old thick Dutch Bible and if I could I would like to snuggle close to her and lie on her lap while she read a chapter from the Bible. Mother's lap always had a mixed smell of cob smoke, bacon, pancakes and home baked bread. The kitchen stove also always produced a variety of smells. At times the stove had cow barn smells coming from the clothing lying behind the stove. The stove also had a warming closet, where we dried our gloves and kept them warm and dry. The reservoir also was kept full of water to enable us to wash our face and hands with warm water.

These are some of those kitchen odors future generations may never experience because of our instant foods and microwave cooking. On cold nights after supper there was a race for the oven door to warm our feet. We had to take turns and were warned every night not to get our shoes too deep into the oven or we would burn the leather. I could never describe the beauty of the pictures that Jack Frost painted on the windows, and they were so decorative. The snow-covered frost will never have anything that will equal its artistic qualities.

Dad went to look out of the door. He had to push the snow away from the outside door to get the door open. He said, "You know Ma, this storm looks just as bad as the year we got married."

Our house on this farm had only one bedroom down stairs and three small bedrooms upstairs. We always took a lantern upstairs to get undressed and blew it out before going to bed, if we didn't forget. Sometimes we left it burn on purpose. Our beds were slid right against the roofline and we would hear the wind howling, along with a few mice scampering over the plastered walls in the attic.

There in the attic is where Dad had his next year's seed corn stored; still on the ear just as he picked it. "I bet we won't have school tomorrow, so the kids will be home, then if it is still storming we will start picking the bad kernels of corn off of the ears and get the corn ready for hand shelling." Then we put the kernels of corn through a corn grader, which selected the kernels by size. The reason this was done was to enable my

51

father's corn planter to drop the proper amount of kernels. Our corn had to be carefully selected for the following year's planting.

The next morning I could sleep in, but my older brothers were called up before daylight. Dad already had the stove hot and the coffee percolator pot on the back of the stove. He had already enjoyed his first morning cup of coffee. He set coffee out and some of Mom's cookies. There was never a better smell in the morning than that of fresh brewed coffee.

Dad's morning ritual was to put in his daily journal the events of the previous day, the market prices, where he went and whom he visited with. This was always done between 4 and 6 o-clock in the morning.

Dad said, "This morning put your big overcoats on over your jackets and wear these scarves (which he already placed by the stove) over your face, the wind is bitter cold and snow is drifting very badly. The snow is so high I can't see the barn door. I brought all the grain scoops in the porch last night so everybody wait until we all go together." The drifts were so high that it was like climbing mountains to get to the barn. All the roads were closed; even horses couldn't get over the snow banks. So my brothers dug a tunnel through the mountain of snow that separated the house from the barn. The bank of snow was so high that a horse could walk through the tunnel they dug to get from the house to the barn and so they could get the horses to the water tank.

Farmers couldn't get to town and the milk cans were full of milk. So the milk was put through the separator. They put their cream in washtubs and washing machines until they could to get to the creamery in town. We made butter with a lot of our cream when all our containers were full.

A train with a snowplow was trying to move a snow bank north of town and got stuck. The conductor walked back to town to get all the workers of the creamery and any available person to scoop snow so they could try to free that train. Farmers were desperate. They would organize neighbors to try to scoop their way into town. Collectively they would bring in their cream and eggs and try bringing supplies back. They would cut through the fields and if there were any fences they had to cross they would cut the wires and crisscross anywhere they could get horses through.

I have several very vivid recollections of that winter. The first one was when we went one evening to a surprise farewell party for neighbors Bill and Bertha. Dad hitched the horses to the sleigh and we zigged and zagged through the fields. But when we got to our neighbor's grove the snow was frozen so hard and the banks so high that my older brothers had to hold the telephone wires up in the air so the horses could walk under them.

After spending several weeks at home on Sunday, when the weather began warming up, Dad said, "I'm hitching the horses to the sleigh today and we will all go to church." We were all happy to go because we had been cooped up so long already; to get away once again was a treat. Mom cleaned us up, dressed us in our hand me down clothing and Pa hitched his best team of horses to the sleigh. He also put a few straw bales in the sleigh. He tied the team to the pump while he got dressed. We went to church without incident. When we got there, a lot more farmers had the same idea and there were lots of other teams with sleighs.

While in church the snow began to thaw and the weather became bright and sunny. We were just a mile west of town when we saw a family whose bobsled had tipped over and the two men were trapped inside. The wife and daughter were screaming for help. So Dad and my brothers ran up the hill to help lift up the wagon box to get the men rescued from under the box. The men were quite heavy and both men had sat on one side of the bob sleigh; a sleigh runner cut through the snow and tipped them over.

We got about one half mile from home and were going over the top of the snow when suddenly one of our horses fell through the snow and spooked the other horse. The downed horse struggled but couldn't get up. After a lot of work Dad managed to separate the horses but the downed horse had a broken leg and hip. Talk about a sad day. This was my dad's favorite team that he always took when he wanted his best work done. The men always bragged about their best horses so when they went to church or to town, they always took their best team of horses. Not a word was said as we walked all the way home. Mother showed such pain. Dad said, "Hurry up boys, get your clothes changed, we've got an awful job to do."

Dad had no choice. A horse with a broken leg had to be destroyed. He hurried back and put that horse out of his pain. That was how I remember the painful years of T*he Depression*, financial hardships, hardships from the extreme elements of nature, and I saw a father with determination like steel.

He was going to stay and he would succeed; he wasn't going to quit. No matter what, he wasn't going back to the city for factory work and he had confidence that the Lord would lead us through this and other future hurdles too.

Cream Separator: This is the author, on his father's farm, in the milk barn, tending the cream separator. He is separating the milk from the cream of the 26 milk cows. At this time it was accomplished with power from electricity. Earlier years we had to turn a crank to power the cream separator.

Chapter 4

World War II Years

Things during World War II weren't the same at home; everyone took on a different view of life. First came the registering of all the young men for the draft. Then came the physicals and those who passed it. Their names were then put in a big fish bowl. The local draft board would pick names to fill the quotas of the men needed.

The draft board stepped up their quota because of that awful "Day of Infamy," Sunday, December 7, 1941, as President Franklin D Roosevelt called it. We had just come home from our Sunday afternoon church service. When we turned on our battery radio in the house, suddenly the announcer interrupted the regular programming and we heard the news directly from President Roosevelt. He announced that Pearl Harbor had been bombed and hundreds of our men went down inside their ships.

That evening as we sat around, our ears were attentive toward the radio to hear latest developments (most radios at that time weren't always very clear). No longer was it a war being fought in distant Europe, now we were more directly involved in it. Now our territory was attacked. At this time our enemy thought we were at our weakest. As I remember it, our country had to establish a new strategy. The US as a country would not have the ability to produce or ship rubber. All the rubber tires that could be produced were needed by the military. The tires were rationed and only the essential civilian tires would receive an allotment by issuing tire stamps to the buyer, before they could purchase a tire. Tires for personal use were not given; only a limited amount was given for agriculture. I remember it well. In fact I can still feel the way our neighbor's small Ford tractor rode with the steel lug wheels.

Dad Was Always Willing to Lend a Helping Hand

Our neighbor living north of us bought a Ford tractor but it only came in steel wheels with big lugs on it. It was nearly impossible to ride on it. We shook and bounced a lot. Our neighbor had 80 acres of land to work. He had stomach cancer and that rough riding tractor was killing him. Dad noticed that our neighbor was having a difficult time so he sent me out there to disk his fields and plow the land. When I would come home at night my pockets were full of ground and I looked like a coal miner. It was difficult for me to see this neighbor slowly fading away as he suffered from that dreaded disease of cancer.

Dad would be firm about not permitting any family member to accept money or anything as pay or reward for helping someone in need. Early in life he instructed us that this was far more than a requirement; it was a responsibility for Christians to help those in need without receiving pay. It was our privilege to reach out to help those who are in need.

I guess for me it was the first time that I was daily made aware of the fact that we as humans are not immortal. Here was a young man with a family, who was slowly dying, and he would never get to see his children grow up to be men. I'll not forget how this fact hit me hard at his funeral, as the organist began playing and I followed along in the hymnbook. Then I realized that life is uncertain and not everyone would live out his or her life to an old age.

To get back to my story, the next ration notice that really affected us was that of sugar and gas. The government was going to give each person a small amount of sugar and gas. This could only be bought with stamps. Every family had to go to their school district and report how much of these supplies we had in our home. They deducted from our stamps the amount that we reported that we had in our home. The amount of gas we were allowed was four gallons per week per car. If we had a truck, we were given more gas. We were given a stamp called a *T Stamp* that could give about as much gas as we needed, but we didn't have a pickup or truck so we only could have four gallons per week per car.

Rumors were everywhere about people quickly storing 100 # sacks of sugar in their attic. But did this cross my dad's mind? Never. He went to the cupboards and when he found any sugar in the sugar bowls he emptied it all in a bowl, weighed it on a scale and reported it. He measured the gas in the barrels and in the gas cans and reported how much we had on hand.

When we told Dad about the people we heard that had stored sugar and gas up ahead he said, "If the boys in the army need my gas, oil, tires, and sugar they are going to get it, we will be honest in all our dealings, end of the discussion."
What a powerful example for us, not only an example in words but we saw it in our father's actions.

My prayer is that by writing these experiences, the readers might follow my father's example. That what is honest, right and true is the only way to live a life, "End of discussion."

Although my Dad loved sugar in his coffee; he was going to set the example for his family and not use sugar in his coffee, but he did come home with a jar of imitation sugar called saccharin. What a bitter taste that stuff had. We would try to use it on cereal and for all our other sweeteners but our food wasn't the same without sugar. Dad let Mom save what little we had so she could keep baking bread and an occasional cake. We were able to get some honey and corn syrup but to this day I don't like food or drinks that contain saccharin.

Every school district had an air raid warden and when the fire whistle blew in town and the party phone line rang seven short rings that was our signal to put all the lights out. The air raid warden could arrest anyone who disobeyed. We would sit in the dark not saying a word until the "all clear" was sounded. Dad would cover over any light with a heavy coat, which came from the fire in the stove. Even though the threat in Iowa was very minimal, it made all of the adults and children mindful that our nation was at war and we all were to get behind the effort. In rural areas if they had small planes they would load up small flour sacks and from the air, throw them on houses that were showing any light.

One by one my three older brothers had to report for physicals. My oldest brother had high blood pressure and failed his physical. Then when the twin brothers had their physicals, one brother was chosen and the other failed because of an enlarged heart.

One brother was soon called to the army. He trained for joining in with a mule artillery pack in the mountain range of Pikes Peak in Colorado. They were called, The Ski Troops and their artillery pieces had to be hauled up by mule train. They were being trained for fighting in the mountains in Italy.

Back at the farm, we were farming 360 acres of land with horses and we had a small Model H John Deere tractor that would pull a two 12-inch bottom plow. Every time we traveled across the field we would cover two feet of land. This meant we had to keep that tractor going all day and all night. We had on the tractor, two tanks of fuel, one and a half gallon of gas and a five-gallon tank of kerosene.

We started the tractor on gas and when it got warm we switched it to kerosene. We switched drivers when they had worked five hours, so the driver could eat a meal and rest. We also refueled the tractor every five hours. The tractor only stopped for Sunday or when it was too wet to be in the field. We also used seven horses on a two 16 inch bottom plow, but only worked the horses on two shifts from sun up to sun down. Our farm, when I was lad, consisted of 20 to 26 milk cows, five hundred chickens, and we raised about 200-250 pigs. We also raised the little calves that were born to our milk cows.

My Attempt At High School

I had graduated from the eighth grade in country school and Dad wanted me to go to high school. Dad had hoped that one of his sons would go into the ministry and he made no bones about encouraging me to get an education. I decided to go to high school, and Dad informed me that it would not be an easy road. I would be needed to help milk the cows and do the chores especially when they were working in the field. Because of the gas rationing, no bus service was available and I would have to walk morning and evening the four miles to and from school. I was expected to work on the farm every spare moment that I could. I was prepared to go along with those conditions so I enrolled myself in school and started attending high school.

Now that was quite a shock. First of all, I was used to a one-room country school with the students all from our neighborhood. I knew ever since 1st grade that attending country school was a sheltered environment compared to high school in town. Now I was being thrown together with 30-40 other students in each of the four grades with a mix of city versus country boys. Needless to say those first weeks of school were a test of wills. The challenge was going to be who would "rule the roost," the country boys or city kids. The country boys, though outnumbered, were not going to allow themselves to be pushovers. The school system also lost a lot of their younger teachers to the draft. That left little, or at times no supervision on the playground. They also removed from their curriculum every subject except that which they termed as essential because of the shortage of teachers.

Walking Home Very Sick

During my second or third week of school I wasn't feeling very well and the playing on the school ground was exceptionally rough that noon hour. When the bell rang calling us back into school, the horseplay carried over into our music class. We had a new young teacher who was boarding at my aunt and uncle's home. When we finally were seated, she asked if anyone had a favorite song. One of the wise city kids suggested we sing, "*It was my last cigar.*" First the teacher doubted that there was such a song but the wise one said, "It's on such and such a page, we always used to sing it in the lower grades." Of course that was a lie and when the class tried singing it she knew she had been "had." She became very angry and some of the city kids in the class thought it was very funny and laughed at her. The sparks flew and she said, "Every student will stay after school a couple hours to learn that in my class you'll have respect for music and the person who is teaching it. Class dismissed until after school. Then we will have our music."

As the day progressed I started to really feel sick and went to the bathroom and vomited several times. I stuck it out until the last class. Then I went to the music teacher and told her I was sick and had to go home. She said, "You will stay after, no one of that class will go home until they learn to respect their teacher." Even though I had killing pain, I stayed. I don't remember anything of what she taught us. I remember walking a half block to my aunt Martha's house and found no one home. Then I walked to the drug store where Uncle Ray worked but he was off for the noon hour. The storeowner called to my home and got no answer. He tried for Aunt Dina's house and got no answer, so I started walking those four miles home. I made the first two miles but vomited in the ditch several times. I remember curling up in a fetal position and passing out next to a bridge a mile and a half from home. I woke up later and somehow made it home. I made my way into my parents' bed, which was downstairs.

Meanwhile, that morning, my brother who was in *Mountain Ski Troop* training, had called home that he was leaving the states for Italy. He told my folks that he was at a nearby train station and could have the afternoon and evening at home. Mother quickly called all the relatives together to go to Maurice and have a farewell for my brother at our uncle's home. That was why none of my relatives were at home; they were all at my brother's farewell. When my parents got home, Mother and Dad felt my forehead and realized I had a burning fever so they called our doctor. At that time when someone was very ill the country doctor would make house calls. He came to our home and informed my parents that he was very afraid the appendix was ruptured and I would need emergency surgery as soon as possible if I were to survive.

I was taken to the Hull, Iowa hospital that night or very early the next morning. I don't even remember Dad was with me in surgery and my mother was riding along with the other brothers to bring my brother to the train to go overseas. I was placed into surgery very early in the morning. The only thing I remember was as I was lying on the operating table, an elderly nurse (whom all the patients disliked because of her lack of compassion and sarcastic attitude), threw a wet cloth soaked with ether over my nose and shouted, "Just blow Richard, just blow Richard" I was going under, feeling like I was spinning around in a giant mixing bowl and that wicked old nurse was telling them to blow Richard around in the circle faster and faster. "Just blow Richard, just blow, just blow." I was going

64

around and around in my mind. When I woke up confused, there was that horrible nurse looking into my eyes. I blinked and then saw my folks and the doctor staring down at me. Oh how I hurt! I was so dizzy and my stomach ached so. I had to vomit and I couldn't. I asked myself, "Why didn't I die, why am I still here?" The doctor said, "You had a big surgery, but you made it this far. You will have a slow recovery ahead of you, but you are going to pull through." With that he motioned to my folks to step out of the room where I could hear him whispering to them.

The next day when they changed the dressing, I learned that I had a long tube inside me. The tube was used to try to drain the infection and pus out of the area where my appendix broke. Every other day the battle-ax nurse would come into my room and say, "Richard, I have a surprise for you." Then she would peel back my dressing and jerk the tube out a short way without any sympathy.

My first visitor was Joan, a classmate from school. Her mother was seriously ill in the same hospital. She came into my room with a large scroll of drugstore wrapping paper, on which almost all the class had signed their names and wrote little greetings and notes. At the school's 50th class reunion in 1999, I brought that scroll of notes and signatures for the students to observe and reminisce.

My aunt Grace came to visit me and brought me a book entitled, "*What Would Jesus Do?*" by Charles Sheldon. It was a book that challenged me to examine my life in respect to that phrase. What would Jesus do if he were lying on this bed and he were me, what would he do?

I have asked myself that question time and time again in many different circumstances in my life.

I was feeling worse instead of better, and again was getting a high fever. I started to pass a lot of blood in my urine. The infection had gained a foothold in my kidneys.

The nurse brought with her the younger brother of my doctor who was practicing in another small town. My folks came and that afternoon the two doctors came along with the doctor's young son who had just graduated from medical school.

This young doctor told them about a new drug that was doing wonders for the soldiers with infected wounds. Maybe they could try that drug on this infection.

Dad gave his okay to try this drug. This was in a time when no forms had to be signed. If a person gave their word to go ahead, that was even better than a signature is today. In those days your word was gospel and people trusted each other.

They started to give me the new drug called *Sulfa,* although my parents realized that for a person who had ruptured appendix many times it was fatal. I had signs of peritonitis and blood in my urine.

My pastor came to me and had words of encouragement and prayer. I also had a dear nurse who was a pastor's wife. She would give me back rubs, hold my hand and pat it with her other hand and say, "I will keep praying for you," and she would wink at me and would say, "You are going to be okay."

At the end of the fourth day my fever broke, my kidneys slowly started to clear up and I was on the mend. I asked myself many questions. Did I witness an answer to prayer? Was it a miracle or was it a miracle drug? All these questions were turning in my mind in light of what I was reading in the book, "What Would Jesus Do?" After being in the hospital 21 days I finally was permitted to go home by ambulance and had to remain in bed for another week.

My Return to School

"Well," Dad said, "If you are strong enough to go back to school I will bring you. If you can take it, we will look for a place for you to board so you won't have to walk back and forth for now."

The school class room was up one flight of stairs before we got into the school building, then two flights up to get into the class room. I started up and made the first flight and on the second flight I couldn't climb any more. I was too weak and sore. Dad helped me down the steps and we went home. I never got upstairs to clean out my desk or return to my homeroom.

The next year the war was even worse. School officials took away shop and agriculture classes. There was still no bus transportation and I was not able to find housing in town. Gas rationing was still on and I was dreading that four-mile walk. I said, "Dad I will stay home and work for you instead of going to school." I know that was a disappointment for him but he understood how difficult it was to continue, especially since my friends were now all one grade above me. Also I had been away from studying for over a year. My parents reluctantly agreed it would be okay for me to stay home.

The war years left my parents hurrying to the mailbox waiting for news of my brother's welfare from one letter to the next. At times while reading a letter, Mom would go off to the bedroom and cry. They always had the question on their minds, "How is our son faring in battle?" Mother would stare in the distance a lot.

My brother wrote about the mud, and the difficult time he had, trying to keep moving his gun emplacements. He enclosed in one of his letters a clipping that told about his unit giving him a citation for bravery. The act of bravery took place when an enemy shell fell on the ammunition dump. He quickly carried off the live ammo, while the fire was burning around him, to save their weapons and ammunition.

We all went once a month to community prayer meetings where all the churches gathered together to pray that the war would end and for the safety of our service men. My parents aged a lot during those war years.

They were so thankful when the announcement came that V E Day had arrived. There was joy everywhere; the church bells were all ringing and our soldiers who struggled so long would soon be coming home.

But in many a home throughout our small towns were gold stars in the windows, representing the loss of a loved one and they only would feel even deeper the heartache and emptiness at the return of the other soldiers. My brother was coming home from the military service.

Dad got a permit to buy lumber for a new home that we needed desperately on the farm. Our old home had no indoor plumbing and we still used the outhouse. We got the permit because we were housing a returning veteran. Our old house was too small and too old to remodel. Even though he had a permit, he still had to find the lumber and all the lumberyards' supplies were completely depleted.

We could now buy gas so every morning Dad would go out with a list of his lumber needs for the house. He would hook up his trailer to the car and go from town to town to buy supplies. That year, Dad spent all day driving just to keep the carpenter supplied with lumber. While the home was being built we lived in our old house, which had been moved off the old site, and it stood on blocks about four feet in the air.

Then, I believe it was the summer of 1946 on a hot humid June day that the following incident took place.

We were haying a 20-acre field of alfalfa and putting the hay in the barn. We picked up the hay off windrows and the hay loader put it on the wagon. We would fill the hayrack with three slings to fill one hayrack load. We pulled the hay slings into the barn with horses and a haymow rope with the use of pulleys. This went very well since we had the new tile barn built in 1941-42. The door was larger and all the equipment was quite new.

While having our usual afternoon coffee break the air was so burning hot. Dad said, "Boys, be careful not to get overheated. You have to also watch the sky because this weather is bound to bring up a storm." In fact there were already deep thunderclouds forming in the far west.

We went out with our John Deere hay loader and loaded another two loads of hay during which time the sky became very dark with rolling clouds. Dad came out of the milk barn where he was milking. He said, "Quick, get the haymow door shut and the horses in the barn!" We just got the door shut and the horses inside when the air became deathly still, not even a chicken feather would move on the ground.

Dad said, "Get Mom and Wynn out of the house quick; I don't like the way the sky looks. Get ready to all go into the barn cellar." Mom came out of the house and Dad said, "Carrie turn off your stove and get in the barn cellar." We could see the clouds twisting and rolling and in the distance a funnel cloud dropped out of the sky. Dad said, "Kids get down the cellar quick!'

He and one of my brothers stayed until the tornado got close and a few shingles were falling on our yard. After a short time they went out to look and discovered that a farm that was on a hill west of us was gone. Dad could see the funnel cloud drop southwest of us and to the east as well. Then came torrents of rain.

After sitting in the barn a while he said, "What if the neighbors need help, we better hurry over and check." We all piled into our 1937 Ford and in the downpour started out for our north corner. There we got stuck in the mud and the boys pushed us back on the center of the road again.

We got to the neighbor's farm and discovered none of the buildings were left. We saw that a horse was picked up and carried a long way; about one fourth of a mile and dropped on his feet up to his stomach in the deep muddy grassland.

A car front end was on top of a 55-gallon gas barrel standing up right.

We saw a chicken tail feather halfway into a tree so tight that it couldn't be pulled out with pliers. I later figured out that the tree twisted so much that the wood opened up enough to permit the feather to enter. When the wind let go it twisted back and left the feather locked in the tree.

They had enough help at that farm but another neighbor had a pullet house destroyed and all the young chickens were drowning in the rain. We went there and spent that evening running after and catching wet chicks, drying them up and putting them in a fenced area of the barn that had a small part of the roof left over it.

That night there were seven farms destroyed and lots of buildings damaged. So we spent all our spare time that summer first helping to clean up lumber from the fields, repairing buildings and constructing new ones for people.

With all of this damage there was no loss of life; only one child was injured when the home they were in was destroyed while they were huddled in the basement. The baby was sucked right out of the mother's hands and was injured.

The baby's father went for the car but it was gone and he had to run a half of a mile to get help. When we looked at all of the destruction and heard the people's stories, I realized it was only through some providential miracle that no lives were lost that night.

Cross Examined By Mrs. Agnes Te Paske

At the age of 17 my folks permitted me to join the Christian Endeavor. This was an International Christian Youth organization that our church was a part of at that time. When we joined we were asked to take part in the program.

When I got our schedule, to my surprise, I was to read Scripture but it was for the Easter sunrise service. Now this would not only be before the young people but a lot of the congregation would be in attendance. The speaker was Attorney Mrs. Agnes Te Paske. She was a person who loved the Lord. She spoke very slowly but always with much wisdom. She had to choose the scripture that was to be read.

So I drove to her home. She invited me in and asked what I thought we should use. I was no help to her, so we didn't decide that day and after two more attempts still no scripture was chosen. Time was getting short so I went back there again. She invited me in. She picked up a Bible and gave me one too. She said, "Richard, I want you to read the story about the men as they were walking on the way to Emmaus in *Luke 24:1-32*" So she had me read the story and when I got through the 32nd verse she said, "Read that 32nd verse again slowly." So I read very slowly,

> *"And they said to one another, **did not our hearts burn within us** while he talked with us by the way and opened to us the scriptures?"*
>
> *Luke 24:32 KJV*

Then when I had finished, Agnes in her soft-spoken voice asked, "Richard, have you ever had that burning heart when Jesus walked and talked with you in the way?" She waited as I started to shift in my seat. Then she said, "Think about it." As I drove away my first thought was, "The nerve of that woman."

But the words of that 32nd verse of Luke 24 began to burn deep into my heart and soul. Yes, I have had that burning heart of Jesus; when I felt the healing touch in the hospital, when I read the book "*What would Jesus Do?*" and when I saw the power and the effects of the tornado with no one lost.

That was Jesus walking along side of them and me personally. I have felt that burning heart. Later, I met with the elders of the church and made my stand for Christ.

I read the scripture that Sunday with a new set of eyes and the picture of the two men walking to Emmaus. After Phyllis and I were married, we hung a picture in our living room of the men walking on the road to Emmaus, because for me it had special meaning.

My First Attempt At Speaking

Now the New Year's program of Christian Endeavor came out and I was listed as being on the schedule to take charge of the Bible topic. This was the responsibility that we had when we became a confessing member.

I was shaking in my boots. I wasn't part of the popular crowd and some of boys made a habit of poking fun of the person who had to lead and this would make me nervous.

As the time got close I had a plan. I got the nerve to go to Rev. P.A. De Jong and I asked him if he would lead the scripture discussion for me. He asked, "Why can't you do it?" I thought for a minute and said, "I get so nervous that my voice shakes, my papers shake and then I can't read." He thought for a minute and said, "Sounds like you are trying to do it in your own strength.

The apostle Paul says:

I can do all things through Christ who strengthens me.

Philippians 4:13 (KJV)

Richard, you have to stop trying on your own strength and begin to rely on the strength of Christ who dwells within you. I will tell you what I will do. I will be at the meeting. You prepare your message and if you can't deliver it I will take over and discuss the scripture that you have chosen."

"Okay Richard," I said to myself, "you didn't find an easy way out, so now what?" I had no choice but to search the scriptures to try find a topic.

The Korean War was already going on and older guys from the church were already in the service. I knew that I would soon be drafted.

In view of that I began to search the scripture for a topic for my Bible study. I found and chose the story of the Apostle Paul found in *Acts 28* about how, as a prisoner, he was shipwrecked on an island and was now in chains heading for his trial and possible death. Fellow Christians at *Three Taverns* met Paul.

"And who, when the Apostle Paul saw them,
"Thanked God and took Courage"

Acts 28:15 KJV

Those five words I used for my topic "Thank God and Take Courage." I was able for the first time to experience the Holy Spirit help me prepare and deliver a message with power.

It was far beyond my ability and it left me no doubt that what I had just experienced was that through Christ's strength I could prepare and deliver a topic in front of people. Maybe Rev.

De Jong was right. In Christ's strength I could do anything as long as Christ was in it.

I would find out later that I would have to go through experiences I never would have dreamed about then. Through each of these experiences, step-by-step, I was beginning to discover Gods wonderful attributes, through the study of Scripture and through my personal daily walk with my Lord.

Leaving loved ones behind was difficult

This was taken before I was drafted into the service.
Here I am with my attractive girl friend Phyllis Bolkema.

Chapter 5

Uncle Sam Wants You

It was a fall day. I was working on Dad's farm that at that time was called an Iowa diversified farm. The farm consisted of all types of livestock except sheep but also included various types of field crops.

The corn harvest was finished and brother Bill and I were getting the livestock ready for another severe Iowa winter. This included the job of insulating the water tanks and fountains and putting burlap bags in front of the hog house doors. This we did so the pigs could go out and in without losing so much building heat.

Some of the pullets that we grew in the summer growing houses located in the pasture were already caught and carried to the laying house. The trees were still full of pullets that refused to go inside at night. They had to be caught one at a time which was always a nasty time consuming job. To remove the pullets from the trees would require many nights of poking the birds with a long pole to push them out of the trees, then running them down and catching them before they could run away too far.

When our hands were full of pullets we would leave for the layer house that was about a city block away. We would have to repeat these trips successively until we dropped of exhaustion or were finished rounding up the chickens, whichever occurred first. At times our hands felt like they were stretched to the ground, they were so sore and tired.

Dad was already suffering with a severe asthmatic heart condition and completely unable to work. This condition developed several years earlier while we were in the process of rounding up the chickens during a snowstorm.

I will never forget how he gasped for air and how we had to half carry him inside the brooder house so that he could get his breath again. This was the last day he worked because he couldn't be out side anymore, which left my brother and myself to manage the family farm.

It was dinnertime and Mom called in her usual way, "Boys come to dinner now and get the mail for Pa." I ran to get the mail before coming to dinner. All Dad could do since his heart attack was sit at the window and watch us work outside.

But Dad always was well informed of the world situation because he kept up with the news by reading the daily Sioux City paper.

By this time we had the mail at the end of the driveway, thanks to Farm Bureau's effort. As usual I would walk slowly to the house to see what letters or bills came in the mail.

What? A letter addressed to Richard Van Regenmorter from the Sioux Country Draft Board. With shaking hands I opened it. My mind started to rush from thought to thought.

Surely they won't need more men. Just last night the radio said the fighting in Korea was only a *Police Action*. But there it was, a message from the President of the United States. The President asks you to report to the OK Cafe at Alton, Iowa,

8:A.M. December 5, 1951. You must board the bus for Sioux Falls at that time for induction into the US Army.

As usual Dad said, "What came in the mail today?" The usual answer was, "Not much." But today trying to be brave I said, "I got a letter from the President of the United States."

Brave or not, that was all that Mom needed to hear. She remembered all too well the time my brother got this letter back in World War II. I am sure that her mind flashed back to those many hours she spent with her ears against the radio trying to get the latest reports on how the battles were going.

I remembered those long nights Mom and Dad sat in the dark, in prayer for their son, at the same time saving electricity, as well as doing everything they could that might be of help to speed the end of the war.

Mom dashed off to the bedroom where she could try to gain her composure. After some time she came out with a fresh apron on, It was her way of saying I'm going to do all that I can to keep a good front. I recognized the signs, but her inner pain she couldn't hide. It was heard by the way she mashed the potatoes with the old style potato masher. It hit the bottom of the pot with swift aggressive strokes.

It's okay, I thought; she is trying to get rid of her emotional pain. That noon meal was a very quiet one. Dad said nothing, but his mind was active, and that affected his ability to eat.

I knew what was going through his mind and through the minds of many parents. The question "Why?" had no answer. Why do we have to permit our sons to be used as cannon fodder, to be shot at to protect people we don't know?

Dad finally had to admit he wasn't hungry any more; even his favorite food had no taste.

My brother Bill and I were always keeping Dad up to date on what we were doing and plans for the future but that afternoon nothing in the future seemed important to any of us.

I remember that afternoon we didn't accomplish much. There we were, a working team with our minds miles away and my future on the farm was shattered.

Needless to say, my mind was also on the fact that I was in the beginning of a relationship with a young, but pleasant girl from Rock Valley. It was the first time that I cared about a member of the opposite sex.

Every time we were together she made me feel like life had a lot to offer us and I thought a great deal of her. Now what would happen to this relationship? What would be the best that could be expected of this relationship with a two-year separation?

By the next day Mom and Dad, but mostly Mom had my next weeks planned with a whirlwind of places to visit. I went to a lot of lunches during the day, and evenings to dinners with relatives, saying good-bye to friends, uncles, aunts, and immediate family members. As many nights as I dared, I asked Phyllis, that special girl friend from Rock Valley, to go along. Phyllis was still in high school so we met with a lot of resistance from her dad.

Thanks to her mother who intervened on our behalf more than once, she did go with me sometimes.

After all those good-byes, the time had come: tomorrow would be the day. Dad and I had one of those father to son talks that will always be remembered.

Dad knew that his health wasn't getting any better. Each asthma attack was worse than the last.

Gripping my hand he said, "Son, I may not be here after the war is over and I want you to have a start in farming. I won't be able to give you a start but I want your brother to farm the land when you are in the service. Then when you get back you can continue in a partnership."

For Dad this was second best even though it was his dream that one of his sons would go into professional ministry.

Being that I was the youngest, and the other family members had already chosen their careers, Dad was now resigning himself to the fact that his dream might not be fulfilled. Dad was broad-minded and was always willing to accept what each child chose for their profession and didn't interfere in our decisions.

Dad's dream was fulfilled (even though he didn't see it in his lifetime} when his grandson entered the ministry.

I went to bed that night, but the morning didn't seem to want to come. I tossed and turned all night thinking about leaving in the morning. When morning finally came, I hurriedly put my shaving gear and one change of clothing in a bag.

Mother fixed a big breakfast, but few words were said as my brother drove me off the farm that morning and headed down the road for the bus at Alton, Iowa. As far as I could see, my parents at the farm kept waving until we were out of their sight.

81

At Alton *OK Café*, the Sioux County Draft Board secretary had roll call as we went on the bus.

As we were leaving she said with sarcasm in her voice "Have a good time boys, have a good time." That was all we needed to arouse deep anger towards her for the way she said those words.

At Sioux Falls, SD. a man approached the bus. This person couldn't have been born of a woman. This brute of a man didn't speak; he only barked orders at us.

We were treated like cattle at the stockyards years ago. He was herding us around into a sweaty non-ventilated room.

The room was filled with smoke and smelled like an old gym, which was never aired out. We were put at desks and he barked at us, "Fill out these forms!" If anyone asked questions or talked to anyone he would howl obscenities at them.

"Time is up!" He bellowed, "Finished or not take off all of your clothes, put them in a bag, put your name on the bag and you must begin your all day nude march."

After being poked in every conceivable part of our body, if we had any dignity, we lost it all by the end of that day.

There was an assembly line of so-called doctors. If we called them doctors we would be really disgracing the profession. One looked in our mouth, one at our eyes, one looked at our feet so he could count our toes. But I doubted if he could even count to ten.

Then there was the infamous guy who says, "Bend over and hold your ankles," while he jams a head light into our behind. Then he gave us a slap on the rear end and says, "Okay, next."

My mind flashed a thought. This guy has a job that has to be very exciting. What would he talk about to his wife at night when he came home from work? What do you think he counted when he went to sleep at night? Certainly it wasn't counting sheep.

If there had been HIV and AIDS in that day, every prospective soldier would have had a case of it. The last doctor in the line up of doctors was to listen to my heartbeat and check my lungs. As he listened to my heart he noticed an irregular heart beat. He listened again and said, "H---they all sound alike, at the end of the day you will be okay."

Then came that brute of a man again. He ordered us to get dressed. Then we were loaded in old broken down railroad passenger cars. We stayed on those sidetracks what seemed to us like an eternity. Finally hours later, they hooked up those cars to a locomotive and moved us a little way, then we stayed standing on the side tracks for several more hours.

While we were sitting on the sidetrack the train had no ventilation. Well, you guessed it, all these fellows were nervous, but believe it or not, nobody was going to admit it.

I took a look around the rail car and you ought to have seen how the fellows were dragging on cigarettes and cigars, especially those who wanted to prove that they were men.

All evening they would light one cigarette right after another and before long I was getting sicker than a dog of all that smoke.

To make matters worse we were still parked on the sidetracks and the toilets were locked up. In those days the toilets were locked up in the towns and opened up while traveling in the country. Guess where your waste went. You guessed it, right on the tracks.

When we started to roll, a conductor came aboard and unlocked the door of the toilet. He saw my face and how sick I was. He quickly stepped aside after he opened the toilet room door. I thought that a volcano was released. That night all I heard was the clickity clack as I was looking through the hole of the stool at the rails below. I stayed in the bent over position until I was almost too weak and dizzy to stand up.

The conductor stopped by several times to say, "Soldier are you okay?" I didn't tell him that the bent over position over the rails listening to those rails going clickity clack, clickity clack, was the only place that I could get a breath of fresh air and get away from the rail cars that were saturated with smoke.

The word got around that we were going to Chicago via St. Louis and that it would take us three full days to get there.

Then on the noon of the second day the conductor came with household ammonia and I had to take a deep whiff of that bottle. "That will settle your stomach," he said. I don't really know if that ammonia helped or that the guys ran out of cigarettes. They were now buying them from each other for $5.00 a pack. (That was an awesome price in 1951) Then on the third day the smoke was getting almost non-existent. I believe the price of cigarettes had a lot to do with the lesser amount of smoke in the air.

I never figured out how it can take three days and nights to get a train from Sioux Falls, SD. to Chicago. The distance by car or bus would have been about 550 miles. I guess it took three days and nights because we sidetracked for every freight train that came through. Those side rails were all very boring and the toilet would be locked up until we were in the country again. I sometimes believed it was the Army's training exercise to stretch the bladders.

Finally we saw signs of the big city. We were going to stop and disembark at Fort Sheridan, Illinois. This was known as a *Troop-Processing Center.*

Now what were they all going to do to us at this place? Well, we would find out all too soon. First, another loud mouth brute, whom I wonder if only a mother could love, met us. He had with him a few foul mouth cadres who would try to bully any person they chose to make a fool of.

The first stop was to get our clothes. When we came out of there, every one had a perfect army fit (either too baggy or too tight). Then we had to put our name and rank and serial number in all our clothing plus our boots and belt.

How I longed to have a short name like Jones or Smith. Almost everybody would be finished and I wouldn't be, because of my long name, so I got punished for taking so long to get my name in all my clothing.

It didn't take long to know that the army wouldn't be treating anyone fairly and everybody could be subject to harassment in one form or another. The next stop was for us to get our first set of shots.

We were told to take our shirts off, put our hands on our hips and keep on walking. Bang, from this side, and then bang from the other side. In those days they would only change the needle when it was too dull to poke into our arm by using all their force. Needles weren't replaced with every shot like they do today.

Every once in a while we would hear another thud, and another person had fallen to the floor in a faint: The soldiers who passed out were dragged off to the side and were embarrassed when they woke up on the floor because they fainted getting a shot.

In the morning we woke up with a noisy sound of a whistle. When we heard the whistle we had to be dressed and out on the street in three minutes flat.

Oh, were my arms stiff that morning! I couldn't raise them above my shoulders. The spots where I had the shots were all swollen.

To start out the day we had to empty three big warehouse buildings of mattresses and carry them into other buildings. All day we carried mattresses with our hands above our shoulders trying to balance those mattresses. We had to carry them about three blocks from one building to another.

I really believe that every day a new group of recruits was ordered to carry those mattresses, one day from here to there, the next day from there to here. Is that what the army calls efficient? I believe that is the way they got the troops to exercise their sore muscles after those shots.

We were told that the next day we were all going to separate. Nobody wanted to go to the infantry basic training centers. We had no choice but to wait for our name to be called out for our orders.

That night I couldn't help but think about Dad and Mom, and what a long distance I was from Phyllis. The big question was, what does my future have in store for me? One thing was sure; I wasn't too much in a hurry to know what would happen in the future. There was in all of us some inner fear about our future because the news we would hear about what was going on at the front lines in Korea wasn't very encouraging. Would I be one of the soldiers who would be shipped to the advanced infantry training camps? Who would go to Europe and who would go to Korea? Would I be lucky enough to stay in the States after my training?

That night I picked up a Chicago newspaper. The only thing that seemed to be important was, what labor group was going on strike to ask for higher wages and more benefits? I had to search and search for any news about President Truman's so called, *Police Action*. If the war news wasn't important enough to put in the newspaper then why were we fighting there in the first place? This was the question going through my mind.

I decided I had better finish my devotions and get some sleep for no one knew what would happen tomorrow. I would have to be very tired before I fell asleep, because sleeping with a couple hundred men, all snoring a different tune, wasn't conducive to getting a good night of sleep.

Chapter 6

Basic Training

Left, Right, Left 1,2,3,4, Hut, Two, Three, Four

I found myself in an army camp, stuck in the Infantry outfit for the sixteen-week course, eight weeks of basic training; and then eight weeks advanced infantry training. I can still hear the non-commissioned officer reading off the names of those who would be going to Fort Riley, Kansas. Finally he came to that long name, Van Regenmorter. The sergeant chopped up the name so badly that no one could recognize it. Not even my father who gave me my name would have been able to recognize it. Then out of frustration he called out, "Serial number US 55 239 521." Then he said, "I am not going to say anything about your name, it is a curse enough, come forward. All I'm going to say about a name that long; it ought to give you some interesting times in the army.

Get a move on, into that bus, it will take you to the train that will take you to the 10th Division 87th Regiment, 1st Battalion, G Company, 4th Platoon, Fort Riley, Kansas." After the train ride from Sioux Falls to Fort Sheridan, this ride was a piece of cake. It was on a regular passenger train and the ride went all too fast. I was really scared because of all the stories I had heard about what the infantry basic camp was like. I wasn't too anxious to get started.

But on the plus side, the camp was only 360 miles from home. And that meant that it might be possible to come home sometimes. Another plus was that there were other Sioux County, Iowa guys going there also.

The first sight of the camp wasn't something that left a good impression. The barracks had been under water for some time. The bottom floors of the barracks were made of wood and were covered with musty moldy mud, and because they had been under water for some time, the edges of the flooring were all curled up. The footlockers were rusty and the hinges broke off when we opened them.

But the worst was yet to come. That was when I looked down the barrel of the rifle and found it to be totally rusted.

The barrel and the rifle had been standing in water and the barrel was rusted shut. I didn't think it could be cleaned. I said to the supply sergeant, "Look at this rifle, it's no good." His reply was, "Why, this rifle only needs a little cleaning, go to work on it." "Go work on it," was what I mumbled all the way to our barracks, "shine it up inside and out. Gee, thanks." I thought.

When I tried to clean the rifle there wasn't a hole through it. I took it back to the supply sergeant and I said, "This rifle is plugged." The supply sergeant took the rifle and said, "No, it's okay, now sign here for it, one complete rifle."

Little did I realize how much trouble that signature would cause me later.

When we finally had our equipment, we heard someone outside scream, "Fall out to Company Street." FALL OUT meant-- everybody out on the Company Street in formation in a few seconds time.

I was soon to find out how I was going to hate that term and all the harassment that went along with it. I still hate that phrase today and it is over 50 years later. "Too slow!!" the sergeant would bark, or, "Cadre get back in your barracks and try it again, and you better be faster next time."

Then after the 5th time he said somewhat better, "But tomorrow morning we will work on it some more, and if you don't fall out fast enough I will make you fall out with your foot locker on your shoulders!"

The next morning from the time the whistle blew in our barracks, we were to be fully dressed and on Company Street in just two minutes. Well, you guessed it; we were too slow according to the platoon sergeant. So he said, " We will work on this some more because we will be the first of the four platoons of this company on the street each morning waiting for the others. DO YOU HEAR ME? So march back in the barracks and this time I want you to fall out with your footlocker on your shoulder!"

So every soldier was to be out in Company Street with their full footlocker on their shoulders in less then 10 seconds in complete formation.

What the platoon sergeant didn't understand was. that upstairs was a group of fellows from the Chicago area that were sick of his games of going back and forth upstairs.

They closed the doors behind them when they went upstairs to get ready to rush down the stairs with their footlocker on their shoulders.

Nor did the platoon sergeant realize how very ticked off at the sergeant these Chicago fellows were.

When the sergeant blew his whistle they came down those stairs all in a row on a full run; they hit the closed door like a bomb-- the door and doorpost all went flying into a hundred pieces on Company Street.

When the sergeant saw the mess they made, he even lost his ability to use swear words. His mouth moved but no words came out. He was responsible for the fourth platoon as well as the condition of the barracks. What would the captain say when he would see what was left of the barracks?

That night when our captain came over from our platoon he was so angry his face got red and he screamed at us.

He started his speech; "This morning we had some violence in 4th platoon that was not called for. At 1700 hours (9 PM) tonight every member of this platoon, including the sergeant and cadre will all be in full field pack and we will have a forced 10-mile march.

The commander who spoke to us had a jeep and driver, but even our sergeant was carrying his full pack. The beer that was in the sergeant's blood really came sweating out of him as we went on that 10-mile forced march, supervised by the captain riding in his jeep. Needless to say, that was the last time we had to fall out on Company Street with footlockers on our shoulders.

I have to explain what our drill sergeant looked like. He had a sunken upper jaw in which 80% of the lower chin stuck out past his top jaw. The sergeant looked like he had a comic strip face and when he was mad, his jaw would stick out beyond the chin like Andy Gump or Popeye. He was a heavy drinker and every command carried a new swear word. Anyone who dared so much as to have a smirk on his face, he would be take out of the ranks and make him do 20 push ups and run around two blocks.

The training those 16 weeks was a whirlwind of activity. Every inch of where we went, was with a forced march, we went nowhere by truck. After our morning PT, (physical training) we had classes on the various weapons, and then we had to march out to the field and test fire them. This was repeated until every weapon was learned so well that we could take them all apart blind folded.

We were constantly under harassment from the cadre, who would tell combat stories that would make goose bumps all over your body. He received his jollies in making the troops afraid for what might happen in their future. I believe the only fighting he ever did was in the chow line to fight his way to be the first one in line.

The second 8 weeks we had advanced training that included 75 hours of hand to hand combat training with the bayonets on our rifles. We were trained how to disarm the enemy in hand-to-hand battle. This was good training and I later found it to be most helpful. Through it I've learned to disarm an opponent and found that I needed to use that training sooner than I expected.

The next phase was crawling under a barbed wire obstacle course with live machine guns firing over our heads. This exercise was done after a week of continuous rain. This made the area that we had to crawl under like a muddy cattle yard in the spring of the year. We had to keep our rife clean and in firing condition while going under the barbed wire crawling on our bellies in the mud. No one dared to raise his head or butt out of the mud because we could see the tracer bullets and hear them whiz over our heads.

I stopped once to roll over because my belt wasn't tight enough and I was scooping mud in my shorts. The instant I stopped moving they were hollering at me, "Keep moving foreword; move with out stopping." But I had to stop. The mud was scooping up by my loose belt and it was dragging me deeper and deeper into the mud.

This wasn't an exercise for the faint hearted. It was bad enough to do it on dry ground but try it after a lot of spring rain with all those soldiers crawling; the mud gets deeper until you are in mud up to your elbows. I also later learned that it was not unlike the conditions we faced on line.

Next were the night marches with only a compass and rifle to guide us. We had to find several locations. Every soldier had a different location to find in this wooded area. The day before the instructor attempted to teach us how to use the compass, but he was boring and very dry with his presentation so before he was half way through, most of the class was sleeping.

During the night when we were out in the wooded area we were all given different compass readings. That reading was supposed to get us to an assigned target, and then our final reading would get us to the base camp. Some soldiers were so lost they ended up on an unknown highway and came walking into camp the next day. Those who didn't find their way back to camp in the proper time had to do it all over again.

The second eight weeks also gave us an opportunity to go on week-end passes. That was also an experience for a country boy from Iowa whose biggest event was to go to Riverside Park at Sioux City on the 4th of July.

The nearest town was Junction City, Kansas that was a soldiers' hang out. The streets were alive with drinking establishments, gambling, and prostitution. I believe that town had more corruption per square mile in 1951-52 than any mile in New York or Chicago. The only way to get from the camp to town was by bus. The majority of the soldiers were hung over on the trip home and vomited all over the bus.

I wrote to Dad and explained the condition. He sent a letter back asking if it would help if I had a car at camp. We couldn't have one on base but I could park a car at a gas station on private property.

I soon found out that Manhattan, Kansas was a nice college town and not too far from camp.

The next week we were marching back to camp from a field exercise and my location in the column was that of a road guard. As the troops were crossing the highway my job was to run ahead and stop the traffic. Whose car did I stop so the troops could go across safely? Wow! It was my brothers and Mom in the old 1948 Mercury with a Colombia overdrive. Wow, what a surprise!

They followed the troops to my company. I went in to my sergeant to ask for a pass for a weekend but the 1st sergeant wouldn't let me have a pass.

My brother Dick, who was a WWII Veteran, went in and asked the directions to the Inspector General's Office. The captain said, "What do you want to do that for?" Dick stood right up to him and said, "There is no reason for not giving my brother a pass when he does not have duty this weekend, and his mother is here." The captain gave me a pass for that Saturday and Sunday, but going over the sergeant's head didn't make my life easier with the sergeant.

This was the first and the last legal pass that I had. Any time before, when I left the base, I would sneak out of camp. The car would make it much easier now. We made arrangements with a small oil station just outside the camp to store my car and have it ready on weekends for me.

The first week I went to Manhattan I met a Mrs. Elders at a Methodist church who invited me to Sunday dinner. After dinner she had me drive her around the college campus and other sights around that city. It was like heaven to be with Christian civilians again, away from all that cursing at us. I went to her home any time I was able to sneak off and the weather was too bad to make the trip home for the weekend.

Mrs. Elders had a son in the military in Texas and she said, " If I want someone to treat my son well, then I must treat some other person the way I want my son treated."

Part of the excitement of my time in Fort Riley was sneaking off base. It was like a game and they trained us well, even though the training wasn't intended for us to use it to go AWOL (absent with out leave). To get a pass was impossible because my rifle was rusted and awfully pitted; I never did get that rifle to pass any weekend inspection. Never would the barrel shine no matter how much I worked on it. So I resigned myself to the fact that if I ever was going to get off the base it would be by sneaking off.

One of my area buddies was a sergeant from South Sioux City, Nebraska who wanted a ride home and he would help plan the strategy. This sergeant, who was from a different platoon, was able to find out if we were to have any work duty for the weekend. Then during the week as many of us who could, would get passes and would take off with me to Iowa.

The buddies that bunked around us that didn't have passes, would help make up our bunk to look like someone was sleeping in it. They would take our boots; duffel bag and a stick mop to make up our bed for the bed check. The platoon sergeant would make the rounds with a flashlight every night and do a bed check and look if every bed had a lump in it. Then as soon as bed check was finished they would take the things out of bed and redo it again Sunday night. When we got back late on Sunday night we would sneak back in after our weekend in Iowa.

I always had to have a plan to get our gear to the car that was off base. I needed my shaving kit, dirty laundry and change of clothes. If one of the soldiers had a pass he would take all our gear in a duffel bag, take the bus to the car and wait for us to come. Then when the coast was clear we would sneak out the back door into a large irrigation ditch that they built after the flood. This ditch was deep enough to hide a person and there was some earth moving equipment that was just sitting there. So if we got caught we would climb on the Caterpillar and pretend we were looking it over.

This excuse always worked, mainly because we didn't have anything with us and we were always dressed in our fatigues. As soon as we got to the car we would change clothes in the filling station and take off for our homes in Iowa. Then I would rush to Phyllis's home. This was only the beginning of the extremes risks that I would take so I could get to see the girl with whom I knew I was plunging headlong in love.

Saturday night Mom would faithfully have all my clothing washed and pressed and waiting for me. We would worship together Sunday morning, eat a quick dinner, round up my buddies who came with me, and away we drove like speed demons.

I often wonder, the way we drove, how we made it back to camp. I am sure that the reason for the success of trips home was Mom and Dad's constant prayers for our safety and the Lord must have been sending his guardian angels to protect us.

This fact of my parents praying for me I understood better when we had children that we knew were driving on the highways going back and forth to college.

Our traveling experiences were always full of excitement. In the 1950s, most states had no speed limits except in towns and cities, which we observed religiously. When we traveled open country the speed limit was called reasonable and proper as the legal speed limit. We had a problem in Nebraska. The state patrol and we, never agreed what was reasonable and proper and sure enough we never got across the state without having a bubble flashing a light and a siren behind us. They always gave us one warning ticket. The ticket was given to the driver not the car. So every weekend we would designate a different driver,

That car was geared up for high-speed police work and could go 80 miles per. hour in 2nd gear overdrive. I never found out how fast the car would go in high gear. I believe the car would have been air borne before we reached the limits of its speed. I know why we had every patrolman watching for us. The way that red car streaked by the patrolman was like a bull chasing after a bright red cape.

Even with changing drivers each time, before basic training was completed we had accumulated quite a handful of warning tickets. We didn't fool anyone. The patrolmen especially around Lincoln, Nebraska knew what we were doing.

One cold rainy Saturday we had to march in a parade in the morning and three of us were going to try making a quick trip home. We were still in Kansas and we rode past a hitchhiker. Elmer, a buddy who lives in Jasper, Minnesota was riding with me to see his wife and he said, "Pick up that poor guy." He was wearing an army jacket but was out of uniform with the rest of his clothing.

Our first mistake was to let this guy in the back seat alone when we sat with three of us in the front seat. I took off and was accelerating hard to make up some time lost and looked in the back seat through the center rear view mirror. I saw the hitchhiker put his hand into his inside jacket pocket and I noticed that he was pulling out a pistol.

While I was driving but without giving it a second thought what I was doing, I reached my arm back over the seat and grabbed the pistol, twisted it out of his hand and threw it

98

on the floor in the front. It was loaded so I said, "When I pick up hitch-hikers the first thing I want is their pistol."

Now remember, we just had completed a couple of weeks of hand-to-hand combat, 75 hours of it to be exact. In this training we were taught to disarm our enemy. I realized was that this training caused my impulses to respond automatically. It happened so fast even before my mind let me realize that I should disarm this hitchhiker. To say the least, this hiker was nervous and started to spit and stammer out a lot of excuses, all of which were a bunch of garbage.

We kicked him out of the car and looked at each other a while. It had happened so fast we hardly realized what had happened. We laughed out of fright and nervousness.

Now what do we do with a loaded 45 pistol? What if it was stolen? What if he had already killed someone with it? It might also be so hot that we could spend a lifetime in jail because of it.

Suddenly I started to drive slower. Here we were, soldiers from an army camp who were absent without leave, no papers, and speeding with a hot pistol in the car. We decided that this was not a very good scene if we got caught with this pistol on us. We decided the best thing to do was dispose of the pistol. We determined that it would best to dump the pistol over a bridge into a large stream of water. We threw it so hard that it would bury itself in the mud. So at the next bridge we crossed, that is what we did.

I thought that was the end of the story. But 20 years later my brother-in -law was filling silo with the help of his neighbors, and they were talking about hitchhikers. It so happened that the buddy from Minnesota who rode with us that day, told about this episode of the hitchhiker being disarmed by the driver of that car. Elmer said, "I lost track of that buddy." My brother-in-law said, "What is his name?" Then he told Elmer that the driver of the car married his sister. So subsequently Elmer came over and we had an interesting talk because we hadn't seen each other since our basic training.

On one trip during the spring rains, we turned on the car radio as we started for home and we heard there was a big flood. The Missouri river was wild and over flowing it's banks by a couple miles wide. And all the Missouri River crossings were flooded. This was before the dams were built on the Missouri River to prevent flooding. I soon learned that the bridge at Sioux City was closed.

We stopped at the patrol office even though I had no pass and a bad-driving record. I told them I had an emergency and had to get to Northwest Iowa. Could he route me where I could across the mighty Missouri?

They did some calling around and found that the two-story bridge at Yankton, South Dakota was open on the top deck only, but that the water was going over the road at the bridge approaches.

So we rushed all the way around to Yankton, SD. When I got there my heart sank, because water was not only running fast there, but also it was up to the car floorboards and our feet were touching water.

There were several cars stalled, but my Mercury was a tall one with big white walled tires I don't remember who was with me but I said, "Are you game to try it?" He said, "What do we have to lose, we are going to Korea anyway."

So we slowly crept across the water. We finally made it on the top deck of the bridge but the other side looked worse. Water was all the way around the stores in downtown Yankton. We crept along praying that the car wouldn't get wet or float off the road.

Whew! We made it, with sweaty hands and a lump in my throat that I couldn't seem to swallow.

Love and courtship is a wonderful thing but it doesn't always work smoothly by mail. That was what Phyllis and I were experiencing. We would read into letters-- things that weren't there. We were at this time in some sort of misunderstanding. I knew that no matter what happened, I had to talk to her about it. Never did I see and ride through so much water but there was this love relationship, a broken relationship that needed fixing that was driving me foreword. The next thought was, could we get across the Sioux River? When we got there it was just passable and from there I went to a place called *Perkins Corner* seven miles from my home that was at that time a kids hang out. There I dropped off my passenger whose wife was already waiting to pick him up.

From there I called Mom." Do you want me to bring you the wash before I go to see Phyllis?" Mom thought I was fooling her. She said, "Where are you?" I replied," Perkins Corner." She said, "All the roads are closed, it's impossible."

I said, "But I'm here." Since she knew I wanted to see Phyllis she said, "Then I will do your wash tomorrow morning early." That was the first time I remember Mom ever doing wash on Sunday and I believe also the last. I am sure God forgave her for that one time.

That Saturday night Phyllis and I had a short but very important evening together talking over the misunderstanding. Sunday noon I called to Sioux City. They said emergency traffic was being pulled across but only if it was an emergency.

We rushed to the bridge where the National Guard soldiers were helping only emergency traffic. I went to a corporal standing there and told him the truth that I was AWOL from camp and if I didn't get back I would be in big trouble. He yelled at the captain and said, "These soldiers have an emergency." The captain motioned the amphibian to hook on and they pulled us through the water, all the way past where the Iowa Beef Plant stands today. Water stood on the car floor up to the brake pedal at times. They helped start the car on the other side because it was too wet to start without drying off the points.

I am sure it was love, because no person in his or her right mind would have taken such risks or gone through such extremes if it wasn't love. Oh, by the way, we did patch up our differences that weekend.

Now in a few weeks I would know for sure where the army would send me. Rumors had it that some would go to Germany. We would have to wait for the orders to come out. I hoped I would be a lucky one, it surely is a lot better than the other alternative...Korea. Every day we would train while we waited for our orders to come down.

There were a lot of rumors floating around and those rumors would get to us. It was those days we could feel the pressure mounting, but all the soldiers were carrying a brave front. While we hoped in our heart that they wouldn't send us, yet we knew our training was designed for our tour of duty in Korea.

Whenever we could get near a radio we found it even hard to find a station with up to date events about the Korean War. Yet when we met veterans who just returned from there they talked about the cold freezing winters and the rainy muddy monsoon seasons. The men who were in the infantry talked about the large amount of casualties they suffered.

The lack of news on the radio and the stories from the troops coming back didn't seem to make sense. It didn't seem to be important to the civilians back home. Where was the public support that the soldiers of WW II experienced?

Chapter 7

Harbor lights

The last weeks of basic training went by very fast and as the time drew near for us to receive our orders, it became very evident that there would be only a few who would go anywhere but to Korea. This is what was called the *Korean Police Action.*

As this became more and more apparent, we became more bold, and the more we dared to face the corruption that existed in our company.

At first when we arrived in the basic training company we were told on the first pay day that every soldier would have to do K.P. (kitchen police) and the only soap that we had to do it with would be GI soap (lard & lye base soap) But if everyone would contribute a dollar every month, they would buy detergent soap and life would be easier for everybody. Guess what? Sixteen weeks came and went and we never did get soap in the kitchen. The money was used for cadre parties.

The second rip off was with cadre at the end of the pay line. They would say, "We want you to donate to the Red Cross fund. Where you are going you will need the Red Cross so you better make a sizable donation." Then came the division report what was given to the Red Cross and our company was listed as having given next to nothing.

It was interesting to note that the company officers and cadre were having great weekend parties with money to spare. The average number of soldiers in our company was 240 to 280 men. Now that gave the cadre a good-sized party each month with the so-called *Red Cross Money*.

Another deal that made me very angry was--- the cadre would have some of the trainees clean their quarters, polish their shoes and wash their cars in exchange for weekend passes.

I, a country boy, was not going to stoop so low as to bribe my way out on a pass, but these guys received and parceled out passes that belonged to all the troops instead of to the few who did favors. So because of my principles I didn't get a pass, but my system of sneaking through the drainage ditch to get off the base worked quite well too.

The last thing that broke the camels back as far as I was concerned was that on the last day, we were promised that when we were through cleaning all our equipment, those who passed inspection would get a pass. Well, here I am with that rifle again and that rifle wouldn't pass inspection no matter what I did to it.

The word also got to me that when we received our rifle, we all signed for **"a rifle complete,"** which meant in the butt of the rifle was a combination tool and oil case. The supply sergeant took them all out, hid them in a box and charged everybody $5.85, payable in cash because they said we lost the combination tool and oil case. This was another cash rip off that our unit officers pulled off.

The plan was for us Sioux County boys, who were all going home together, to have our gear loaded up in my Mercury. After my rifle had cleared inspection, we were to gather in a building to get our orders and our tickets to our new duty station and get home as fast as we could. Well, they told me to turn my rifle into supply. There they hit me for $ 5.85 cash for a tool and oil case. I said, "I am sorry, there wasn't any in here when I got it" and he showed me my signature to *Rifle Complete.* "Now pay up," he said, "You lost it, pay up or you don't leave this post."

That did it. I blew up. "No way, I am sick and tired of this outfit's corruption. Before I pay you $5.85 I am going to the inspector general and tell him about your soap deal, and the way this outfit skims off the Red Cross funds." Needless to say, he was all shook up when I talked about the soap money, he let me go, but that wasn't the end of it. My Sioux County buddies had the car all loaded and waiting at the assembly room where we were to get our orders, travel tickets and money. This place was three blocks from where I turned in my rifle.

When I got there, my buddy Willard was waiting at the door to give me the keys to the car. I said to him, "Do you have the car locked up?" He said "No." So I ran and shut the windows and locked the doors and ran back to where the troops were gathering.

As I was going in the building the captain grabbed me by the shoulders and said, "Soldier, *YOU HAVE BEEN DRINKING* and I want you to sober up real good and I'll keep you here for a week to scrub those four barracks. Then you ought to be sober enough to go to your new unit station without a leave."

How the supply sergeant got to the old man so quickly I will never understand. But he was after me. I said, "But sir, I never drink liquor, nor did I now." He said, "I saw that you went to the car and you have been nipping. It is too dangerous to let you drive that way."

The providence of God was on my side. Along came the sergeant that I always took to South Sioux City when we went home. I said, "Sergeant, come here." He said, "Van what's up?" I said, "The captain is accusing me of drinking and being drunk. I am being falsely charged. Will you testify that I never drink liquor? If the captain detains me, will you go to the IG (inspector general) for me?"

"Sure I will," said the sergeant. The captain was red with anger and said, "All right get in the building, but let me warn you, one miss move and Ill have your *###* rear end." Whew! That was a close call.

When we left with our orders and travel money I said, "One of you drive, I am still shaking and be careful until we get off base."

It wasn't until we got off base and riding safely towards home that I looked at my orders. The orders read: **"Report to a camp in Seattle Washington, May 1, for debarkation to Korea."** Then it hit me that in two weeks I would be heading to a war zone.

The time at home was one of all kinds of mixed emotions. My dad's health was deteriorating and he was positive that this was the last we would see each other on this earth. It was an issue that Dad could talk about but with some emotion. I knew it was difficult for him because whenever he got excited he stuttered a lot. But for Mom it was almost impossible to face the possibility that she would lose her beloved husband and have her last born overseas in battle. Mother always managed to picture the worst probability and that thought was too much for her, so she left the room when Dad talked about his impending departure.

The time that Phyllis and I had together was limited because she was preparing for graduation from Western Christian High School in May 1952. Explaining the feelings we had during the time together is not an easy matter. Phyllis had the excitement of upcoming graduation and preparing to go to Grand Rapids, MI. to Calvin College and the hope of an exciting future.

I was full of the sober reality that my future was not going to be too bright. My training was in hand-to-hand combat in an infantry company, and that was a sobering thought.

These emotions were miles apart. I wanted to share in her excitement, she wanted to comfort my fears and for the two emotions to blend together was an impossibility. Even though we cared for each other a lot we had a lot of hurdles to cross before we could say we understood each other's emotions. Even though we tried to understand, the reality was entirely different.

When I was to say good-bye my heart was broken because I knew that things would never be the same again. If I were to return, would I be able to adjust to the changes that would happen while I was gone? There would be changes in both my parents and what Phyllis and I had together. Would that survive the time apart?

The bus ride to Seattle went quite well until we got to Butte, Montana. The Greyhound bus drivers went on strike. The bus company was one of many other industries that were on strike. Here we were, without a lot of money, walking the streets. I doubt if you could call what we were walking on, streets. This western mining town's streets were a far cry from streets, as we knew them.

When we were walking towards the town, a limousine pulled along side of us and a well-dressed man wearing a cowboy hat stepped out and said, "Boys where are you going?" We answered, "Nowhere the way it looks." We then told him about the bus strike and that we were going to Korea. He appeared to feel sorry for us and looked as though he was truly friendly. He then invited us into his limousine. After we were in, he told the driver to take him home. This man's home was a mansion on a large hill. Before he left the limousine he handed a bag of silver to the driver and said, "Take them out to see the silver mine, feed them, show them a good time and get them some lodging for tonight. Then tomorrow put them on the train that will take them to Seattle."

That night we had thick steaks, a nice hotel room, a good breakfast and a ride in a limousine to the train station. We learned the man was an owner of a silver mine. He arranged for our tickets and off we went by train to our camp, ever so grateful for the kindness shown to us by that stranger.

We also had a bus agent's signature stating why we were late coming into camp. Who paid for the train ride I don't know, but every thing else the owner of the mine paid for with the silver he gave to the driver.

We arrived at the army camp and found that the camp was nicknamed *The Snake Pit* and we soon knew why. The barracks were all temporary, arranged on wooden posts.

There was nothing at the camp that was pretty, but there were billions of dandelions in full bloom. With a camp full of soldiers with nothing to do while they waited for their ship, the army chose for us to pick all those dandelions every day. While we waited for our ship assignment we would daily check if our name was listed on the bulletin board for our departure time.

The list with my name finally came. I would be boarding the liberty ship, called *Pvt. Joe Martinez*. Now that I had my orders and date that we would be leaving, I wasn't in the mood to pick dandelions. How can I beat the system? Where can I go? I am sick and tired of picking dandelions.

I remember sitting on a ridge watching the sun go down and Seattle lights come on. There on the other side was the bay and beyond it the harbor and it's lights. My thoughts weren't there. As I sat there the words of the current popular song came to mind. I hummed the tune over and over again.

* One evening long ago, a big ship was leaving.
One evening long ago, two lovers were grieving,
A crimson sun went down, the lights began to
glow across the harbor one evening long ago.
Chorus
I saw the Harbor Lights;
They only told me we were parting,
The same old Harbor Lights
That once brought you to me
I watched the Harbor Lights
How could I help if tears were starting?
Good-bye to tender nights

Beside the silvery sea.

I longed to hold you near and kiss you just once more,

But you were on the ship and I was on the shore,

Now I know lonely nights

For all the while my heart is whispering

Some other Harbor Lights will steal your love from me.

* Written by *Jimmy Kennedy and Hugh Williams and published by Chappel & Co. New York in 1937

I repeated those words over and over again. I remember being on the ridge alone, with the camp below with its noise and circles of card players. The night was so quiet except for those who were playing cards and an occasional frog making a croaking sound.

But slowly the lights in the barracks started to go out and everybody was in bed. Then it hit me like a bomb. The time I have left in this my beloved country would be less than a week. Then what? I was going to the unknown.

My thoughts were racing all over the place as the camp became very quiet and in one week and I would be out of touch with my dear ones.

The moon was now shining on me brightly, and I remember that was the first time my emotions got the best of me. I had carried a big front all the time but tonight I choked while sitting on that ridge under the moon. I cried. Was I home sick, was I afraid, or was it self-pity? Was it those good-byes, the lights, the song, the moon? Yep, it was a little of all of these. I knew that I couldn't go to the barracks with red eyes.

111

So under the stars that night I felt like Jacob of the Old Testament on the stone at Bethel. I looked up at the moon again. It was now deathly quiet except for the singing of the crickets and the splash of the fish. The moon was smiling at me. This was the same moon that my parents were watching and the same moon Phyllis and I watched during our last evening together. We weren't separated. We had things in common: the same moon, the same God who hears and answers prayers was watching all of us.

That night was my Bethel where I knew that there was much more than an intellectual knowledge of God. My parents' prayers were answered that night as the moon was winking at me, telling me that God was with me.

The Scriptures that I remembered from the time when I was young came back to me, and even though the night air of early spring was cold I felt warm all over my body. I remember winking back at the moon as I headed for the barracks. I said to myself, "Tomorrow I am not going to get depressed if I have to pick those dandelions for an additional day. That night I slept like a log and before I knew it there was a sergeant with fat cheeks and with a whistle in his mouth, trying to wake us up.

At breakfast that morning I met a soldier from South Dakota and we talked about picking dandelions. He said, "I sure hate to do that for a week." So we decided to sneak off the base by crawling 75 feet straight down some tree roots that were bordering the bay side of the camp. Now if we could get down those roots we could walk along the bay and not be spotted.

My sleeping quarters already had roll call before breakfast so that was all the accounting they would require until the next morning.

As we were walking along the shoreline feeling as free as a bird, I spotted a sign just around the bend. It read, "RENT- A- BOAT- CLUB." We went to check it out.

"What do you guys want?" We stammered back, "We want to rent a boat for a day. What do you get for a small boat and motor rental for a day?" Thirty dollars." was the reply. "Do you have some fishing gear that you can throw in?" So he filled up the boat with gas and gave us some extra in a can and off we went, leaving a trail of blue smoke.

Here we were, two green horns with no life jackets and not able to swim a stroke. That described me, and believe me the other fellow knew even less than I did. Off we were to a day of adventure that turned out to be an experience that we would never forget.

We took the boat far enough away from camp so that nobody would see us. The water was calm and without a ripple. My partner for today (I didn't even know his name), decided to do some fishing. While he was fishing I decided it was such a beautiful day that it would be a good time to get in a few ZZZs. Because of my late night up, I was tired and sleepy. I pulled my fatigue cap over my eyes to block out the world and was soon off to slumber land.

After what took place last night, it felt so good to rest without anyone yelling at me and I was really sleepy. The last I heard him say was, "This sure beats picking up dandelions."

Somewhere along the way my buddy didn't catch fish so he fell off to sleep too. How long we slept I don't know.

Suddenly I felt that we were rocking like a cradle but not as gentle as one. Looking up and around I didn't see shore. There were high waves all around us getting rougher and rougher. I woke up my buddy and said, "Do you know where we are?" "No." he said, and his face turned white as a ghost.

My training came back to me and I said, "The sun is on that side and it is 3 o'clock so camp is that way." I hung onto the boat with one hand and with the other hand I tried to start the motor. The stupid motor just sputtered but wouldn't start. I found pliers and I reached over to turn the spark plug out. I got it out, and while I was wiping it off with my shirt a wave came along and water went down the spark plug hole. The only thing to do now was to row and keep the boat in line with the waves. But we seemed to be going out further and further from any sight of land.

We were going nowhere fast and becoming worse off by the second. Rowing didn't work because we kept going backwards no matter how hard I rowed.

What are two stupid country kids doing in an ocean without supervision? We were in the same predicament that the disciples were in on the Sea of Galilee when they cried, *"Lord save us lest we drown."* That incident from the scriptures was on my mind. But would the Lord calm these large waves?

My long distance sight has never been the best, but my buddy thought he spotted a boat pulling skiers where we thought the shore was. The boat appeared to be circling around with skiers behind it. So we got the idea to take my tee shirt

114

off, tie it on the oar and while I held my friend, he began to swing the oar with the tee shirt. Finally the boat stopped and we could see it as a speck on the horizon and it was gone. Our hopes were lost.

What a way to go, drowned in the ocean and no trace of any bodies. Who will know what happened to us? Did we pray? I don't know about my buddy but I sure did. I also remembered what the Lord said when the disciples were in a boat when a storm hit them on the Sea of Galilee. *"Oh ye of little faith"* Jesus said to his disciples, and so it was with us out on that stormy sea in that little rowboat.

"Do I see something?" asked my buddy. I thought, "He is so scared he is seeing things." But no, it was true. A boat was coming toward us with high speed, waves spraying all over it and we were breathing a little easier.

The boat coming toward us was a coast guard cutter with a bunch of sailors on it. When they came near, they came to us slowly so as not to capsize us.

The captain hollered, "What's the trouble, can't you guys get back to the bay? Are you guys in trouble?" We told him, "The motor won't start; it's one from the RENT A BOAT CLUB by the camp. We confessed that we were AWOL because were tired of picking dandelions every day, and that we had played hooky to get away from the camp. "We are both going to Korea next week if we ever get out of here."

He threw us two life jackets and said, "Can you hold out a few minutes while we get a new motor for that boat?" We said we would try, but the bottom of the boat had already started sloshing water back and forth. The *Coast Guard* shot away, water spraying in all directions. It seemed to us that it took eternity for them to get back to our boat.

We were so scared our hands were sore of holding on and we were lying down to keep the boat from capsizing. They brought us a motor, held our boat against their big boat and put on the motor.

The sailor said, "You drifted out here because the tide went out and you could never row against that." He started the motor and said, "Follow us." They broke the waves for us and when we got to calmer water they hollered, "Have a good tour of duty in Korea."

When we got back inside the bay and the calm water it was for me the same as when Jesus said to the disciples, *"Peace be still."* He didn't calm the waters, but he brought us into the calm seas and we were thankful that our lives were spared.

We brought the boat back. Then began the hard climb up those tree roots. After what we been through, climbing up those tree roots was a piece of cake. We made it for chow that evening. My friend, while sitting at the table, said that he decided picking dandelions wasn't so bad after all.

This was going to be my last Friday night in the States. I wanted to see Phyllis' sister and a cousin who were teaching at Mount Vernon, Washington.

If I would use the tree roots as my route of escape again maybe I could get to a bus depot, spend some time with her sister and come back Sunday evening.

Now what could happen to me if I got caught? Lets see, they say, "We'll take a stripe away if you go over the hill." That they couldn't do because rank was frozen so I had none to take away.

If I got caught they could send me to Korea, so what's the big deal. I am going AWOL (Absent Without Leave) to see Phyllis's sister. It all worked like a charm. I got off the base and found a ride to down town, went to the bus station and caught the next bus out.

I found Phyllis's sister and her cousin, who were roommates in Mt. Vernon Washington. We all went to church together Sunday. A member of the church, a former veteran, gave us his old car, which was a 1946 Dodge. So the three of us drove to and around Seattle. That evening they took me right through the front gate without any problems getting in. I realized how much I needed to get away from that *Snake Pit* for the weekend.

Tuesday we had armed forces day. They were having tours of the camp so that was why we were daily on dandelion detail.

This was also the day I was to load on the ship for Korea. The loading area was not a place for a romantic send off but the dirty old docks were the last things we saw of the good old continental USA.

It was painful to say "so long" to those harbor lights and the country that I was leaving. It would be 14 of the longest months that I would ever experience. Little did I know that what I would encounter would change my life forever. It was a blessing that I was spared from any knowledge of what I was to go through in the months ahead.

When we left sight of the shore on that small liberty ship, we soon found out that it was like a bathtub converted to carrying far more troops then it was designed to have on it.

We all stood outside watching those harbor lights disappear in the distance. That really made the words of that song become authentic. How little did I realize how much I would long to see the shores of my country again.

Yes, this was my country that called me to fight, to protect the freedom of South Korea from Marxist aggression.

Yes, we needed to protect people I didn't know. Praise the Lord I didn't know how much physical and emotional pain would be squeezed into the next 14 months. Maybe if I did they would never have been able to pull me off that ship.

Chapter 8

Storm at Sea

SPLISH SPLASH. ROCK and ROLL

On board the ship, the first thing we were given was an assignment number. That would give us everything we would need while we were on board. The first number was the deck level. The second number was the time our group would receive our meal. The third and fourth numbers were the row of bunks that we were in, and the fifth number was what height our bunk was off the ground. First we had to find our deck, our area, and then our row. It was like following a mouse maze, everybody running through each other.

I thought the army was mismanaged. But this was an old tub they call a liberty ship managed by the Merchant Marines. The ship was used as a freighter and converted to a troop ship. It wasn't designed for troops, but by bolting poles upright, they could then hang beds on these poles, six beds with one above the other. The ship could then be called a troop ship.

My bunk was way up on number five on the pole with one more above me and the distance between the bunks was so small that if we laid on our back we couldn't put our knees up or we would push the person above us in the back. The person above me was from Shakersville, Ohio. He was from parents who were very rich and had a lot of culture. I soon discovered that he was even more scared of being on the ship than I was, if that were possible.

We both were on our first big ride and it didn't appear like we were going to enjoy it especially after my experience with boats at the *Snake Pit*. The ride on the ship didn't seem like it would be any worse then the thought of not knowing what we faced upon leaving the ship; that had no appeal either.

The person from Ohio was the first person with whom I was able to talk boldly about my faith in God. As you may remember I had made a stand for Christ some time earlier. Here on that long voyage I had an opportunity to share my faith with someone who was facing death without hope for eternity.

This new friend would talk about what would happen to us if we were killed in battle. This gave me a chance to share what I believed, how that Christ died for me, that he would give me eternal life and that my death would not be death but be everlasting life, and that all believers and I would be united with Christ in heaven.

Other than our discussion, it was a rather uneventful day on the ship with a lot of irritation-- standing in line three hours to get dinner, that was a plate of beans and a dry piece of bread.

We could see that the officers and ship personnel had fruit and ice cream and a bun with meat on it, as well as our usual beans.

It took six hours of our day standing in line to get our two meals a day. It took us an hour to find the toilets. After getting there, we stood behind seven or eight guys that were ahead of us all staggering like drunken sailors.

The toilets were forward in the ship and towards the end of that second day it was getting rough riding. Taking a step towards the urinal, one would have to hold fast because all the soldiers were so sick that they vomited their beans on the floor before they got to the urinal or stool.

Now for a land lover who had never been on a ship, it wasn't getting any easier. The public address system would use the words that had no meaning to me like, starboard, aft, stern and galley. These were all strange terms to most of us.

The word came down the public address system that we were going to prepare for a storm and everything by our bunks would have to be "buttoned down." I finally realized they meant "tied down" when they said "buttoned down." I thought it was bad already and the storm had not yet begun.

They were calling up guys for various duties and my name came up just when a soldier came back from duty where he had to clean up toilets. They finally sent him back to the bunk because he was contributing more than he was cleaning up. I was scared to death that they wanted me to take his place.

So when I got to the officer in charge I said that I would like to volunteer for guard duty. The reason I wanted to do that was because cleaning toilets wasn't for me.

"Well," he said, "Van, you will get a four hour shift starting at midnight. Your duty station will be the kitchen proper where the stoves are. It will be fire and safety guard duty." "Piece of cake," I thought. Surprise!

The storm hit at it's worse about 10 o'clock that evening and we had to hold on to the bunk to keep from being bucked out. It was like sitting on a rodeo horse.

121

Needless to say the whole sleeping quarters became one big toilet. Midnight came and I managed to get my clothing on. Then on hands and knees I got to the steps and worked my way up to the kitchen to my guard station. When I got there, I found that the person I was supposed to relieve was already gone so I went into the kitchen.

When I walked through the door of the kitchen, I fell on my bottom and went sliding back and forth in bacon grease that had been rendered out the night before for the morning breakfast. The grease was in a round sunken pot in the stove and with all the swaying the pot tipped and the grease poured out onto the deck.

This was joined by a hundred pounds of potatoes that broke out of the sack and were all rolling in this grease as well as most of the pots and pans.

Here I was on hands and knees on the deck trying to get up while covered with bacon grease. The potatoes, pots and pans in the kitchen were all-sliding back and forth on the floor along with the grease and potatoes.

It was literally splash, splash, rock and roll, back and forth, and sideways like a tilt-a whirl at the fair, but this one wouldn't quit. When I finally slid to the doorway again I grabbed the doorpost and hung on for dear life. I pulled myself out of the kitchen. I had already lost my cookies twice in this ordeal.

Was I ever a mess! Grease from head to toe.

I said to myself "What am I doing here?" I was heaving until nothing would come anymore. I was attempting to leave-- figuring the worst they could do to me was to send me to Korea if I got caught. At the ladder by the hatch there was a big navy person trying to shut a hatch that was breaking loose. He opened it up to slam it shut, when along came a big wave and soaked us before he got it shut.

A couple of flights of steps below, a soldier was trying to sleep on the top bunk and when the wave came in, it hit him full blast. He grabbed his life jacket and up the steps he came hollering, "We're sinking, we're sinking!" Like a wild man he flew past me.

The big navy guy who was on the top step grabbed him before this soldier could open the hatch. The sailor said, "Help me hold him down or he'll get the hatch open and we'll all drown." It took us a while to calm him down and get him to understand that we weren't sinking but water was rushing over the decks because of the waves.

I sat my entire time on guard duty on the steps trying to get control of my stomach. The air was much better by the hatch than in the bunk on top of a pole in quarters where every one was vomiting. The storm lasted for three days but that night was the worst. The reports from the ship's newspaper were that the ship made no progress for three days and during that time the captain had turned the ship into the storm in order to weather the 40 to 50 foot waves that accompanied the storm.

To our surprise this storm happened when we were not very far from Adak, Alaska.

We were told that we would stop and refuel, that the port there was full of lonely Eskimo women and that we would find one behind every tree. It was announced that the soldiers who wished to go ashore could do so.

My stomach was still very sore so I chose to stay aboard. There was not a tree on the island, only rocks. So those who signed up to go on shore were put into formation and were to run as fast as they could up and down the barren streets, all in formation. Those who left the ship had to board the ship again without ever stopping to see anything and they were really mad about that. We were there for five hours to load up some supplies because we lost three days in the storm.

The rest of the trip was a piece of cake. The main problem was that it took us, what seemed forever to get the ship clean. We never did get the smell out of those bunks. The sleeping quarters always smelled of vomit and sweaty bodies.

On this ship we had no sweet water to wash or take a bath, we only had a limited supply of sweet water to drink. Salt water causes the dirt to roll up on your skin and the more soap you use the more your body feels like it's covered with rubber and dirt.

I visited with a merchant marine on the ship. He told me that last trip they hauled was a load of weapons and ammunition that was made in the United States, picked up in Great Britain and unloaded in Hong Kong.

They had been hauling used rifles and military equipment that was sold by someone in Great Britain to be delivered to North Korea to fight against us. This was the equipment we were to face later.

The army had told us that the North Koreans captured these US weapons from wounded and killed Americans. I knew better. North Korea got their American made equipment from our friends who were making a profit at our expense.

I thanked this person for his encouragement. He said, "This is the difference between this war and *World War II*. There, it was everybody against the enemy and here, anybody who could make a profit would do so at the expense of American lives."

One morning we heard a bunch of noise out side and rumors were flying that someone saw land. We began to see some smaller fishing boats with Japanese fisherman so this was a sign we must be going to Japan.

We finally did land at *Yokohama Harbor* where we were met with trucks and army busses that took us to a compound where we were processed for our trip to Korea. We spent a week getting our personal rifles, the big old M-1 rifle.

Also, our shot records were brought up to date. Those who had poor teeth had them pulled. We were issued helmets and bayonets and had to turn in all class A dress clothing. I am convinced that later those who were going back to the States picked up these uniforms.

We were all outfitted with backpacks, bedrolls, duffel bags, some blankets and some overshoes. No one was permitted to call anyone, or leave our barracks.

Then one night we loaded up in a ship and were off to Korea. We were to land at *Inchon* near *Seoul*, but because of a possible lack of security once we landed, they took us to the southernmost port of *Pusan*.

There we were ordered to put on our combat boots because it was rainy season, and anyone who had any extra gear should dispose of it. We were to disembark the ship over the side, climbing down nets into the landing crafts. While at

Yokohama, Japan they briefed us on what to expect, but I wasn't prepared for what we were to see as we got off the ship and on the land.

It was the beginning of the rainy season or monsoons, and it was raining quite hard. The ship had to be unloaded with two landing crafts. The docks were being used to unload other ships with war supplies. The process took about seven hours.

We were then assigned to our company assembly area that was running in mud and water and human waste coming from the hillsides and about to the top of our boots. There we stood, for hours in running sewage water. All that time we were holding the duffel bag with all our worldly possessions and our blankets, with full field pack that included our rifle.

There was no place where we could set our duffel bags down. The streets were full of sewage and wall-to-wall water. As long as we had any strength we would keep our belongings out of the filthy water.

On one side of us was a tumbled down old storefront and looking out the window with broken panes was a *mamason (a Korean term that we used for mamma)* without a blouse on. A boy was standing next to her nursing from the mother. The boy, at least six years old was standing right up to his mother looking at us with his eyes on us and holding a nipple in his mouth at the same time.

The first ones off the ship stood in that sewage for seven hours. We were told we were waiting for a train. After standing that long, and no train in sight, we were ready to take the landing craft by force and load back onto the ship. At first sight none of us believed that this country was worth saving.

It didn't take long and we started to chant, "Load us back on the boat and get us out of here." I had to wait to load on the train four hours. Those who waited seven hours finally had to drop their bags in the sewage and let everything inside get dirty. I won't even mention what some of the soldiers from big cities were saying. The paper of this book would burn up if I printed it.

When the train finally came, the officers had a tough time keeping order. Everybody was wet, dirty, tired and angry. Everyone wanted to hurry onto the train for a nine-hour ride to the staging area near the front line, thinking at least the nine hours would be better.

We had no idea what the train ride would be like. We were expecting the same type trains like we had in the United States, troop trains. This was considerably different, which we would soon find out.

Chapter 9

Terrors of Old Baldy

When we got on the train we had a big surprise. It was a very narrow train with wooden seats. On the seats there was room for only two persons on each side of the narrow aisle.

When we got in them they were so low to the ground that our knees stuck out with no legroom in front of us, so everybody with long legs had them all curled up. To make matters worse the one person sitting on the inside had to have a part of their ham sticking in the aisle because there wasn't room on the seat. Now we are wondering, what do we do with those wet duffel bags?

The conductor said, "No bags in the aisle." Either they had to be under the seat, or on our lap with us. I looked at the fellow next to me and said, "There isn't room for both of our bags underneath so one of us must have one on the lap." So we worked out a deal. The person sitting on the inside near the window had his bag on the lap because his one ham wasn't sticking over in the aisle. We agreed to change places every hour so we would be able endure the long ride.

It didn't take long after the train started for the guys to really grumble about our accommodations. Everyone in the whole rail train car was complaining.

About that time a sergeant, whom I never met before, got tired of all the complaining and he said, "AT EASE. I want to remind you it doesn't get better than this. Before this week is out you'll be wishing you had a set of wheels under you." I found out this sergeant was wounded and was coming back to the line from Japan to join his unit.

Do you know what? He was right on target. How we wished many times for any ride, even if it had square wheels.

We rode the train most of the night and saw Korean beggars along side of the tracks everywhere. They would run after anything that was thrown out, always looking for a bite to eat. We then saw what the real effects of war are like on children. They were cold, hungry and lacking adequate clothing and housing.

Very early in the morning we arrived at *Second Infantry Division Headquarters*. This would be my division that was called the *Indianhead Division*. I was assigned to the *23rd Infantry Regiment, Easy Company*. What a laugh to call it *Easy Company*. In an infantry no company is an easy company.

It didn't take long for rumors to fly. They were separating all those who were friends and those who came from the same area into different units. So my close buddies were all separated.

Word was out that we would have a week or two at the most, and then we would go to *Old Baldy*. It was said to be the place where the most activity was immediately developing on the line.

Suddenly one morning, I don't remember the date because every day ran through each other; we were all rushed out of our tents, and put on a road with all our stuff in one long line for a special inspection.

Slowly the word came down that the colonel from the Regimental commands was blown up in his bed by a shape charge that was located under his bed. The *Military Intelligence* was being flown in to hunt for clues and find the guilty person.

We stayed on one spot for three days with one meal a day of old C rations while they went through our stuff with a fine tooth comb hunting for clues, and for the person who was so angry at the colonel that he would blow him up.

Rumor had it that he had pushed around some of the men too far and someone became angry and decided to blow him up. I don't believe they ever did find who did it and the colonel was considered a war casualty.

We got a new colonel whose name was *Joseph W. Stilwell.* He was a grandson of the old *Vinegar Joe Stilwell* of WW II. The colonel took each soldier by the hand, looked him in the eye with a piercing look, and said, "Welcome on board." He shook hands with every soldier and gave each person a blue silk scarf. He let us know he expected us to fight to the last man. But he wasn't going to pick on anyone, and everyone would be treated fairly. He truly was a tough fighting man who later started the green berets fighting unit in Vietnam. I believe he got killed there.

We soon learned, when in combat, arguments were settled in the dark with a rifle bullet in the back or a hand grenade thrown at you. We had the most trouble with those who came to us from the *States* and had gained their rank with a college degree. Then they were given a short basic training and were sent to us green as grass. We called them, *"90 Day Wonders."* Their training never taught them the principle of how to treat soldiers like humans, because if you don't, you yourself will go home in a basket. They would treat the men under them like children because while they were in training, and they received their 2nd Lieutenant bars, they themselves were treated the same way. You can imagine how that went over with seasoned combat veterans. I will try to tell you about that later but now I must get back to my platoon at *Easy Company*.

The first two weeks after we arrived, the company time was spent learning to work together as a company, platoon, and squad.

Let me break away from my story to explain how the military infantry company was structured during the Korean War. I'll start with the level of a squad. The squad is generally composed of 9-12 men with one of them being the leader, and one an assistant squad leader with a possible rank of sergeant and corporal. There are four squads of about 9-12 men each in a platoon with one squad of the four being the heavier weapons squad. A 1st or 2nd lieutenant generally led these platoons of about 40-48 persons. The assistant leader is generally sergeant first class. Four platoons make a company led by a captain. These three companies make up a battalion. Three battalions make up a regiment, and three regiments compose a division. Those are the figures as I remember them.

The tactics used in Korea were to have each battalion unit place two units up front on line, and one unit in reserve in training in case of an enemy break through. Then the reserve unit would fill in the spot.

Our battalion was in reserve to fill in their ranks with new recruits. When we joined it, we were given training to work as a unit. Day after day and night after night we would have a hill we would have to pretend to take from the enemy, using live ammo, working as squads to move up on the enemy.

This was hard work because I was placed in the fourth squad and was assigned to a machine gun. I was the gunner and was responsible to set up supporting fire as the other three squads moved up. Then they would set up supporting fire so our three man machine gun crew could move forward to set up their supporting fire again.

Our training went very well because we all had sixteen weeks of basic, training and at this point there was no enemy shooting back at us, nor any artillery dropping shells in our back pockets.

I wasn't too excited about being a machine gunner because the word is that the life expectancy of a machine gunner in battle isn't in hours, the life expectancy is only minutes. I had excellent men on my machine gun crew and at times our crew had two Korean ammunition carriers. They joined our squad when we lost a lot of soldiers on *Old Baldy*.

At that time I couldn't speak a word of Korean and they knew no English but they understood the word "chow." To make matters worse at that time, I didn't trust them and I couldn't distinguish them from the enemy in the dark. Their names were Kim Do Chun and Lee Hi Mien. I later came to accept them as fellow soldiers.

I certainly wished that I would have had some training and understanding of their culture before we were tossed together like we were. Living in the same foxhole, eating from the same chow and sharing one sleeping bag with two foreigners were not easy adjustments.

After we did squad tactics all day, we would use our nights to train on how to maintain our machine guns. First, we would replace the barrels in the dark and adjust headspace. This is done so that when the barrel gets hot it doesn't jam the gun. Then we would take the gun all apart and repair it blind folded. I worked and worked at it until the assistant gunner and I had the ability to assemble all the parts of our machine gun blindfolded. Little did I realize that this training would have so much importance in our survival before the week was over.

By the way, when we weren't on line at this time we lived in 12-14 person squad tents. Of course we had no electricity and we had bottles and cases of the chemical DDT in oil suspension for mosquitoes.

So the soldiers improvised light in the tent by cutting up old socks, putting the strips of socks into the bottle of oil based DDT and light them for candles. We always had to hide the light from being recognized in case of air attack, so the tent flaps had to go down to hide the light and we would choke in that DDT smoke. This was the only light by which we could write letters and do any personal things. Now, do I need to wonder why I have a lot of difficulty with my breathing? Maybe all that DDT contributed to my losing some lung capacity.

I am sure it never did our bodies any good inhaling those DDT vapors. We also had to strip entirely every week and get sprayed with DDT to rid our bodies of lice that the Koreans carried with them. When they went home they would come back to camp with body lice on them. I believe all that DDT did have some lasting effect on our health.

It seemed strange to me and causes me to wonder about the fact that the American agriculture department would not permit the use of the DDT on farm animals but the Army was using it on our troops.

To help keep the lice down we would also cut our hair often. This was accomplished by forming a buddy system. "If you cut my hair, I will cut yours," and most of the time it was far from a professional haircut, but we got by.

Early one morning as we went for chow we noticed they were digging in poles for volleyball nets. There was also a notice posted that the *Protestant* and the *Catholic Chaplains* were going to hold services on the grounds at 0800 hours. Now that was strange. Chaplains never showed up on base and our chapel services were held only on Sunday. Then the Sunday services were always held at Battalion or Division Headquarters in the rear. At the service I soon learned from the manner of the Chaplain's prayers that we were going to be moving into a very hot spot on line.

Now I became aware of the reality of it all. This war was beginning to stare in the face. We were beginning to understand what I had trained for since Dec. 5, 1951. But I had no idea of the impact and the effect the killing and injuring of other humans beings would have on my life. These were individuals and people that I didn't even know, or for that matter didn't even hate.

I was one who was trained as a child not even to think about killing. Would I now be able to go against everything I was taught?

On the day of July 16, 1952, " This is a day for you to enjoy yourself," was the Captain's announcement at breakfast, "Volley ball games, relaxing or do whatever you wish to do. You will all be on *Company Street* at 1400 hours (2 o'clock) for additional announcements." I wrote letters to my folks, to Phyllis and to friends that morning because I knew it would be some time before I would be able to write letters again.

You guessed it, the announcement at 2 o'clock was, "Pack your gear, and strike tents, we will be moving to an unknown assembly area." We were to be loaded on trucks just before it was dark. We had to leave our duffel bags behind and we carried only the minimum of gear.

Down the road we went, on dusty trucks, bouncing towards the noise of exploding shells and flashing lights. We unloaded in a clearing where the trucks could turn around and we watched them leave. We had the same feeling inside that a child has when their parents desert them.

Then we started walking up the road and as soon as it was dark, moved forward in staggered columns trudging forward, with none of the foot soldiers being in a hurry. The officers tried to keep us moving at a fast pace so the transfer could be made before the morning sun would give away our troop movements and positions.

We could all hear the noise of the artillery shells as they were leaving the tubes. Then a short time later we could hear them explode and see the flash of lights. This was the real thing, no more war games. These people are out to kill us.

Get that in your head, this isn't the Iowa farm noise. It isn't a *Police Action* like President Truman says it is. This is pure and simple war. That saying was only a Presidential cover up for entering into war without congressional approval.

We could feel in our hearts the tension building up, the pounding was getting faster and the breathing was getting heavier. I was breathing in short fast breaths. Why do I have sweaty hands and forehead, I remember thinking and yet the night air was cool? Everybody was quiet, only the sergeant gave commands and those feet kept shuffling onward over each hill bringing us closer and closer.

The field packs and our rifles we were carrying were heavy, as well as our machine guns that were broken down in three pieces to make them easier to carry. All that weight being carried for several miles and all that gear, was beginning to weigh like a ton of bricks on our backs.

I remember climbing up a steep ridge and passing out momentarily with some of my buddies helping me up and carrying some of my load.

Things were different now then when we were in basic training. We were a unit and we were all buddies and every body now was looking out for each other. We were not individuals like in basic training. On the front line our survival depended on teamwork. Our welfare also depended on how well our teammates performed. Any break down meant a hole in the defenses, and endangered the rest of the platoon.

Under the cover of darkness, we were slowly moving into our positions. All the jeeps we met were driving in the dark; so dark they could only see a few feet in front of themselves.

There we were, finally at the base of the main line of resistance. Our platoon leader was a lieutenant and a good person. He stopped us and said, "This is it, and you have worked, played and prayed together, now we have a job to do. Let's do it to the best of our ability, good luck, and God bless each one of you."

The platoon sergeant took a US dollar bill, broke it into 48 pieces, gave each one of us in the platoon a piece and said, "Now it in your responsibility to bring it back when we come off the line into reserve. We will have a party and those without the piece of the dollar bill will pay for it.

July 17 and 18, 1952 is a date that I will not forget. Usually the days were a blur as far as the progression of time-- one day ran into the next. But those two days would dramatically change the way I looked at life.

The squad leader took each of us to our fighting bunker. Ours was a bunker dug down about three and a half feet deep on the forward slope of the hill blocking the valley leading up to "Old Baldy." We were faced by a large sector of the enemy positions.

The bunker was connected to other bunkers by trenches and these bunkers were about 300 - 500 ft. apart. Our bunker had some logs over our heads and three layers of sand bags all around the front, back and on top. These bunkers, if they took a direct hit maybe would collapse, especially if it were hit with an artillery shell on the right place. But shells that landed

137

nearby would give us protection from getting shrapnel in our bunker.

We were replacing the 45th Division in this position. They were so happy to see us they couldn't wait to get off the hill. I had to really talk fast to get them to explain where the enemy was located and where the routes were that the enemy might use to come up when they attacked. The pat answer we got from them was, "You will find out soon enough."

The night was soon disappearing and the men from the 45th hurried to get off the hill before the darkness would leave and be replaced with the rising of the morning sun.

Now here we were. None of us in this squad had been in combat. Now we were on our own.

When morning came we soon found out that we were not alone in that bunker. We had quite a number of the Iowa variety of Norway rats, and they were already combat veterans. The only way we had of killing them was to shoot them when we saw them. They would look at us, waiting for us to open a can of C rations and there they were. We would reach for our rifle and they would be gone before we could get a shot at them.

Those rats were hiding in the sand bags of our bunkers and moved in from a village that was vacated by the Koreans when it was shelled. They were so pesky; we stayed up until we were so sleepy that we dropped off to catch a few winks. The rats would either scratch sand in our face from the bunker top or they would scurry across us hunting for food. Even when someone else was standing guard, we never did get peaceful rest.

This, our first morning on line, was very quiet, not much happening. So I left my buddy to watch with the machine gun and went exploring to see the lay of the land and where the neighboring bunkers were located.

But as you would expect there were no provisions made for toilets. So I found a tree and dug a hole and commenced to squat over the hole. Then I heard what sounded like a rifle fire and then some dirt kicked up on my right. I looked at it and continued what I was doing. I heard another rifle shot and then dirt kicked up on my left.

My mind then kicked into gear and I knew there was someone zeroing in on me with a rifle. I jumped forward into a trench, pants down and all.

As I was jumping in the trench I heard the third zing go over my head and then a sound of a rifle shot. When I had the courage to look, there was a bullet hole in the tree right behind where I was sitting seconds before.

Thank you God for the poor aim of that enemy soldier as it took three shots to hit the target. Thanks for waking me up to the fact that there never is a time that we are safe from enemy snipers.

I then gathered some sticks which I needed and kept my body in the trenches with my head down. After I had enough sticks, we started to test fire the machine gun to mark the places with sticks under our machine gun barrel.

To mark the positions we used tracer shells and hunted for spots that the enemy might use to come during the night and attack us. Those shells glowed red as they traveled to the target and would show us where the shell hit. This was the way we could establish our field of fire.

We set the field of fire on a road or a pathway on the slope coming off Old Baldy. These were normal routes that the enemy would use to approach our positions.

We then put a stake under the gun barrel so that when we needed to locate the desired target at night we could find our target by placing the gun barrel on top of those stakes.

As the sun was setting that evening of July17, 1952, we saw some movement on the North Korean side of the line. We were told that nighttime was when all the activity took place. This was our first nightfall so we had no idea what normal activity was. We were all very tired. We missed a night of sleep because we were up the whole night before moving into our positions. The evening started with a lot of artillery shells coming in and they were scattered around the line a bit.

What we didn't know at the time was that they were zeroing their artillery weapons and marking those positions for a full-scale attack.

It didn't take us long to tell by the sound of the shells coming in, if they were going over our heads, or if they would be close to our bunker.

We also soon could distinguish if it were artillery shells or from their direct fired guns that were fired from tanks or half-tracks. Those shells came in with a swish-bang and the artillery came in with a whistle. Then the bang and the mortar sounded like they were flipping end for end as they came in.

As it got darker the shells started coming more and more and then at ten o' clock everything broke loose. We could see in the flares and the exploding shells that the enemy was coming up the hillside. We started firing at them coming up the slope. They were coming up like ants up an anthill, on the slope of our outpost named *Old Baldy (hill 266)*.

The sky was red of all the artillery shells exploding. There were so many incoming rounds that the whole hill of *Baldy* was smoke and dust. Some reports indicate there were 4400 rounds of artillery fired on that small hill in a 24-hour period.

*Old Baldy (hill 266)

On July 17, 1952 the night sky was lit up with flares, artillery, and mortar shells. Everything broke loose as the enemy attacked on Old Baldy (hill 266). The sky was red from the constant rain of these shells.

* Picture from 2nd division history in Korea 1951-1952

We kept blazing away with our machine gun, but the machine gun barrel was so hot it would get red and jam up. The company located on the top of *Old Baldy* fought and fought. We could see the enemy, wave after wave, coming up the hill. The enemy, who were expecting us to send help, ambushed F company platoon that was sent to help the soldiers on *Old Baldy* as reinforcement. This happened not too far from our machine gun nest and the soldiers never made it to *Old Baldy*.

The night sky was red, all lit up with flares, and the shells were bursting all around us. These shells, along with some flares in the sky that were sent up by the artillery, gave us the light to see the enemy coming towards us. They were in such large numbers; they were like flies climbing around a molasses barrel.

The enemy sent wave after wave of soldiers. We soon discovered that the first wave had burp guns, the second wave came with only ammo and used weapons they picked up from the dead, and the third wave carried grenades.

The question we faced was, "Were these troops we saw coming toward the main line all enemy, or were some of them our troops retreating off the outpost Old Baldy. We were firing down the slopes at the enemy. That was the only way F Platoon could get to the main line. With the kind of odds they faced, they must have known that they couldn't hold the outpost.

A question I asked myself time and time again was, "Were we with our machine guns shooting at some of our own troops who were retreating?"

If anyone left Baldy they had to go through our field of fire from our machine guns. How many men in the heat of battle were killed with our friendly fire that night we will never know. I may ask the question, but we will never be able to find the answer to that question.

Even though there is no answer, the question has a tendency to come back to haunt me. There was more than one night that question prevented me from getting a good night's sleep.

We do know that those who were retreating had no way of communicating with our line, because the shelling destroyed all communication. Nobody had the means to communicate with each other.

We, on the main line, were experiencing a lot of trouble because at the rate we had to fire our machine guns the barrels were getting red hot. The barrel would become red hot and stick out like a neon sign saying, "Come and get me." The enemy soon spotted our machine gun placement and started to zing in shells close to us trying to knock out our machine gun.

We then started to pull the tracer shells out of the ammo belt and replace them with regular shells. The reason we were removing the tracers was because they produced a lot of heat for the machine gun barrels, and the enemy could trace our position by seeing where the tracers were coming from.

My assistant gunner was working on replacing those shells in the ammo belts as they came out of the box. While I was firing the machine gun my assistant gunner said, "Van, help me with this shell, hold the belt as I try to jerk it out."

144

We were both on our knees trying to remove the shell when all of a sudden swish- bang, a 76 mm shell swished through the aperture of our bunker right where I had been standing firing the gun just an instant before the shell became stuck.

The enemy's 76 mm shell went through the front of the bunker and into the second layer of our sand bags in the rear of the bunker. It didn't blow up until it was in the second layer of bags at the back end of our bunker.

The shrapnel that flew through the air and a large jagged piece tore open a case of C ration cans on the floor right beside where we were pulling the obstinate shell out. We were dripping with sweat and were thrown to the floor with the concussion. We both had nosebleeds as well. Our eyes were blood shot and our whole bodies that at first were numb, ached and burned.

I said to my buddy, "I am hit and hurt, see the blood." He also had a nosebleed. It must have been the shock and the concussion that caused the bleeding and the blurred vision.

Then my buddy said, "Van, you are okay, get back on the gun and get back to firing before they run over our position."

It wasn't until some time later that we realized we had witnessed a miracle. We bent way down and got on our knees to remove that shell and we were both close to the ground just at the same time the enemy shell passed over our heads, exploded, and both of us escaped with no life threatening injures, but with some severe concussions.

I've asked myself the question then and many times since then, "Was that God's special protection by sending a guardian angel to get us down on the ground to pull the stuck shell out?"

This was the second incident in the first two days in battle, and I was to witness many more in the months that would follow. Every time it I witnessed God's care over me it reinforced the passage taken from Psalms

> *"Because he hath set his love upon me, therefore will I deliver him: I will set him on high, because he hath known my name. He shall call upon me, and I will answer him: I will be with him in trouble; I will deliver him, and honour him. With long life will I satisfy him, and show him my salvation".*
>
> *Psalms 91: 14-16 KJV.*

Old Baldy: Blood, Sweat and Tears

After we got back on the base of Old Baldy we had to rebuild everything. Trenches had to be dug. We uncovered several bodies that had been buried by the powdery dirt.

*Bottom picture is of personnel carriers from <u>2nd Division History Book</u> 1951-52

That night we burned up our 2nd machine gun barrel and we were on the 3rd and last barrel when things began to quiet down.

It was then we were told that the enemy had taken control of *Old Baldy*. They stopped their assault short of trying to control the main line. The stray enemy soldiers retreated back to the out post that they had captured. Our company was ordered to regroup and counter attack before the morning and try to retake *Old Baldy*

We were given the assistance of a tank to give us firepower, and a personnel carrier for support to carry the wounded and supplies up the hill.

Some of us were ordered to walk along the side of a tank to protect the tank from the enemy that might still be along the road, from throwing grenades at the tracks of the tank. The concern was that the enemy would cripple the tank by destroying the tracks with grenades.

This was a difficult assignment because the tank was always the target the enemy tried to knock out first.

It all went smoothly until we came to the place where a large number of a platoon was ambushed on the road. The road was littered with bodies. It appeared like they were ambushed and were scattered all over the road. Most of them were dead and some were dying. The tank driver couldn't go around the bodies because of soft rice paddies and the only choice he had was to ride over the bodies scattered on the roadway. I will never forget the sound of the bodies crushing as the tank tracks passed over them.

It was a mistake in my opinion to have our unit try to retake *Old Baldy* that night. We were too tired and badly disorganized by this time. The shelling by the enemy was extremely heavy with unbelievable force. We weren't strong enough to be able to have a successful counter attack and the enemy was already too entrenched to route them. We had a staggering amount of casualties, and many were wounded.

We were coming back from being pushed off the hill and I asked my platoon leader where to go. He said, "To your old positions." He was wounded in the hand, had lost some fingers, and was in a lot of pain.

We went to our old machine gun position and waited for the sun to rise. When the sun came up there was destruction all around us. *Old Baldy* (hill266) was in front of us and only sticks were left of the trees. Records show that on the small hill in a 24-hour period over 14,000 rounds of artillery were fired. The casualties were awesome on both sides and all for a worthless piece of ground that wasn't bigger than two square miles.

The sight of the death and destruction will never be erased from my mind and the pain of that night will always be remembered because of our comrades who died. What a price to pay.

In short, there is no other way to describe the price of war, other than to say it is "Hell on Earth," and I certainly agree.

I felt guilt that morning and a lot of responsibility for the death of other human beings. Was it because I wasn't hardened to the effects of war? Was it because I was taught from a child that to kill was to break a command of God?

The following article was written in the book, HISTORY OF 2ND INFANTRY DIVISION. KOREA 1951-52

The 23rd Regiment, the first to relieve, moved into the left half of the division sector. It was soon apparent that Old Baldy was the center of activity and proved to be the repeated target for concentrations of enemy artillery and mortar fire. At 2200 hours on 17 July incoming rounds reached a devastating rate. During a 20-minute preparatory fire a battalion of Chinese overran the positions of F Company, the unit occupying the crest. E Company quickly formed a counterattack. When the unit reached the hill, the crest had been lost but a successful counterattack placed elements of E and F back on Old Baldy by 0345 on the 18th The Chinese quickly retaliated. Supported by heavy artillery and mortar fire, they were able to win back the crest on the morning of the 18th.

In the next four days the hill changed hands a number of times. A provisional battalion of I L and B companies and later by K and, G companies temporarily regained it. Each time, however, the Chinese used the tactics of withdrawing, plastering the hill with barrages and following closely with counterattacks. On 22 July the 23rd withdrew from the outpost. Continuous artillery concentrations and air strikes were directed against the enemy on the scarred slopes of Old Baldy five-day siege of heavy rain beginning on 26 July hindered operations for both sides and permitted the 23rd

to prepare for its next counterattack. It came on the night of 31 July when the First Battalion, with A and C Companies leading, moved up with a double envelopment which successfully seized Old Baldy and put the 23rd there to stay. The enemy suffered more than 1,150 casualties during the two-week engagement.

The reports do not list how many American casualties there were. From that report and the picture of the hill *Old Baldy* you can get an idea what tremendous death and destruction was all around after this battles.

Early that morning I went behind the hill where our command post was located to hunt for food to replace that which had been destroyed during the night by the shells, but there was nobody there. Every body was gone. Why? Nobody told us. We were told to go to our position and hold the line.

What I didn't know was that our sergeant was wounded or died, and that our lieutenant was hospitalized.

The next morning our platoon had only a few men left that were able to fight and the company had to reorganize because of their losses. The company evidently withdrew to the rear and the unit that we just replaced packed up from the blocking positions to fill our holes.

Because of the confusion with the dead, wounded and missing no one knew we were still in our bunker on the forward slope. A basic training friend was in a company that was adjacent to ours. He came to check and discovered that I was considered missing in action because I did not come off the hill.

We had no choice but to hold the hill because we thought reinforcements would soon be there. Talk about being scary. I found some C rations and my assistant gunner and myself had these rations to eat. This was such an empty feeling to have no support around and be faced with an enemy that was unpredictable.

After the morning meal I took the sweat soaked *Bible* that was still in my pocket. I opened it and to my surprise, as I read, these were the words that I read from it:

> A *thousand shall fall at thy side and ten thousand at thy right hand but it shall not come nigh you, only with thy eye shall you behold it.*"
>
> *Psalm 91.KJV*

God was with us even now giving comfort at a time when everything was at it's darkest. In my discouragement that morning I had been wishing that I had been one of the lucky ones who didn't have to face war any more. God was with us even now giving comfort at a time when everything was at it's darkest.

Top row: An enemy soldier. Note how he was dressed.

Middle row: Our machine gun nest, and battle weary author

Bottom row: A direct hit on our bunker

We had tank support when we tried to retake Old Baldy

153

How was I going to stand a year or more of this? This was only my first 24 hours on line. Was this what I would have to face every day? I remember saying, "God, why didn't you take me?" But instead of taking me, God gave me His assurance of His presence. The Lord would watch over me as a mother hen watches over her young chicks and takes them under her wings.

God showed me that morning that everybody was not gone. His presence was with me, He had a plan for my life and I would be able to carry on no matter what the future held. At that time everything was so confusing. Was everybody gone'? Where were they? After reading that Psalm I realized that we weren't alone. Everybody was not gone. Our Heavenly Father was with us all the time watching over us.

There in Korea was a war, now almost forgotten, in which men were wounded, died, and many are still missing, We are the men of that war who served in a grand division, the 2nd division. By writing these painful memories, we want to make sure that the memory and the ideals of that war still live on.

HISTORY OF 2ND INFANTRY DIVISION. KOREA 1951-52

July 18th E Company was selected to attack shortly after midnight. By the time E Company reached the hill, the crest was in enemy control, but a successful counterattack pushed back the Chinese in the early morning hours. Two successive enemy counterattacks hit Old Baldy that morning and the second was able to wrest control from the hard-hit E and F Companies. The Third Battalion had now been called up from reserve. K Company was ordered to counterattack, with tanks and personnel carriers in support. A rain of mortar and artillery hampered their movement to the hill in daylight hours. A handful of men were able to reach the remaining elements of E and F Companies, but the Chinese tenaciously held on to the crest.

On 22 July the 2nd Reconnaissance Company relieved the few men still on Old Baldy The unit was later driven from the top but stayed in position on the right finger, a part of the hill, which had never fallen to the enemy. At this time a heavy rain beg which slowed activity considerably. The main thought of the infantrymen became existence in the downpour. Bunkers caved in and those that did remain standing were knee-deep in mud. The slow-up in the action gave the 23rd a chance to plan a new- counterattack that would drive the Chinese from Old Baldy permanently. In the meantime air strikes and artillery barrages were directed at enemy positions on Baldy and strong points to the north and west.

Parts of the following article were taken directly from the 2ND Division Book "SECOND TO NONE". [July 2, 1953, Page 3]

DISTINGUISHED SERVICE CROSSES TO BALDY HEROES--FIVE INDIANHEADERS CITED FOR ACTIONS

"The countless battles for outpost positions, which have characterized the Korean war since 1951, have, in a sense, become historically routine, But after such engagements the dead lie just as dead, the ground is just

155

as devastated, and the infantryman's efforts are no less heroic than if he had been part of the most spectacular battle of the war.

'Old Baldy' was one of these outpost positions, west of Chorwon and the southwest of the northern most knob of the infamous T-bone Hill, the rise of land has a history of glory as its former name 'Bloody Baldy' implies.

Five men of the 2nd Infantry Division wrote part of this history during the summer of 1952 when the Indianhead sector included 'Old Baldy's slopes. All five were recently awarded the Distinguished Service Cross, cited on the same Department of the Army General Orders Number 37, dated 29 April 1953.

The nation's second highest award for valor was given posthumously to 2nd Lieutenant Richard R. McCullough, E Company, 23rd Infantry Regiment, (i.e. McCullough was from my unit and was a friend of mine) and Pvt. Miguel A Vera, E Company, and 38th Infantry Regiment. The living DSC recipients were Sgt. Victor H Espinoza, A Company, 23rd Regiment, Sgt. Eddie L Bouknight, G Company, 38th Regiment, and Sgt. Francis L.Schwartze, G Company 38th Regiment.

The Indianhead Division had just relieved another American division on 'Old Baldy' when the Chinese struck on the night of July 18. It was during this action that Lieutenant McCullough gave his life for his country. Lieutenant McCullough was leading a counterattack on Old Baldy when one of his soldiers became separated from his carbine. The lieutenant quickly replaced the

156

warrior's headpiece and weapon with his own weapon and continued to lead the assault on the hill. As the attacking unit neared the crest of Baldy, the enemy showered concussion grenades upon it. The lieutenant caught many of the grenades and tossed them back inflicting many casualties.

Although wounded, Lieutenant McCullough engineered a limited withdrawal and set up defensive positions, exposing him to mortar and artillery fire. The Indianhead officer moved about the perimeter, encouraging his men, distributing ammunition and coordinating the holding action. He was hit again but continued to organize and spearhead a counterattack, directing, organizing and spearheading, until he lost his life. The Chinese clung stubbornly to the battered 'Old Baldy' and remained in control until August 1, 1952"

The following article was taken from the _VFW Magazine_ December 1991

Counting Casualties

America paid a heavy price for its noble crusade in Korea. More than 90% of non-Korean UN combat dead was Americans, many of whom died during the "talking war." U.S. forces suffered 62,200 causalities, 12,300 KIA in the war's last two years in establishing the DMZ at Line, Kansas.

Some 103,284 American servicemen were seriously wounded, requiring hospitalization and. twenty-two percent of all wounded in action died. Chances of Survival *from wounds were greatly improved in Korea, however, once they reached the hospital. There, only 2.5% died.*

Perhaps the greatest lifesaver was evacuation by aircraft. Beginning in January 1951, helicopters—"flying ambulances"—were introduced for this purpose. Equally important was the first-time use of special medical units. As Maj. Gen. George E. Armstrong, then U.S. Army Surgeon General, said, "In Korea, Mobile Army Surgical Hospitals (MASH) have been the big factor in lowering the mortality rate of the wounded."

Another category of U.S. casualties did not fare so well ---7140 American POWs. A tragic number— 2,701, or 38%—died while in captivity because of inhumane conditions in North Korean prison camps. In addition, 8,194 GI'S are still listed as missing in action or unidentified from Korea."

CHAPTER 10

The Long Night On Patrol

NOTE TO MY DECEASED ARMY BUDDY FROM THE KOREAN WAR

I was given an assignment by a VA psychologist, who himself lost his leg in battle in Vietnam, for my individual therapy, to write a letter to my deceased comrade telling how I felt about the experience that lead up to his giving his life. This friend was a company radioman who went out on this patrol in that capacity.

The task of writing this letter has proven to be one of the most difficult things I ever attempted to do. The letter follows. His name was not included in this book in order to protect my comrade's widow from suffering any additional pain.

Dear comrade;

I have before me a very difficult and emotional assignment. My assignment is to talk to you about how I feel now and what I felt that awful night on our patrol.

You were not of my platoon, but I knew you were attached to our company and we rode to chapel together whenever we could go. I believe you were with the third platoon and in the position of a radio signalman. You volunteered to go along and give us the needed radio communications.

I don't know what your reactions were when we got together for the briefing for the patrol.

Nor do I know how you felt when we were told that the 2nd lieutenant, who was fresh out of Officers Candidate School, was going to be our patrol leader.

I was really afraid to go out with him. After all, he had just been placed in our company and wasn't familiar with this location or anything. Most of the men must have felt the same way as I evaluated the looks on the faces of the other members of our patrol. Everybody sat together. No one spoke a word. But it didn't take a rocket scientist to figure out that every one of us who were going out that night was affected.

Remember how he set forth his plan whereby we were to follow the drainage ditch all the way to the Chinese line and then return the same way we came? When he asked for questions about the patrol, I said, "Sir, the enemy is known to be able to hide in that ditch. They will be able to ambush us anywhere along that route." The lieutenant's hair came straight up like an angry dog when I questioned the wisdom of his plan. His response was, "You are second in command, but I am leading this patrol. I know my way if we follow the drainage ditch." Remember I said, "Sir we can safely go through the rice paddy. We'll all get wet but no enemy will be hiding in the water soaked paddy and it will be much safer."

He snapped at me like a snapping turtle. "I want to let you know before we get started that when I am in control I will call the shots. Is that clear to everyone?"

Wasn't this typical of those 90-Day Wonders? They never knew beans from buckshot, yet treated the non-commissioned troops like stupid school kids.

When I looked over to where you were sitting, I felt so sorry for you, because you were so heavily loaded down with the big radio and that battery pack on your back. I thought, why did they ever choose such a small-framed person like you to carry that heavy load?

Then the lieutenant said to me, "Since you are second in command, you take the M1 rifle with the grenade launcher and a hand full of crimp cartridges with the signal flares."

Everyone hated those crimp cartridges because it is impossible to defend yourself if there is one of those cartridges in the chamber of your rifle. Then we couldn't shoot regular shells.

I knew there wasn't much love flowing between the lieutenant and me. It was very noticeable the way he sneered when he gave me that assignment.

I'll never forget those uneasy looks on everyone's face when we assembled that night, as it was getting dark. Nobody felt secure with a green horn from state side in charge. I remember you whispered to me, "This is going to be something else; it's going to be a long night."

Did you have the feeling then already that you wouldn't be coming back alive?

Remember how foggy the night was? The cool fall air was moving in and I can still feel the chill go down my spine.
Every detail about that night causes me flash backs and nightmares. Foggy, misty nights especially, will still get to me. They give me a chill.

How often I recall that night. I can still feel the eyes of the enemy trailing me; I still can feel them moving in the fog just outside of my clear vision.

I bet you were glad that night when we made it to the enemy line without incident. You took off that heavy radio pack completely exhausted. Could you, like I, smell the garlic at different spots as we walked along the route? Remember how the North Koreans and the Chinese always carried a ball of rice and garlic cloves with them?

That night I am positive the enemy had scouts that were observing our route and reported each move to their troops on line. I was so afraid every time when I would smell that garlic. My body would shiver and shake, because at any minute I expected to hear the zing of bullets going by from one of the enemy burp guns.

You will, no doubt, remember how we all lay on the cold grass in a semi-circle very close to the enemy's line. I was close enough to their line to see the Chinese digging in two 76 mm guns, mounted on half-track. I plotted their positions according to a nearby tree. The wind was coming up and the moon was starting to break through the clouds and the fog was starting to lift. Do you remember I whispered to you, "We got to get out of here; we will be sitting ducks in a half hour?"

I made it to the lieutenant and told him what I knew was happening. Our mission was complete and we should pack up and move out. His reply was, "We are going to stay until 0300 hours and then leave." I said, "Sir, can't we go now? We will soon be sitting ducks." "We will leave at 0300 hour, and take the same route we came," he said, "Do you understand?" "Sir," I said, "Can't we go through the rice paddies? It will be safer and I know my way back to our line anywhere in the rice paddy. I'm afraid of an ambush if we take the same route back." He replied, "I have had enough out of you; when we leave you will be last person of our column! I hear that the enemy likes to take prisoners off the rear of the column."

We waited until the moon was full bright and shining on us, a clear silhouette for the enemy when the lieutenant told us to start out at 0300 hours.

We went along side of the drainage ditch again and the smell of garlic was all around. Every step we took I felt we would be stepping into mine fields where everything would break loose.

Then we came to a point and a curve in the ditch. I heard the sound of a machine gun bolt being pulled back. I was a machine gunner and could distinguish the sound of a machine gun bolt being pulled back.

In fact, in my sleep at night I still hear the sound, and wake up shivering. Remember that night when I heard that sound, I screamed, "Hit the dirt!" as I dived for cover against the rocks.

But you couldn't dive into the rocks. It would have damaged the radio. And the radio and battery pack were too heavy for you to move fast. As the machine gun opened up on us, those who didn't get down quick enough were hit. You were like a sitting duck. That hollow sound of bullets tearing into bodies and some zinging past will always stay with me.

Along with you and the lieutenant, at least five more men were hit badly by that first burst from the enemy's machine gun. You didn't have a chance. The radio didn't permit you to dive into the rocks for cover.

It was the big guy with the beard that we called 'Hatch' who was carrying a Browning automatic rifle that put out the machine gunner. He did this when the gunner was reloading another belt of ammo. He stood upright and got the machine gunner, but by that time the backside of the ditch that we were walking along side of, was loaded with Chinese that were shooting down on us and throwing hand grenades in our direction. They kept us pinned down and were attempting to surround us. One was within ten feet of me as I was hollering for Corporal Hatch to keep his head down. I thought it was a bush but the bush back of me called, "Hatchee, Hatchee, here."

I couldn't shoot because I was using my rifle as a launcher to send signals. Then that young kid who was just 16 years old--- we called him *Slim*--- spotted at the same time I did, that the bush was moving towards us from the rear. Slim lifted his M2 carbine, mowed the bush down and inside the bush was a camouflaged Chinese. He was within 10 feet of me when Slim dropped him. This Chinese was throwing concussion grenades and trying to take prisoners.

They were now throwing concussion grenades from all sides trying to disable us with them. I was shielding my face with my arm when I saw a grenade coming over the drainage ditch. The grenade went off so close to me that a piece of the plastic canister lodged in my hand and under my arm.

Then I remember crawling on hands and knees getting to you to check how badly you were hit. I saw you were hit in the stomach and wounded very badly. Your eyes were pleading for help, and you were thinking clearly. Do you remember my saying to you, "We are going to get you out or go down together?"

164

There also was a hole through the battery of the radio where the shell pierced through you and into the battery. The acid was leaking out of the battery. I had sent my signals with the flares that we were hit and hurt badly. Remember you said, "Van, don't let them take us. Here is the radio, call for help." I noticed that it was a hopeless case. We were out numbered and suffered the loss of most of our patrol.

There was a disabled tank nearby that the artillery used as a base target point. I had visited a lot with the artillery forward observer who was attached to our unit. He told me the tank was their base point for fire missions.

He told me if we ever needed artillery support while in the valley, we were always to use the tank as base point to call for directions.

Your radio was still working and I called in artillery to hit 450 feet to the right of the base point. I was trying to get the shells to fall on top of what they thought was our position.

I heard that you and I would be better dead than to be prisoners of the North Koreans. I couldn't see us suffer like that. I had given up all hope of surviving. A short time later the incoming shells started whistling in. I was figuring on this being the last for all of us. Remember how the ground shook when the shells come whistling in, the flashing of lights and the ear shattering noise?

After the barrage of shells ended, I discovered they all landed on the enemy side of the ditch. We had just witnessed what I considered a miracle. It couldn't have been anything else.

From the screams that were coming from the enemy side of the drainage ditch they had been hit full blast and not one of those shells hit on our side. As you may remember I didn't use military procedure. I was just screaming in the radio, "Fire, fire, fire for effect, you are getting the Chinese pinned down!"

The radio went dead and no more would it hum when we pressed the speak button.

But the shells were coming and coming and coming, and again all the shells hitting perfectly on the enemy's position.

It was then I shouted, "Let's go, leave the dead, pick up the wounded and all the weapons and head for the rice paddies. Stop at the first ridge and regroup!" I was counting on breaking free while the enemy was still shattered because of the shelling. When everybody was on the ridge, I gave the order, "Fire at the enemy with all you got, then move over and fire again." By doing this we would look like we had joined a larger group.

I remember carrying you. We dropped off your radio because it wasn't working, and I set you down to fire. Blood was all over both of us. You were in and out of consciousness. You knew we were no longer pinned down and I told you to hang on, that no Chinese would get you.

When we got to the base of our line it was still dark, and the men on line were so jumpy that when our troops heard noises they started to shoot at us. I set you down in a ditch where we were down below the range of the bullets, which were now going over our heads.

This gave us time to examine our wounded. David was trying to make the lieutenant comfortable, but he was having difficulty breathing. He took a shell in the lungs. You were hanging on, but it wouldn't be long if we didn't get some blood for you soon.

We heard noise behind us. It was several men walking in the rice paddy in the tall grass. I motioned the rest of the remaining men to line up in the ditch to be ready to fight. Suddenly I remembered the password for that night. I said, "EASY," and an answer came back, "DOES IT"

This was an answer to prayer. A friend from basic training came in response to my panic radio transmission and his captain told him to organize his patrol and go help us. His radio worked and our line soon notified the troops who we were and that we would come through. Soon the shooting from our line stopped and became quiet so we could climb that steep slippery hill to our position.

The lieutenant said, "Boys, please carry me up feet first it will give me less pain." And as David did that, the lieutenant died by drowning in his own blood. We were very near our line and you were getting so weak. But suddenly you, with full voice looked up, smiled at me and reverently said, *"OH MY GOD WHAT IS HAPPENING TO ME!"* I was no longer carrying you but only the remains of your body. Your spirit left your body and you were carried to your eternal home. I will never forget that moment you left this world. It was like you saw the angels coming; they were picking you up out of my arms.

By that time it was about morning as it was just getting light. The company commander met us, and after seeing we didn't have all the dead with us, he ordered those who could walk, to go back with some fresh helpers to retrieve the others. I believe there were five more bodies.

I was soaked with your blood, emotionally shot, and in such emotional and physical pain. The thought kept running through my mind, if I would have stood my ground that night would this have ever happened?

I said to our company commander, " Sir, they are dead, they aren't there, and I can't go one more step without screaming. I am soaked in mud and blood. My loss has been too much already to risk the rest of my men." Then David stepped forward and said, "Give me enough fresh troops that are ready to fight, with stretchers and body bags, and we will bring them back."

They rushed out to beat the daylight while the rest of the troops fired on the enemy line to prevent them from sniping at our soldiers who were going to get the bodies.

I retreated in a bunker alone and sat with those blood soaked clothing and cried. The loss was too much. I thought about you and the dreams your wife had for your return and your dreams of being with her. You used to say you would disappear with her for a week just to make up for lost time.

I was still sitting in a daze when the captain walked in with a nicely written story from battalion that he wanted to have me sign as a witness. It was about the lieutenant and how he fought to protect the lives of his patrol and gave his life doing it. This letter was recommending him to receive the Silver Star for bravery.

I blew up! "Never! Never! That lieutenant was not willing to listen to advice, He didn't protect the men, he led them to their death and for that he will receive a silver star? Never! The silver stars belong to guys like Hatch, Beldfelt, and

Justman. No, in all respect this would be wrong for me to sign that. For the rest of my life he will be a murderer in my eyes because of his stubbornness!"

The captain walked away, but soon sent a messenger to tell me he had a truck waiting to bring me to a shower point to clean up and get new clothing, I have never been able to wash the smell of blood off my body. Every time I see blood or smell it, I think of what you gave that night so all of us could enjoy freedom.

Oh, I need to tell you, when we went off line for a short period to rest, they had a battalion formation for our patrol and flew the flag at half-mast for you and the others who died.

The battalion commander gave each one of us another stripe in honor of our being able to break free of an enemy ambush. This was at a time when President Truman froze rank of all the service men and women. This was called a *Battlefield Promotion* when we received our stripe.

A few days later the captain did come to talk about that night. I apologized for blowing up about that Silver Star, but that my position hasn't changed. The captain said all the survivors of that patrol felt the same way about the Silver Star so he would drop it.

Then I asked if he had the address of your next of kin. He gave me your wife's address in Wisconsin. I wrote several letters explaining about how reverently you spoke as you left this world and that it was as if I could feel the angels come and get you as you said, *"Oh my God, what is happening to me?"* I am assuming that you saw something that we could not. But I knew without a doubt you were taken from my arms into eternity with God.

It was like your face lit up as you left your body and I knew you were leaving us for your heavenly home. From that point on, I knew that I was only carrying the empty shell of your body. I did feel very sorry for your wife. She wrote how much she suffered because of your leaving her. She loved you and she had a terrible time believing that you weren't coming back.

For me, it was all like a bad dream that would be gone in the morning, but this dream never leaves.

Comrade, if I had the time, we could talk about the many awful days and nights that were spent after that night and the losses we suffered. It hurt that nobody back home knew or seemed to care what was happening in this part of the world.

They were having their steel strikes and their wage battles when we were struggling to get enough artillery support because lack of ammo.

The true facts never hit the press because we weren't supposed to be at war, we were only *Policemen* for our country.

That's why if there was any news of the war, it was on the back page of the daily newspapers. Maybe someday we will get the real message on the front page of the daily newspapers. It may seem strange to you that I talk to you, but night after night I relive those horrible days and nights.

Some day we will have a big reunion in the sky, you and I and all those from 2nd Division, 23rd Infantry Regiment, Easy Company that left us that year. Maybe someday we will have the answers as to why we had to have all the pain, fear, frustrations and anger.

My prayer is that it won't forever be on my mind, that those noises and sounds I hear won't remind me of those awful sounds of battle. I pray that some day it will be gone forever and never bother me again.

But, I guess we can't block out certain painful parts of our memory without affecting the other parts as well.

I am reminded of the *Apostle Paul* when he asked for his thorn to be removed. The Lord's answer was, *"MY GRACE IS SUFFICIENT FOR ALL YOUR NEEDS."* So I understand in HIS strength I will be able to carry on until He comes again.

Until we meet again.

Your buddy, Van

Chapter 11

Back to the Slopes Of Old Baldy

In the military we had to be able to make major adjustments or we would not survive. When we withdrew to reorganize, the replacements were not available to fill the loss of men that we had experienced. To my surprise, and my anxiety, they appointed me to be acting person in charge of a machine gun squad. This squad now consisted of three soldiers from South Korea who spoke only Korean, three soldiers from Puerto Rico who spoke only Spanish, and the other soldiers were Americans who spoke only English. There we were, one squad with three different languages, and me without any training in language other than English. I was given an armband that showed a sergeant's stripes when I was in reality only a private first class.

In theory, the foreigners were supposed to be ammunition carriers. On line we would man three gun emplacements and assign two men to each site. The three words the foreigners learned very quickly were *chow, mail call,* and *you're dismissed.* It was frustrating for me, but also for them. They soon learned that if it were a dangerous assignment they suddenly didn't understand English and therefore didn't understand my instructions.

The Korean weather was loaded with extremes of nature; the winters were very bone chilling cold and the monsoon season would bring day after day of torrential rains.

We were just into the monsoon season when we were ordered to go back up on Old Baldy. We were loaded up on trucks and brought to the base of the line where we stumbled along a deep rutted road. The night sky was blacker than coal. We were loaded one squad at a time on a personnel carrier. This was like a tank with some armor, but was designed with an open top to move people if necessary to where we could duck down behind the sides and not be hit with rifle fire.

Our platoon was chosen to take up positions on the finger of the rear slope of Old Baldy. The Chinese and North Koreans held the top of Baldy and the reverse slope. They were again by now well dug in. The personnel carrier, which we were riding, stopped at the base of Baldy. The driver stuck his head out of a small porthole and said, "Hurry, grab your gear and run like hell or you'll get it."

What a reception! We expected and received our welcoming party that we knew that night was going to be Chinese/North Korean soldiers. The hill wasn't that large and then to be occupied by both the enemy and us wasn't going to be like a Sunday school picnic nor was it a pretty sight.

The soldiers from the 2nd Division Recon whom we were replacing came running to the personnel carrier. They didn't look like soldiers; they and their equipment were just like balls of mud. One soldier told me as he was trying to load up, "Get all the hand grenades you can, that is the only way you can keep those #@## Chinese out of your bunker and they will try every night."

We found that the trenches were so shallow they were less than up to your waist deep and some spots were half full of

173

mud and water. Our bunker, that we needed to occupy, had inside, some water soaked GIs that we had to replace.

Their machine gun looked like a chunk of metal full of rust. The GI took up his machine gun and said, "After a few days the only thing you can use your gun for is a big club, because it won't fire." My machine gun was still oil soaked and I set it up in the water soaked bunker. The bunker was so shallow that we couldn't stand up in it. Like the soldiers before, we had three empty ammo boxes where we could sit on.

The water from the side of the hill would run in the trenches and the mud would flow into our bunker. So all the time our feet were in water up to our ankles and some times the water was higher.

Remember this hill, *Old Baldy*. It had been shelled with 14,000 shells so there were no more trees, only powdery dirt on top of the ground. The place stunk of decaying bodies that were buried very shallowly by the dirt dug up by the shell craters. On the night that we took over the hill we didn't experience an enemy probe but the troops we replaced had fought them off earlier that night.

It drizzled all night and a heavy fog hung over the area. A messenger came to our platoon area and said, "We will have a 100% alert every night," which meant everyone would be on guard all night long. We were to guard all night and during the day as much as we could, especially if it were foggy. We would dig these trenches deeper and work to try to get them to drain. That morning we got a shovel and a pick ax. We were digging in that rubbery soil when suddenly my pickax fell into a concave and out came a bad odor.

I uncovered a body that was covered when a shell apparently blew up close by him during the attack on *Old Baldy*. After uncovering the body we discovered it was an American soldier. We put one dog tag between the teeth and sent the body to the rear area. It was nearly impossible to eat food on this hill. We only had the water from our canteen to drink, no wash water, only muddy water coming off the hill, and our hands smelled like dead bodies.

That night, like every night following, we would get scrutinized and probed by about ten to twelve Chinese who wanted to push us off the hill. The first sign that the enemy was close in on those foggy nights was the smell in the air. The smell of garlic would alert us to their coming, and then we would see shadows coming out of the fog. As soon as we fired the machine gun we were sprayed back with bullets from their burp guns. If we didn't get them with the first shot, we knew we better duck real fast until the Chinese unloaded their clips of ammo.

After the first week we also were having a lot of trouble keeping our machine gun firing because the ammo would soon get muddy. We soon learned to spread out in our make shift trench upon signal, all fire or throw our grenades at the same time as the men appeared in the shadows. We would wait until we would see the Chinese coming through in the rain and we would heave a bunch of grenades at them.

One night they were determined to push us off the hill and they had several waves of troops that kept coming. One of the guys who joined our unit was a southerner from the hill country and also a professional bootlegger. The first time he wore shoes was now in the army.

He was an extremely nice guy until you made him angry. The Chinese kept coming and our squad and I were trying to keep the machine guns firing. The rest of the guys were throwing hand grenades. A soldier, who also was from the same area as the Ridge Runner, was next to me throwing hand grenades. He had a strong arm and could get them way out there. He pulled the pin, reached back to throw it; the grenade slipped out of his muddy hand and fell in the trench between us. He knew that he didn't have enough time to throw it again so he threw himself on top of it. He shielded me from that grenade but gave his own life in the act of protecting me.

At the same time when the hillbilly, or ridge runner, as he was called, saw his buddy get killed, lost it, grabbed a machine gun, took it off the tripod, and jumped out of the trench. Like a wild man he started running after the Chinese hollering you dirty #######'s, all the while spraying them with bullets and all the while dragging behind him a machine gun belt with shells. He was then unprotected by the trench that we stood in. Then in front of us, out of the fog came a Chinese and sprayed him with burp gun slugs. The Ridge Runner came running towards me, threw the machine gun at me and said, "Get those dirty Chinese, they got me, here Van, get them." The Ridge Runner fell in the trench near his dead buddy. He turned the tide and the enemy retreated because they were afraid of an all out attack when they saw him running at them.

I sent one of my ammo bearers to quickly get a medic and a couple of stretchers while I tried to help Ridge Runner who had a couple bullet holes in his chest. One hole appeared to be through his lung. We hurried to get him on the personnel

176

carrier but as we were loading him he said, "I will be back. I am going to get that dirty Chinese. I tell you Van, I will be back." Two months later he refused to go to the states. He said, "Send me back to the line to my old outfit because I have a score to settle."

While I was on line my folks and my girl friend wrote to me faithfully. Mother or Dad always sent along a sheet of paper and an envelope and would tell me, "Just drop a note so we know you are still okay." The next day I was feeling very blue sitting on a wet ammo can with my feet in 14 inches deep the mud I hadn't had my clothes off and had only taken my boots off once in about two weeks. My hands were always wet, my boots were always in the mud so my toes looked like wrinkled prunes and were already turning blue.

I was really feeling down that I had lost two excellent warriors the night before. I couldn't help but think about how my squad member gave his life to save mine.

All I could think about was what happened to him when he threw himself on the grenade. **"Oh Lord, how much can we take?"** was my cry that morning. 'I know you again saved me from death last night but what an awful price that our Squad had to pay to defend this little piece of real estate. It doesn't make sense, it isn't worth it."

Then when I was lost in thought I heard someone say, "There's mail for you Van." I hurried to open one from my folks and one from an Aunt Coba. I quickly read the one from my aunt. She told me how she and her Ladies Aid Circle were praying for me and for the other boys in the service. She shared with me how she was having some of my friends over for lunch on Sunday

177

nights; occasionally my girl friend would be there and they were having such a nice time.

Then I got a letter from my girl friend telling me how the teachers would go out roller-skating with the gang on Friday nights. How hard it was for her not to date since her friends were going out on dates. She said she wanted to go out once in a while too. She usually wrote letters that would give me a lift for days.

The circumstances that I found myself in were already more then I could stand. I hurried and opened the letter from my folks to get the paper and envelope that my folks had sent me and sent a sizzling note to my girl friend. In the letter I remember telling her how sorry I felt for her because she was suffering so much. I don't remember the exact words I used but it certainly wasn't a masterpiece. I later discovered she didn't put that letter in her archives for future reference either.

The Enemy Tried to Push us off Old Baldy Every Night

We spent several weeks on line in the July/August monsoon rains Old Baldy reverse slopes. A friend and I were waiting for a ride back to change our tattered mud soaked clothes when a 2nd division photographer snapped this picture. The ammo box was located behind the front line, near the aid station. It felt like sleeping on a feather bed after skirmishing nightly with the enemy in knee-deep water and mud soaked trenches for weeks without rest. (*Photo from: History 2nd Division 1951-1952)

179

After being in that in that dreadful position on the base of *Old Baldy* for two weeks, it was so good to get off. We must have looked just as dirty, grimy and as anxious to get off, as the soldiers were that we replaced two weeks before. The ice cold shower never felt so good, and to change into clean clothing was a treat.

That night we slept in army cots, out of the mud and water, in a squad tent in a reserve area.

One of my Puerto Rican soldiers received in the mail a small recorder that he could wind up and play music. He and three of his buddies played Spanish songs and mambos until the wee hours of the morning. Several of us in the tent had already told him to shut it off. But the usual answer would be "No comprendo"(I don't understand) and after tolerating it just so long one of the fellas said, "Mendez, shut that darn thing off." Mendez said, "No comprendo." One angry soldier reached under his bed, pulled out a carbine and shot right through the center of the recorder. It flew into a bunch of pieces and lay silent.

That night I thought that I would have a killing in our squad tent. I later asked to have the American soldier transferred to a different unit. When I told the captain what happened, he agreed that they shouldn't go back on line together with all that hatred for each other.

We heard that part of our division had finally pushed the Chinese totally off the rest of Old Baldy and that we would have to go back up again to secure it. This was so that the group who took the hill could come down and regroup. We did leave that night, and I was placed with one other American soldier on the forward slope of *Old Baldy* with the Chinese looking down our throat. The enemy was just on the next ridge with a valley between us. In the morning when it started to get daylight, we noticed just about 100 ft. out from the front of our bunker, a little beyond where we had some barbed wire entanglement, lying in a mine field were three dead Chinese. They were either caught in a mine or the machine gunners before us had killed them.

We had the luxury of having strung a wire for a sound power from our bunker directly to the captain's bunker on the other side of the hill. When we told the captain about those dead Chinese he said, "I will get in touch with grave's registration to bury them." They wouldn't remove the bodies until the minefield was cleared. The mine removal crew wouldn't clear the minefield as long as the Chinese were firing on them during the day. They said they wouldn't clear mines during the dark hours because it would be too dangerous. We were on this position, in the heat of August, for 21 days. Those dead bodies smelled worse day by day. We finally started shooting into these swollen corpses to get them to decay quicker. I found in that environment it was impossible to eat anything but C rations wafers.

We were located in front of where an army tank was stationed. It had a big direct firing weapon and also carried a fifty-caliber machine gun. Every once in a while the tank would climb just above our bunker and when they fired at the enemy, our bunker would shake. Then the tank would pull back behind the hill before the enemy would fire back. The Chinese thinking it was us who fired at them, would aim at our bunker and fire shells from a tank.

Captain Marra would call on the sound power and say, "Van, can you get a grid azimuth (range and distance) from where they are firing that tank?" When I could, I would report the tank's location so that out tank could try to silence the tank firing at us." "Sir," I replied, "They are shooting the front off of our bunker; the guys in the tank have created all this fuss. Let them stick their heads out of the tank and find out from where the Chinese were shooting. If we stick our heads out, the next shell will get us." We did at a later time get the location of the tank when they were firing on a different position. Then our tank rolled up and sent a few shells their way. That quieted them down for the rest of the day.

While we were at this position in our bunker, we had dug a cave-like hole at the one end that we could crawl into if the tank started firing at our bunker again. This really helped to prevent the flying shrapnel from getting us. Our tank that was behind us could draw more incoming shells than we could draw flies around a hog-slop barrel in an Iowa mid summer.

After three weeks in this position we were pulled off line and were taking a new type of training. We then had an opportunity to attend chapel. On Sunday morning a bunch of us guys loaded up on a 2-½ ton truck and headed to chapel. We had a very heavy rain all night long and as we were riding down the steep hillside we came across fast moving water on the road.

The driver hit the brakes on the truck and slid into a deep wash out on the road. One of our groups was carrying a Sub-Machine gun (Grease Gun) and as we all fell against the cab of the truck his submachine gun fell to the floor and began shooting and spinning in a circle spraying us with shells. The person, who dropped it, threw his body on top of the submachine gun and was severely wounded and I believe he died. Several of our group had leg wounds.

Top:

We are off of the front line
and in the rear for a short
time. The author and his
buddies dry their clothing
and share a meal together.

Bottom:

Back on line; Tony and I
are ready with full gear to
go out tonight to engage
 the enemy on patrol.

Chapter 12

Road to Koje-Do

POW Detail

We were hearing rumors that we were going to have beachhead invasion training and then land by ship in North Korea. We were given training in using gas masks and a lot of hand-to-hand combat training using the bayonet.

We were loaded on trucks at night and arrived at Inchon Harbor, where landing crafts were waiting to ferry us to a ship.

Nobody knew or would tell where we were going or even hint where we were headed. We discovered that they were taking us around the south side of Korea to the Island of Koje-do. We discovered that this is where all the war prisoners were held. We left the boat the same way we loaded on it by crawling up and down the side of the boat on nets.

The Navy assault boats that opened up from the front took us ashore. They stopped a way from shore and we had to jump into water, (some spots were shoulder high), and still try to keep our weapons dry.

When our platoon was all on shore, we got into formation and marched in our wet clothing and our boots sloshing with water as we headed toward our barracks. We marched past rows and rows of prison compounds with barracks made of stone and mud. There were machine guns in towers on each corner and in between the corners were also machine gun towers.

When we got into our living area we noticed that we had a cot for every person and a dry place to keep our stuff. We also had the luxury of an army PX with drinks and food, a barber and a place to worship. The reason they shipped us to this prison compound was that they were expecting a prison break and we were sent right from fierce combat over there to show not only force, but we needed to control the prisoners with a firm hand. This change for the 23rd was necessary because the men had lost a lot of weight and were very discouraged. Ever since we had arrived in Korea we were mostly under enemy fire, we had lost a lot of our men, and had already suffered so much because of that loss.

While we were at *Koje-Do* we had to break up a riot of striking prisoners who had a sit down strike. No one would move to do any work. This was at the time when *Joe Stalin* died. The prisoners took down an American flag and put up a homemade Communist flag. They made the flag by taking a rain poncho, boiling it on the stove and rubbing all the rubber off it leaving a white nylon base. Then they took Mercurochrome to paint the red circle and with stove suet made the dark color and flew it at half-mast.

They tore their old jeans and made black bows of them using stove soot for blackening. The prisoners tied these bows to their shirtsleeves. This was their way of expressing their loss of the death of Joe Stalin. They even refused to empty their own honey buckets. Their toilets (which we affectionately called, honey buckets), consisted of 55 gallon gas barrels cut in half with a rope handle on them and an elevated platform above so they could sit on top of them. They had to daily carry them to the boat dock where they were loaded first on small boats then on larger sewage ships to be transported farther into the ocean where they were dumped.

We used the prisoner work crews to unload ships that carried gasoline that was in 55 gallon barrels and all the food and supplies that were required to keep that massive prison compound supplied. These ships had on them the supplies that the service men needed for guarding the island from an outside enemy attack as well as the soldiers who were in charge of keeping the prisoners secure.

We couldn't permit the prisoners to get away with this sit down strike. We were ordered to fix our bayonets and to surround the inside of the compound, placing our soldiers 10 feet apart. Then outside the compound we had a few tanks and a group of soldiers in and around the guard towers. We all had gas masks so we could shoot tear gas into their compounds if we had to. I also disobeyed an army rule; I often used my gas mask carrier for carrying cans of chocolate milk, along with my mask, so I had a drink while standing guard.

A Chinese and North Korean translator told the prisoners they all had to go to the exercise area, that was a small ball field. In that field they had to kneel on their knees in rows 8 feet apart. While in that position they were to remove the black ribbons and promise to be willing to go on their work detail. If they didn't, the soldiers were going to force them with bayonets. Then there would be a very bloody end to this standoff. The prisoners were to decide, blood or cooperation.

After we showed we meant it, most of the prisoners moved into the exercise area. Some took the ribbons off, but a lot of them wouldn't. So the translator again told them that they had one last chance to obey or be punished. As you might guess they refused so we were ordered to walk among them and release all those who already cooperated. Then the translator announced again, "You will now remove the ribbons, put them in your mouth and eat them or else my soldiers will discipline you."

We then, with rifle butts over them, ordered them one by one to eat those ribbons. It took some strong blows to the body for some but after a few were really hurt bad they started to slowly take the ribbons off and put them into their mouths. We could watch, as the black stove soot would drip out of their mouths as they tried to eat those ribbons. Those prisoners who were stubborn and held out were also driven through an alley where soldiers on each side of the alley would have to strike them between the shoulders and their rear. This was done with their rifle butts and was used as a form of discipline for not obeying our orders. This had to be accomplished in each compound of 5000 prisoners until we again had control of the entire camp. That day there were several loads of prisoners who were treated in hospitals and again our unit leaders had to report to the authorities because we had injured prisoners.

When our first sergeant came back from those meetings he said that they asked him why his men had injured prisoners. He said, "The prisoners refused to work; we had to discipline them. I told my men to hit them on the buttocks but it isn't my fault that their aim was so bad."

After that episode we had to make raids each night on their sleeping barracks. We would have two guys with M2 carbines and one with a high power flashlight on each side of the barracks. Upon signal we would open the door and flash the light. Then two soldiers had to go inside and walk all the way among the 5000 prisoners and see if anything was going on. We found out they were making more flags and one prisoner was carving from a wooden door-post, a rifle, that looked exactly like our M1 rifle. Another time they were trying to make bullets using soap and lead from pencils. Whenever I had to walk among the prisoners I would have goose bumps until I was safely outside again. It was awful walking down those small aisles with the prisoners sleeping like cords of wood stacked head to foot, side by side, on both sides of the aisles. We were among them without any protection on us. Only the soldiers who stood in the doorway had weapons.

There was a lot of unrest in the compounds, and they had information that there was a possible riot coming down. Then one night at supper, nine of us were told we had to report to headquarters for a night mission. When we got to the headquarters building I was searching for a reason why I was chosen. The only thing that we all had in common was that we all went to chapel and none of us drank liquor.

Before the mission we all had to raise our right hand and swear under oath that what we were going to see and do would remain a secret with us for the duration of the war. After swearing us in, they loaded us up on a semi and took us a long way from camp to a large warehouse building. There we found about 100 South Korean men who were dressing into prisoners' clothing. We were told to start a fight where we had to rough up the prisoners and they also joined in. They were to become pretend or fake prisoners that we just captured and were being dumped into the prison compound. These were South Koreans trained to be CIA. We had to ruff them up to make them appear like bruised and abused prisoners. Then we were to release a few into each compound building as new added prisoners. They were to stay in the POW compound and every so often they and all the prisoners were going to be interrogated individually along with all the prisoners. That way we could find out from our Korean CIA spies what was going on. We needed to know whom the ring leaders were in the prison compounds and separate the ringleaders from the rest of the prisoners.

A few nights after our delivery of spies, we were hearing about prisoners hanging other prisoners in the toilets. Then in the morning we would find more prisoners hanging by ropes in the toilet area. I knew right away that some of the spies were found out and being hung. It wasn't suicide. Orders came out that the prisoners could only go to the bathroom one at a time at night.

A few nights later I was placed in charge of the compound guard. Around midnight a shotgun guard who was walking inside the compound called out, *"Corporal of the guard, Corporal of the guard."* I could hear panic in his voice. When I got there I spotted three guys dragging and half carrying one of the prisoners whom I recognized as a Korean CIA agent. I called all four prisoners to me and in my mixed Korean and English told them, "One person to the toilet at a time." They told me they understood, so I thought, "Mission accomplished."

About 1 o'clock in the morning I again heard in a loud voice, "*Corporal of the Guard, Corporal of the Guard.*" When I got there the same prisoners were coming again. I tried to halt them, but they wouldn't stop. They kept on dragging that CIA agent. So I grabbed the sawed off shotgun from the guard and aimed it low, intending to scare them. I fired a shot; they jumped in the air and ran to the barracks. They were sprayed over their feet with some pellets.

When they turned around and ran for the door, they hit the door so hard that they knocked the door off the hinges with a loud banging noise. The guards in the machine gun towers, who were half asleep, called in that there was a riot in the POW compound. That message signaled to bring up reinforcements and there came the army tanks. Then came the quad fifty caliber rifles mounted on half-tracks; rumbling towards the compound.

When asked why I shot, all I could say was that they were disobeying an order. I couldn't say I was protecting a spy who I thought they were going to kill. At 10 o'clock the next morning I had to report to headquarters. The master sergeant, who was dressed in his finest said, "We have to meet with the North Korean delegation and the *International Red Cross* to fill out a report as to why you shot at prisoners last night.

When I arrived at the meeting building, the wheels were there from North Korea. The Chinese along with the *International Red Cross* officials were already there to interrogate me about shooting at those prisoners.
They started questioning me and I had to be so evasive with my answers. Remember I had taken an oath about putting spies in

those compounds and I couldn't reveal that I was protecting a spy. The questioning went on until noon. By this time the sergeant was getting visibly sick of it all. He stopped the interrogator and said, "May I ask a question of the accused?" The sergeant asked, "Corporal Van, how many prisoners did you kill?" I said, "None sir." The master sergeant became unglued. He had a big book in front of him on prison camp rules from the *Geneva Convention*. He picked up the book, slammed it on the table and said, "What's all the fuss; you shot at them, sprayed them with a few slugs and didn't kill any. Van, you should have aimed higher, now we got all this fuss and we still have to feed the SOBs."

That broke the ice and they dismissed me from the room. The sergeant came out and said, "There will be no charges filed against you because you were following orders." I thought about that later; this CIA agent was a marked man in that compound and his leg wounds permitted him to get to the hospital to patch his leg. So he did not have to go in the same compound again. What happened that night was God's providence at work. I was put in charge of the soldiers, walking compound guard that night, so I could spare that Korean CIA agent's life.

When I worked in the Chinese prisoners officer's compound I had an interesting talk with a Chinese prisoner. This prisoner at one time was a dental student in the USA before he went back to China. He said, "Why do you look so mad at us prisoners. If you went through what my parents did with the Americans you too would be a Communist. When the United States troops had to rush through our land with tanks

192

during World War II, the tanks were traveling over the high way on their way to Burma because the fields were soft. The tanks were in such a hurry that they rumbled into towns and into the town where my parents lived. The streets were too narrow for the tanks, so when the tanks had to turn the corner the tank drivers hit our house and it came tumbling down. The soldiers looking out of the top of the tank laughed and laughed as my parent's house went tumbling to the ground.

We were allies, and that is how your soldiers treated us. Maybe your government paid our country for the damaged roads but it wasn't funny wrecking our house. My parents struggled a long time and never did get that home repaired. If that happened to your parents wouldn't that make you angry?" I walked on saying nothing since our instructions did not allow us to talk with them, but he had given me food for thought.

Maybe he had a point. Many times our service men do act in an ugly manner when they are overseas. I too must say many are very unbecoming and are rightly viewed as the ugly Americans. Later in my life, while traveling overseas, I have also witnessed tourists whose actions I was ashamed of and recognized that some individuals who behaved badly towards foreigners were fellow Americans.

For a few weeks I was assigned to a prisoner inspection program. Before a prisoner was permitted to go on work detail they had to go through our inspection program. Some of the things we were looking for were homemade knives, written notes on toilet paper, pencils and any sharp objects that they could use as weapons.

They were permitted to have 18 inches of toilet paper but they always tried to test us by taking more paper and then writing notes on the paper. They would pass these notes to others from different compounds and in that way the officers would communicate with all the prisoners in other compounds. The Chinese and North Korean officers were the ones who were still trying to control all the rest of the prisoners. They would take the screws out of door hinges and hollow out the heels of their shoes, screw the heel back on, then while on break time take out the note and pass it to other prisoners. When I caught them, I would pry the heels off their shoes and remove the messages in them. At one time a message I took was of encouragement to fellow prisoners to break free and escape. I also caught some of them with morphine needles in their cap visors.

Some prisoners would slip razor blades in their pockets and when we would search their pockets we would get our fingers cut. When this would happen I called a member of my squad, a Korean, whose nickname meant "*small*" (which he was). All I would have to say was, "Please take care of this prisoner." and the sparks would fly. This South Korean became very angry with any prisoner who disobeyed orders. After two weeks they relieved me of the search detail because the POWs complained that I was causing problems for the prisoners, saying that I was destroying their clothing when I was prying the heels off the shoes that were screwed on. They also said that I had torn up their caps when I discovered needles and removed the razor blades.

I was than sent on a neat detail. We were driven up a mountain with a four-wheel drive ¾ ton truck, until the truck would spin out. Then we would hike the rest of the way up the mountain. At this location were a large radio tower and a guardhouse with a power generator and transmitting equipment. The Navy, Army, and Air force would send signals to each other through this tower. We had to provide the security for that tower. For a whole week we had freedom from brass bugging us. Our little detail was for each of us to guard the tower two hours out of every eight. It was a nice detail, and was well located above the smelly prison compounds.

While at Koje-Do I got to know our company first sergeant very well after that episode with the North Koreans. The master sergeant, whose nickname was Mac, was about ready to go to the States and retire after serving his 20 years in the army. He was a rough old salty sort of a guy with a soft spot underneath. We were both going to be on guard the same evening and he was in charge of all the guards. That night we had with us a smart young state side officer, who was the officer of the day, but he hardly ever came around.

The word around the troops was that on the northern most towers, some of the guys had signaled to a Korean prostitute named Rosy to come to that tower. Rumors also had it that soldiers were trading stolen clothing for sex. The sergeant was interested in the facts of the case and wanted to talk to Rosy. The sergeant said to me, "Tonight I am putting you in that tower." I said, "Okay, what do you want from me?" He said, "If I understand right, she will light a fire on the hill, and if it is safe for her to come down, the soldier in the guard tower signals to her to come. You signal to her, and when she comes down the hill, call me; I want to find out if this is true. I want to see what she is like. Maybe I can catch these soldiers who are stealing military clothing in exchange for sex."

So my buddy and I went up to the north tower and occasionally watched for the fire in the hillside. Meanwhile the first sergeant had called two times if Rosy had already come down. After about a half an hour the phone rang, I picked it up expecting it was the sergeant again. I answered the phone "Rosie's Whore House, Rosie's not in." Who should be on the other end of the line but the straight-laced lieutenant. "Who am I speaking with," he shouted. I wasn't even breathing any more. "Who am I speaking with?" he shouted again. "Corporal Van, sir." I said in a timid voice. "Corporal," he shouted, "We will see about replacing your stripes. Then when you are back to a private you maybe will learn proper military telephone procedure. I want you too come to the guard house as soon as you are released from guard duty on the tower." Rosy never showed up that night nor did the sergeant call me again.

Well, I was preparing my defense of course. I had no excuse for the way I talked on the phone. I thought when I answered the phone that it would only be the master sergeant that would call to the machine gun tower. But this rookie lieutenant was calling all the towers, checking if they were secure.

After guard duty I slowly walked to the guardhouse. Over at a desk in the corner sat my master sergeant with a "cat who ate the canary grin" on his face.

I said hello to Sergeant Mac and the lieutenant shouted at me like a basic trainee sergeant would to a recruit, "Soldier stand at attention when you enter a room when there is an officer present!" Then for the next 30 minutes he commenced to chew me out for not using proper military telephone procedure. After he finally caught his breath he said, "At ease soldier," and asked if I had anything to say in my defense.

I said, "Sir, I don't believe you realize and understand, because you are from State side, or know about the conditions we were under before we arrived here. Nor do I expect you to understand that most of us were on the verge an emotional and physical breakdown because of the losses we suffered. We, in part, were sent here to recuperate and a friend and I were having some lighter moments together and you have to read me off for it. No officer would ever call a person down for this on line and if he did he would watch his backside after that. That's not a threat, that is a fact of life. If you want the real scoop ask the sergeant. As far as you taking my stripes away, you have that right, but they were given to me by the regimental commander in a battle field promotion."

The lieutenant turned to Sergeant Mac and said, "Do you have anything you want to add?" "No," he said, "Corporal Van said it all." The lieutenant said, "I want you to be careful to use proper military procedure from now on. Just think what I, your superior officer, would have caught if a commanding general had been on the other end of the line. It would have reflected badly on me." As I walked out the door Sergeant Mac asked, "By the way Van, did you ever have company?" I said,

"No, false alarm," and when back to the guard tent for some shut eye.

Our regiment was once again, after having this short break, prepared to go on line when the rainy season would be past. We would have to prepare for what lay ahead, a cold fall and winter, with the cold winds and the freezing ice and snow, which proved to be challenging for all of us.

Top left: We are loaded on landing craft, heading for the island of Koji-Do.

Top right: Standing on top of mountain protecting the army navy radio

Bottom: Overlooking a POW compound from machine gun tower.

Chapter 13

Listening Post Tragedy

When we left *Koje-Do*, we went again the same way we came, by landing craft and by climbing up the rope netting on the ship that took us to *Inchon* by ship. When we arrived there we went to a line blocking position that was beyond the enemy artillery range. Our mission was to dig trenches and make bunkers in case of an enemy break through on the main line because of the build up of North Korean and Chinese troops in the *Chorwon Valley* sector. We also were able on a short notice, to plug any hole that the enemy punched in our main line.

The weather was getting very cold with a sour wind. My unit had no winter gear and only the light field jackets. I was complaining to the mailman who came in by jeep from Battalion and was wearing a parka, to deliver the mail. He said, "Didn't they issue you any?" "No." I said. Then he told me, "I know where they stayed. Some Korean thieves are selling parkas off of a railroad car at a siding about 7 miles up the road." That took the cake, we were freezing and the Koreans were black marketing our winter clothing. I was so angry that I grabbed my loaded rifle, took another buddy who had a loaded carbine and we stole the mail jeep while he was delivering mail, and we high tailed it to the rail siding. Sure enough, there was a swarm of people around the rail car and parkas were going out right and left. We stopped the jeep with a cloud of dust and jumped out with our weapons pointed and shouted for them to scatter.

Inside the rail car, that was already half empty, were three Koreans with a handful of cash. I ordered them to load 12 winter parkas and winter caps and boots into the jeep.

The leader refused and I pointed my rifle at his forehead and said in Korean, "Load them, or so long to you." He then told his swindling buddies to load our jeep. We hurried back to camp and parked the jeep by our squad's tent. Quickly we unloaded the jeep and parked the jeep back where the mailman left it. Then we hurried to the place where the troops were digging ditches. The sergeant over our detail mumbled that we better get to work because we already were late after our mail call.

The next morning the wind blew in some snow. It was nasty weather with a wet cold breeze blowing. When our squad stood up to be counted for work detail, all of my squad had winter caps, and parkas. We stood out like a sore thumb to the rest. When our Captain found out about it he came to me and said, "Soldier how did you get those clothes?" I said, "Remember how in basic training we used to have moonlight requisition in order to get enough brooms and mops? Well, my men were getting cold and I decided to make our own requisition. The captain snapped back, "Soldier, you will tell me where you got those parkas." I told them about the Koreans selling the stuff off the railroad siding. The Captain turned around and he was off in his jeep. He didn't get any parkas just then but got those thieves put into jail for stealing military supplies.

The captain never took our parkas away because they would all have parkas in a week. When the winter supplies did arrive, it was so very cold that we were also issued winter sleeping bags, one bag for three persons. We had no tents in this blocking position that we moved to; we had to rough it by sleeping out under the stars. I believe this was done so we would be better prepared for the winter on line.

When we were moving on line, it began to snow during the day, and the wind got so cold the snow seemed to cut into our faces. We quit our work on the trenches early, and had a warm meal brought up by the kitchen. After eating, I stamped down some snow with my boots so we would have a level spot to lay our sleeping bag on the ground for the night. All night long I rolled round and round to try to keep warm. When I woke up in the morning I got up, rolled up my sleeping bag and then I headed down the hill for some hot coffee. When we got back from breakfast those who left their sleeping bags lay in the snow found their bags frozen to the ice and snow. They had no choice but to chop under their bags and take with them a bunch of frozen snow that they had to carry with them all day with the ice attached. When we got near the line, we might keep one sleeping bag for every three persons. Those who carried snow and ice with them all day had a few choice words to say when they had to give up their sleeping bags.

On line one person would rest while two soldiers would stand guard. Since we didn't each have a sleeping bag, it was also the beginning of a long infestation of lice that we kept getting from the Koreans. We had already packed up, shipped our tents and were leaving to go to another area, and we were now hiking towards a spot called, *"White Horse."* The ground was covered with snow and it was very cold. The first night we didn't get all the way to *White Horse* so we had to stomp a level spot on top of the snow again to roll out the sleeping bags for the night's rest.

The new position we occupied had a long finger off to the one side facing the Chinese. We set our machine gun sight right in the center of the finger and the other two on each side of the finger to get a good cross fire across that long finger. At the base of the finger, that was about two city blocks away, we had dug a hole in the ground about as deep as the average person's arms. Then we strung wire from this listening post to my machine gun position. From there I had communication to the other machine gun positions as well as the platoon leader's bunker. We were now prepared for a possible attack.

The only major problem was, who would have to sit out in front of everybody in that listening post all night? We agreed that we should rotate, and do a three to four hour shift only during the night hours. So we started by taking turns. I volunteered to be first, but was that ever spooky to be alone, waiting for any enemy to come up. Every bush and tree in our imagination seemed like people moving. After a while, it seemed like all the bushes had Chinese coming out of them.

Our plan was, if we saw the Chinese, we were to refrain from picking a fire fight. We were to report by sound power phone to the machine gun position how many Chinese there were and what their position was. Then if we knew we couldn't get back to the line we would tell them to fire the machine guns and we would crouch down into the hole and hope and pray for the best. After a few nights, where the guys all said it was a tough assignment to be on that listening post, I had a new

203

replacement. A 16 year old came to me and in a bragging way said, "I can do that, count me in tonight."

I gave him the first half of the night and at about 10 or 11 o'clock civilian time, I heard the sound power phone whistle. With a shaky voice he said, "I see the Chinese, can I come in?" "How many did you see and where are they, to your right or left?" "I don't know the whole hill seems to be moving." "Shall I send someone to help you?" " I ca-ca-can't stay here any more." "Wait a minute I'll send someone-- I am sending my partner and he will sit with you for a while." So my partner loaded up some hand grenades and ammo and took off for the listening post. I called again. I said, "My buddy is coming, hang on a little while; he will be there to help you."

After just a short while I heard a rifle crack and fearing for an attack I picked up the sound power and said, "Is everything okay, everything okay?" And then came the weeping voice, "Van I shot him, I shot him, come here quick." I called to the other machine gunners to cover me. "When you see the Chinese coming, start cross firing the machine guns towards the base of the hill."

I ran to the listening post and there lay my buddy with a bad shoulder wound but he went into shock and before we could get help, he had died. I was so angry with myself for sending this kid on the listening post. I was angry for being sent on line without being trained to be able to help someone whose body went into shock. There was no enemy in sight nor was there a sign of an attack.

The young 16-year was overcome with fear and fright. He was so afraid-- he shot at anything that moved even after he acknowledged to me that he knew I was sending my buddy over to help him. This was very difficult, even to this day, to overcome the sick feeling and even maybe I still have some anger at an army that didn't check records and would send a 16-year-old kid on line. In fact, I don't believe I will ever lose the deep pain I felt because of this careless loss. Even as I write about it now, it causes my whole body to shake.

In the winter months the enemy didn't attack us in such mass as they did in the summer offensive. Instead they sent out nightly patrols that would probe our positions and set up ambushes for any patrol we sent out. On one patrol a radioman, which was a seasoned soldier, said to me, "They got us going all the way to the Chinese line." I was helping him carry the extra rolls of wire and he whispered, "Van I am not going to get shot; I am supposed to go home in a week and I don't want to go in a box." So he would unwind wire on a pile whenever he could and when we were getting near the enemy line he ran out of wire.

He said to me, "Van pass the word to the lieutenant that we are out of wire." The lieutenant came to the radioman and asked, "Did you take all the rolls that I asked for?" He said, "Yes." He didn't lie. "How come we are out? Maybe you went in circles or curves in the dark. Well, we can't lose our communications so we will have to set up here." The lieutenant said, "Call in, and tell them what happened, we won't be able to probe the enemy line tonight." When the lieutenant left him he said, "Van, I did it, now we don't have to get our heads shot off just to show the Chinese that we can probe them too."

I was told one morning that I was selected to go out on a very dangerous mission where we were to make contact with the enemy. They told me that I should get an M2 carbine with a lot of ammo, be issued a steel vest, take about six hand grenades and be ready for a briefing at O700hours (5 o' clock civilian time) I had traded my rifle for a carbine. I cleaned and oiled it, checked out my steel vest and gear, and at 5 o'clock went to the command post for briefing. The lieutenant had a patrol of 14. All but two of them spoke only Spanish so our briefing took quite a while.

Our mission was to go as near to the enemy lines as we could and make contact by starting a firefight with the enemy. The enemy would return fire and we were to withdraw. We would then learn the enemy positions, weapons and strength.

We were about to leave the captain's bunker to wait for it to get a little darker, when the phone rang. It was from Battalion for me. It was from my lieutenant who lost part of his hand defending Old Baldy. He said, "Van, I have an opening for someone to go to Non-Commission Officer School. It will be for a couple weeks and is located way to the rear of the line. It won't be easy, but you'll enjoy it. We will pick you up in about 2 hours and you will sleep at Battalion headquarters tonight.
"Sir, I can't go on that patrol tonight. I have had my briefing already. The captain said, "What's up Van?"

I told him that I had a chance to go to school. Then the company medic who was sitting next to the captain, who was an African American said, "I will take your place Van. I haven't been on patrol because I always had to stay back here. Before I go back to the States I would like to try it once." That was okay with the officers so the captain told me to give my gear to the medic and to get ready to go to school.

That night at Battalion I couldn't sleep. I tossed and turned, tossed and turned on my cot. About midnight I heard a jeep come driving up. I looked out of the tent and it was our company jeep. The driver told me Easy Company Patrol was hit and hurt and the last radio transmission was that some were taken prisoners. Before we left that morning I went to the lieutenant and asked him about that patrol. He told me they sent a large group to rescue the wounded, and that the medic who took my place along with six others was killed; the lieutenant was wounded and taken prisoner along with the Puerto Rican soldiers.

My heart sank. I started to shiver and had chills all over my body. Our medic who was to go home in a few weeks gave his life on that patrol. He didn't have to go but he did it for me. They told me later that he took my carbine apart which he had, and as he crawled, he kept pushing pins of the carbine into the mud and as he kept crawling further, pushed other parts into the mud so it could no longer be picked up and used by the enemy.

I was then told that the list of those who were going on that patrol was submitted to Battalion. My former platoon lieutenant who lost his fingers on *Baldy* was the one who read the list and he noticed my name on it. When this lieutenant saw they had a position to fill at Non-commissioned Officers School, he decided to send me. I was pleased to go, but my heart hurt because of this awful loss. It all seemed so foolish. As a footnote, I later learned after the war and through the prisoner release program that the lieutenant wasn't able to keep up with the forced march to the rear. Also that because of his serious wounds he was shot and left along the side of the road to die. Another prisoner from that patrol was also shot for being too tired to move fast enough.

Our training at the Non Commissioned Officers School was to teach us how to lead a unit in combat. This wasn't anything new, and we also studied the code of military justice. This informed us what an officer could do, what a leader and an officer couldn't do, or what isn't permissible under the military code of justice. This course later turned out to be a real benefit to me when a state-side-recruiting sergeant tried to force me to dig a ditch.

The reason for having me dig the ditch was that my squad left the line and went in reserve to prepare our machine guns to be combat ready. This was the first thing we always did so we were cleaning and working on our weapons. Instead, the 1st sergeant wanted us to have polished shoes for his inspection. Because my squad was working on our weapons we failed his shoe inspection, and he was trying to force me, by myself, to dig a sump hole 12 feet by 12 feet by 6 feet deep.

I'll never forget the look on his face when I told him not to tell me about his problems, but to get me a detail. I told him he might not make a non-commissioned officer do degrading tasks when there are privates sitting around doing nothing. If he would provide me with privates, then he would get his sump hole dug. He shot daggers with his expressions and gave me the privates to do the digging. For two days I sat on a bucket supervising the workers while he did a slow burn.

While at the school I met a lieutenant who was an implement dealer from South Dakota. I recognized him by his

Midwest accent and we talked a bit together. One night I had to be on guard duty and to my surprise he was the officer of the day in charge of the guard. He called us all together to pull an inspection and when he came to me he inspected my rifle and asked me my first general order. He said to the inspecting sergeant, "Make this soldier *Super Numerary,* he is really sharp. (A Super Numerary is a military term, which means to be chosen by officers as the best in the rank, and not required to stand guard but be a replacement.) Then he said, "Soldier, I want to talk to you after this inspection."

He told me to get a jeep from the motor pool, and gave me a receipt for it signed by him. He said, "We are going to have an interesting evening. We will wait until dark and we will raid the known places of prostitution. We will be looking for American GIs since these places are off limits to them. Let's find out if any are there, and if they are, let's see them scram when they find us looking for them."

So he put a big temporary MP (Military Police) armband on us. We got in the jeep and off we went to the nearest town. It didn't take him long to find the streets where the prostitutes hung out. We found the street and went on foot. Before long we would hear some one say, "Here come the MPs!" Out of the shacks, soldiers who were hanging out with those ladies of the night would come, flying like a streak. We chased one soldier who had his pants in his hands. He hollered at us as he was running, "You can't arrest me, you didn't see anything." The lieutenant said, "Oh yes we can, improper dress, disorderly conduct. An immediate transfer to the line company will cool you down. Get him Corporal Van, get him" shouted the lieutenant.

When the soldier heard that, he was gone like a jet engine. The lieutenant was laughing so hard at the way the soldier took off; he had to hold on to a door of the building to keep him from falling over. The lieutenant said, "It is a pity that these soldiers think so little of their bodies that they would risk a lifetime of disease and maybe never be admitted back into the United States because they had picked up non-curable oriental venereal diseases."

Those two weeks went by like a flash and after spending several months on line, we were moving to a new location from *Arrowhead* to, I believe, *White Horse Region,* or maybe the other way around. The thing that stands out in my mind about this location was that there was an outpost located a long distance from the main line through a long valley. On that outpost, we would be exposed to small arms fire all day long. The small group of soldiers that had to go on this outpost was chosen by the first sergeant. He chose those soldiers who had ruffled his feathers over some issue. He was the type of person to get even. For me it was the digging the sump hole for our garbage with a detail. Well, when he picked the soldiers for the outpost he chose all the soldiers that he disliked and those of us who would be going home real soon.

He said with a dirty grin, "I wanted to send the old seasoned soldiers who are trained in war. I want to see if you can make it on this hill or to see rather, if you old timers are all hot air." We all started for the out post without an argument, in the dark of night. I guess what burned us up about this guy

210

was that he spent 20 years in soft desk jobs with the last years as a recruiter, Now he volunteered to spend his last 30 days in our unit to be able to wear the combat infantrymen's badge. Where did we find him? Always way back in the command post's bunker with so many logs and bags of sand it would take an A-bomb to get him.

We arrived at the outpost at about 10 o'clock and we were told by the soldiers we replaced, never to stand anywhere more than a short stretch during the day. The enemy snipers could look down our noses and were daily taking shots at those who were on the outpost. We had to be careful during the day to stay down below the ridgeline in our trenches and pretty much out of sight. We were already there three days, daily we received a lot of sniper fire and occasional small mortar rounds. Those Chinese were good with their mortars--they were always right on the money. I often said they could put a mortar shell in your back pocket from a mile away.

It was now the 4th of July. Our 2nd lieutenant, who was with us, received a phone call from the 1st sergeant saying, that he had made 1st lieutenant and was 2nd in command of our company just behind our captain, and over the 1st sergeant. "I have good news and bad news," said the lieutenant, "The good news for you four who are ready to go home, is, you can go home today. The bad news you can only go if you pass a venereal disease examination at battalion rear today before leaving for division rear tonight. The bad news you already know is, you will never make it alive across that long valley in daylight the way the Chinese are firing down on us.

Our anger level at the first sergeant went to an all time high. He had those orders already before he sent us on the outpost. Our lieutenant said, "I have an idea." He went to the phone and called the captain. He said, "Today is the 4th of July, and I have a bunch of troops who are really discouraged because the first sergeant pulled this off to keep them here a month longer." Then he explained what happened. He said he was requesting our captain to call to battalion to ask them if could get permission for every soldier in our battalion to fire all of our weapons and have at least a 30 minute volley on the enemy positions. I believe it will do a lot for the troops morale and send a message to the enemy to not mess with us.

After a few minutes the captain called back and said, "You are approved, get your boys ready to cross the valley while the volley is going on--we owe that to them." The lieutenant said to us, "Take only what you need." and he helped us camouflage ourselves " When it's 12 noon, run like deer across the valley, spread apart, and good luck." I grabbed the lieutenant, hugged him and said, "Thanks!" and four of us who were eligible to rotate to the States took off for the main line, running as fast as we could, not looking back.

We made it across the valley just as our troop stopped firing. When we got back to the rear area, far behind the main line sat the sergeant. I asked him for the papers and as he was getting them, I noticed the mail clerk leaving with his jeep. We hollered at him to wait for us, as we needed a ride back to battalion with him. As the sergeant handed us the papers he said sarcastically, "Boys, did you have a good time on the outpost?" "Fantastic," I said, "and I have a wish for you also. My wish is that your bones may rot in Korea." I know that wasn't very Christian of me, but at the time I was still consumed with anger at what he had done to us by putting us on an outpost just a few days before rotation.

Then to make matters worse, he kept the rotation orders until the morning we had to leave so we had to risk our lives to get to the rear in daylight hours. If it wasn't for the lieutenant's quick thinking of the 4th of July volley we would have to stay another month. I rotated only needing 36 points and I already had 42 points the way it was.

That night we were able to take off our dirty sweaty combat clothing and jump in a shallow pond of water. As we were sitting in the water we could see the artillery shells exploding. It didn't have for us the fear and dread that it had when we first arrived; we now were on our way home. For us to go to sleep on a cot in our shorts without having to be fully dressed, boots and all, was already a treat.

We were processed at division rear and were loaded up on a much larger ship than that with which we came. To my surprise two buddies from our area, with whom I was in basic training, were also on the ship. They were asking for volunteers for workers on the trip back. I quickly volunteered for duty in the cold storage cooler putting the cook's food supply on the dumb waiter to be brought up to the kitchen. That job was like being in paradise, with all kinds of fresh fruit, apples, oranges and bananas. I didn't have to stand in line for rice and beans. Those beans sounded good now, but I didn't need to stand in line. I could take food from crates that were stored in the cooler for the officers' mess.

The trip back was very pleasant. The sailors were to have an inspection on the ship when they got back to San Francisco. Their plan was to get the soldiers, who did not have any work details, the job of chipping the old paint off the boat with chisels. Following that, they planned to have the soldiers painting different areas for them, where the paint was chipped off. The plan didn't work at all. It started with a wise soldier who looked at the chisel they gave him and said, "This chisel is too dull to use," and threw it overboard. It didn't take long and hammers were too round or had chipped heads, and the sailors' equipment was going to "Davy Jones locker in the deep blue sea." A sailor soon caught on, and started to raise cane, but soon found out that a shipload of combat veterans weren't going to do their work. An older army sergeant said to the sailor in charge, "Sonny, I believe if I were you, I would pick up the hammers that are left and clean up your own ship."

When we were a day's travel away from San Francisco, they announced over the loudspeaker that the Korean War was over and the truce was signed. The next day we would be coming into port. That night the top of the deck was loaded with soldiers, lying on pillows on the deck, waiting to see the first glimpse of the good old USA. Before we were anywhere near shore, they were meeting us with newspaper cameramen to get a picture of the first troops back in after the truce was signed. When we did get close to the dock, there was a Navy band playing patriotic tunes for us.

The troops on the ship all went to the dockside, causing the ship to tilt in that direction. Nobody listened to the loud speakers telling us to go to the other side of the boat. Soon the captain came with a bunch of sailors with Billie clubs, telling us to move or they would start clubbing. He had to keep the ship on even keel or he would not begin to unload the ship.

Some of the soldier's wives were at the boat dock to meet their husbands and they were put behind a 10 feet high fence. We were told nobody would get to see their families until they were finished processing at *Camp Stoneman.* It didn't work that way. A few soldiers were coming off the boat when one spotted his wife and climbed right over the fence, carrying his bag over the fence like it was only waist high. Soon other soldiers spotted family and jumped over the fence. It didn't take long and the fence fell down with a crash. They couldn't separate the wives from their soldier husbands. They loaded up the wives and took them all to *Camp Stoneman.* They processed the married soldiers first while the wives waited for them at the camp.

We stood in the hot California sun for a long time before we got inside. When we did, we were issued Class A uniforms, given a quick dental check and given orders to report to camp at Colorado Springs after our leave. I was very unhappy that they were planning to give us another assignment when we were promised that those who spent combat time would be released after the tour of duty.

I wanted to call the folks that I was home in the States, but couldn't get to a phone before we loaded on a train that would go straight through to Omaha, Nebraska. I managed to talk the conductor into letting me write a telegram. He would hold it out to a station manger to grab it as we went past him. It worked. The station manager waved back that he got the Western Union message and sent it on. The message read,

"Have someone meet me in Omaha, contact Phyllis. See you all soon. Rich"

My heart was pounding just as fast as the tracks were going clickety clack, clickety clack. It won't be long now until I will be able to hold her in my arms once more. Will she be the same? It had been 16 long and dreadful months since I last saw her. I will never forget the pain fear, anger and frustrations of what happened to so many of our platoon. I know I have changed. How could it be different? The question that was going through my mind was this, "How has this separation affected her? Will she be the same person or has she changed too? Her letters aren't as warm as they were. Or am I only imagining it?"

Little did the author know that when he left the front line he would have a new battle to fight. The emotional pain suffered while on line couldn't be buried and left behind. This disturbing war would rage on through nightmares and flashbacks.

Chapter 14

The Big Adjustment

As I was riding the train from San Francisco to Omaha, Nebraska that evening, I didn't want to talk to anybody. My mind was reflecting back over what had happened since I left home. I wondered if it was by chance that I was spared from death. Why did so many of my friends have to lose their lives? As the train was winding around the mountains throughout the night, I wanted to shut out the world and ask God a bunch of "why" questions.

Was it by accident on Old Baldy that the machine gun bullet stuck and I bent over as the shell swished over my head? Why did our Afro American medic have to give his life for me by taking my place on the suicide mission? Why would the short southerner from my squad throw himself on the grenade to save my life when the grenade slipped out of his hand in that muddy trench? Why did I hear the Chinese machine gun bolt as he pulled it back, just in time for me to dive between the rocks, when so many of our patrol were hit by those slugs in that ambush? Was it only luck that all of the artillery shells landed on the enemy side of the drainage ditch? Was it accident or skill that those shells pinned down the Chinese so we could escape, (while they were seeking cover) from those artillery shells? Was it God's plan that they stopped shooting long enough for us to pick up the wounded and be released from the enemy's constant firing down on us?

I know God--you were there that night when the radio operator died in my arms. I remember while I was carrying him, he looked up and talked to you as he died, and you took his spirit from his body. Why did I put a young kid on that listening post and Fred had to lose his life with friendly fire? Why did buddy Fred have to go to that listening post instead of going myself and why get did he get shot instead of me? Why wasn't I trained so I could help Fred come out of shock? Why did he have that awful glazed look in his eyes like he was pleading for someone to help him and I failed because I didn't know how?

While reviewing the past 14 months that I survived in combat zone, I realized that there was something more behind my being able to return. It wasn't luck or being fortunate. I had no doubt that the Almighty God of the universe was guiding it. God was setting me apart and calling me for a special task. There must be a reason that God chose to answer the prayers of friends and family for my safety. This was the beginning of a lot of searching to discover God's leading and then trying to follow it.

The sun was slowly coming over the hillside and I was very tired in body and my mind had no rest, only questions. I turned to my Bible and read that day's devotions:

> *"Humble yourselves therefore under the mighty hand of God, so that he may exalt you in due time. Cast all your anxiety on him, because he cares for you. Discipline yourselves. Keep alert. Like a roaring lion your adversary the devil prowls around, looking for someone to devour. Resist him, steadfast in your faith, for you know that your*

brothers and sisters in the entire world are undergoing the same kinds of suffering. And after you have suffered for a little while, the God of all grace, who has called you to his eternal glory in Christ, will himself restore, support, strengthen, and establish you. To him be the power forever and ever. Amen."

I Peter 5:6-11 KJV

Wow! What a powerful passage of Scripture! At that time I didn't fully understand what the passage was saying. Presently, looking back over my life as I am writing this, I think that this is what that passage said to me. It gives me a warm fuzzy feeling to think that the great God of the universe cared enough to encourage Peter to write this passage of Scripture, not only to encourage Christians of that day, but for me on this particular train that morning.

Reflecting back on it, what did the Lord tell me? To stand before the Almighty God in humility, and in his time I would understand the why and wherefore. I was to take all my anxieties and place them upon the Almighty God because he cares for me. I was told by Scripture to discipline myself, to be on my guard because the devil is going to try and rob me of a life of contentment and peace.

How true this Scripture actually is. I never would have imagined how often the devil attempted to devour my life with guilt and anger and discouragement as night after night I return back to those horrible experiences in nightmares and cold sweats. It was no easy matter to function during the day and to try to rise above all the feelings that I was carrying with me both on that train that day, and throughout my entire lifetime. At that point in my life, I wasn't in a frame of mind to be able to receive all the grace that God was willing and wanting to bestow upon me.

As I am writing this book after a lifetime of experiencing God's grace and goodness I begin to realize that I was called by God to live out my life in His service. Christ himself, restored, supported, strengthened, spared my life and established me as his child. The devil will not be able to snatch me out of Christ's protective care even though at times I stumble and fall.

I should get back to my story. As the train neared Omaha my emotions were going in all kind of directions. I would be seeing Mother at the station, and back home, Dad, who was still living and waiting for my return. I was blessed to be able to enjoy my father, although in poor health, for four more years. I anticipated meeting Phyllis at the train and how thrilled I was at the thought of again seeing her. I could close my eyes and feel that warm embrace.

The train pulled into the station and as I looked over the platform for familiar faces I saw that there was nobody waiting for me. I gathered my gear and sat on the hard bench in that dingy depot and waited. Before long I called to my home thinking maybe they didn't get my telegram. There was no answer. So I called my uncle and he informed me that they got a late start but they were on their way.

I paced back and forth to the depot door so I could look outside to see if they were there. Finally my heart pounded when my brother and Mom got out of the car, but Phyllis wasn't there. My mother gave me a hug and began sobbing with

221

emotions that she had held in for so long. She was right to be worried that I wouldn't be coming back and now was overwhelmed with joy and thanksgiving.

My brother, after a proper greeting, loaded my gear in the car and we started driving. "Say, Mom, how is Dad?" Mom answered, "Dad still has difficult times with his asthma and has trouble getting his breath." The excitement of you coming home will be hard on him, but it will help a lot that he won't be worrying all the time about how you are doing."

"I was expecting you to take Phyllis along when you came to pick me up." "We called but she wasn't home, she was at her sister's for the summer," my brother answered. "Do you know when she will be coming home?" I asked. "You know that she will be teaching in Minnesota and school will start again in a few weeks so I suppose you will get to see her before she leaves." he replied. "Well, I can't wait to see her again."

My mother was very quiet and I was reading her expression. I also noticed, when I spoke about seeing Phyllis, she became very quiet.

When we got home it was very late at night and Dad was waiting up. He looked so thin and frail and coughed a lot; he could hardly speak, he was so choked up with emotion.

Mom suggested we all get to bed and get some sleep. I went upstairs to my room. Mother left everything in my bedroom the way I remembered leaving it, even my last Sunday's church bulletin was still lying on the dresser. When I lay down I couldn't believe what a luxury it was to crawl between soft white sheets and lie on a good mattress. I couldn't sleep even though I was so tired. The bed was so cozy and soft.

But I had so many things on my mind and I could hear Dad wheezing every breath and gasping for air. I was so grateful for being safely in my own bed again, even though my mind was asking, why would Phyllis go to her sister and leave the area when I told her I was coming home soon?

The next morning I found my pair of jeans and went outside to help my brother with the chores. It was August. The oats bundles were all hauled off the land and the oats threshing was finished. Bill asked me, "What are you going to do today?" I answered, "Well, I thought I would go right to work, I can't tolerate sitting around, that would drive me crazy." "Well, if you want to work we should bale the straw up around the straw stacks before it rains, and you could help by tying wires on the case hand tie baler. That morning Bill hired a crew to bale straw and we loaded up a couple wagonloads of big straw bales that we picked up around the stack.

We were finished baling. I was walking with the other workers along side the wagon loaded with bales. All at once I heard a loud explosive noise. On impulse I dived head first under the moving wagon, almost getting rode over with the wagon wheels. The wagon tire had blown out. When I crawled under way from the wagon shaking with fear everybody laughed at me that I would do such a dumb thing like jumping under a moving wagon. I had all I could do to control my anger. They didn't understand that I wasn't able to control my reactions to that explosive noise. What I was experiencing was battlefield fatigue and a reaction to the sound of shells coming in.

I was still anxiously waiting to hear from Phyllis so I called her mother to tell her to have Phyllis call as soon as she got home from her sister. It took over a week for her to call me. Something was wrong. She wasn't able to see me until the coming Sunday night because she would be getting her things ready to teach school in Minnesota. Sunday night came and I was all exited about meeting Phyllis. The greeting was cold and distant. It took a lot of coaching on my part to get her to tell me why she wasn't her happy self and somewhat indifferent. She shared that she had met someone and dated that person the last little while. She wasn't certain that she would continue seeing me. I was crushed but was able to share that I had a deep feeling of love for her.

That night I asked her to make her choice between the other person or myself because I wouldn't continue to date her if her heart was with someone else. That was one of the longest weeks that I ever spent waiting for her answer. Then we had a date and she told me she wrote a letter telling the other person it was over and we would continue seeing each other.

That Sunday night some of the youth of our church were having a campfire at Oak Grove State Park and Phyllis and I went there. This park is on a high bluff overlooking a lot of trees and bushes. It was a beautiful night with a bright moon coming up which caused the bushes to throw shadows. I held Phyllis close to me and as I looked over the bushes and trees, I suddenly got chills down my spine and my mind had a flash back to the Korean battlefield. Every bush appeared to me as an enemy coming up the hill. I began to shiver and shake. I was afraid and felt helpless to control my fear. My mind kept searching for my weapons and felt helpless without my machine gun, grenades and personal weapon. Even though everybody was having a good time going up and down trails I said, "Phyllis we have to get out of here quickly. I can't stand it; every bush is like an enemy moving up the hill in the shadows."

She fortunately understood and we left. This was the beginning of a long and difficult process of trying to erase the effects of war.

Each time I was with Phyllis I felt like a new man because she was fun to be with and understood why my war experiences caused me to react the way that I did. When Phyllis went to teach in Minnesota, going on a date meant driving 165 miles one way from our home in Iowa. The long drive home was made more stressful because I needed to drive 55 miles in the opposite direction to be on the job the next morning. My shift started at 6 AM at a packing plant in Sioux City. That made for a short night, only getting a few hours of sleep.

This trip usually went very well except one weekend. While driving home I fought sleep all the way. I was less than a one half mile from home. I relaxed when the farm place came in view and I fell sound asleep. I was traveling at 65 miles per hour. When I looked up, a bridge railing was coming right towards the center of the car. I scared so much that I cramped the steering wheel and braced myself for the crash. In my fear, I pushed harder on the gas pedal causing the front end of the car to turn. The car skidded and turned enough so that the bridge hit the off driver side doorpost, instead of right in front of my face. The car skidded crossways on the road and the bridge railing went flying through the air. When I came to a stop, the car tire was only partly on the bridge. The front end and the whole side of the car from front to the back were pushed back two feet. I managed to limp the car home, woke up my brother and said, "I have to take your car to work this morning. Will you tow my car away? I don't want to even look at it when I get home from work."

I guess it was no surprise that I wasn't sleepy the rest of the night. Later I thought, "If I hadn't been jolted awake at the instant I was, that bridge rail would have come straight into my face." I would have been killed with that bridge railing becoming like a giant spear. This car was only a year old, and there went my army pay, my combat pay, my mustering out pay, all gone in one loud crash as the metal flew in all directions.

Whenever possible, Phyllis and I would get together and really enjoyed being together. We tried to arrange that we could be together generally once or twice a month. Being together more often was impossible because that was about all that I could afford. My job at Sioux City was paying $1.75 per hour, minus deductions. I later took a job at the Sioux Center Co-op Produce that paid only $.75 per hour. The reason I took that job was that I didn't have to travel two hours a day. This local job was a stepping-stone to an egg route job that paid much better. The egg route job was based on commission of how many eggs I brought in per week.

Phyllis and I decided to get engaged. We left for Sioux City early one morning and bought our rings in a jewelry store there. Then we decided to go to Stone Park and relax and begin planning for our future. On the way there, I got lost and ended up driving into a cemetery with all the old upright gravestones.

Phyllis said, "I don't think this is a very romantic place to get engaged. Is this your idea of a joke?" We had a good laugh about it, and we never did find Stone Park that day. We did find a beautiful spot to sit on a blanket on the grass at the band shell in a Sioux City park. It was a beautiful spot and there we set the date for our wedding, the 15th of June 1954.

After our wedding we drove to our honeymoon at Mantrap Lake in northern Minnesota. We rented a housekeeping cabin right off the lake, did our own cooking, went hiking, and canoeing. After hiking in the woods our bodies were loaded with ticks, so we spent hours burning out and picking ticks out of each other's skin. In spite of that little problem, we had a great honeymoon. It was before the busy season at the resort so we had the place to ourselves. It was so good to be away from the hustle and bustle of work, family, and friends so we had such extra special time of communication together.

This was so critical because our courtship was mostly by letters. Now we had a whole week together totally uninterrupted by anybody or anything.

What a great way to begin a commitment of a lifetime. We both felt close to each other. If there was ever any doubt about our love for one another it was all erased when we had this opportunity to finally be together. We knew for certain that we were placed and joined together by God in this special relationship. We soon discovered as we worked together that the area where my gifts and abilities were poor or non-existent, those were the areas that Phyllis' gifts were the strongest. It was neat to discover that as a couple we are much stronger than when we work separately. In a sense, we depend on each other in a unique way, yet we retain our own identity and express ourselves in our own certain way.

We heard various comments from others who observed how we interacted together. Several persons remarked about how they noticed the love that we had for each other, radiated from us to them. As we began our marriage, we wondered what the future would hold. I always felt a heavy load on my shoulders. My mind would not release me of the fact that God spared my life in extra ordinary ways. I felt that God didn't allow me to return only to enjoy myself. I believed God did have one or more designated tasks that he wanted me to accomplish for Him. I began a lifetime of searching what God's plan was for my life.

It took me years before I realized that what God expected was for me to live my life one day at a time, and that I should follow where he leads me today. Tomorrow God will show what steps that I need to take that day. I had a lot to learn about being able to adjust to the Lord's will for my life.

Honeymoon 1954

The author and his beautiful bride Phyllis, enjoying a peaceful
honeymoon at a resort on Mantrap Lake in Northern Minnesota

Chapter 15

Impossible? No, Never

We're back from our honeymoon; I have new responsibilities; now a married man; now faced with an increase in our expenses with a wife to support. Now I need to find the money for house rent.

We rented a house in town from Mayor Te Paske located about where what is now the center of the street, south of the present Dordt College corner stone. At that time, it wasn't a college. It was a smelly mink farm. The farm had mink manure and drainage water running in our basement with every heavy rain. We tried to disinfect that mink waste water in our basement but we couldn't keep ahead of it. The silver fish would snake and zip across our floor at night.

After three months we moved to a nice country home. When I left my packing plant job I earned $.75 cents an hour at my new job. That kind of income didn't cut it to support us.

I was able to get a job on an egg route with the same firm. In the new job of route driver the harder I worked at getting new customers the more my income would improve. I soon learned that some unknown force drove me. I was pushing myself to work from 4 A.M. until 5 P.M., non-stop, six days a week. I would do the egg routes and then rush to the farm and help with things that needed to be done there. I didn't realize that I was working day and night to bury my thoughts. This kept me from having the time and energy to reflect back to

Korea. Also while in Korea, I forced myself to get only a couple hours of sleep in a 24-hour period and now my needs still required only a few hours of sleep.

Phyllis started helping on the routes by each evening preparing four or five ticket books that each held fifty tickets. She would write in the next day's egg prices for each grade of eggs on all the tickets that I would use the following day. As I gained more customers, she would ride with me and carry the empty egg cases from the truck to the farmhouses. By doing this she helped speed me through the route day. Then, as my customer base increased again, she started helping me by carrying cases of eggs to the truck. We soon were hauling two truckloads of eggs per day.

The produce board members took notice of the fact that I was making close to the manager's salary so they took some of my route customers away. This also reduced my commission. I would keep driving myself to rebuild my routes only to have it taken away from me again. I told the manager that it would be the last time I would tolerate having my wages cut because we were working night and day to earn it.

After six months I received a call to come into the office. The manager said, "The board says you are earning too much so I have been told to reduce your rate of pay by $.01 per case."

So I gave the manager my two-week notice and started working on the farm where I already had a working partnership with my brother. Now besides farming 360 acres near the home place, we would work an additional eighty acres from my brother's father-in-law. We also rented another eighty acres of alfalfa from which we harvested three cuttings of hay per season. We had a Case hand tie baler that was run by a large air-cooled Wisconsin engine.

My brother always made those wire tied bales as heavy as lead, so we took turns driving the tractor and stacking bales on the wagon. Both our wives would be tying the wires; one would push the wires through the bales and the other one would tie. They would alternate after a few hours. When our wives tied bales they would get so dusty and dirty we couldn't tell if they were ladies or dust and dirt balls.

My brother and I had given nicknames to our wives. He called his wife *Spoof,* and I called my Phyllis *Snooky,* so from that time on whenever we would call for our wives it was *Snooky* and *Spoof.*

Another farm chore in those days was walking all our corn and bean fields every year. We would have to pull out or chop out the weeds. This was a hard job that took weeks to accomplish. This was before herbicides were used in crop production.

Our livestock program grew large by standards of those days. We were milking 25-30 cows in a 15-stanchion barn with a two unit Surge bucket milking machine. All the milk was dumped into ten-gallon cans and had to be carried into a water cooler bath and be cold before the milkman came at 7 A.M. every morning. We produced pigs from at least 45 brood sows twice a year. All the sows were penned up in individual wooden pens. Along with that we also raised to a market weight of 200-220 pounds at least 500 pigs a year. We had 900 to 1000 laying hens and raised all our own replacement pullet stock. We fed

50-75 steers per year. This type of farming was then called, "General farming" in the mid to late 1950s.

Becoming a New Father

In the fall of 1955 we learned that Phyllis was pregnant with our first child. She was really sick the first trimester, but at this time was feeling somewhat better than when she was first pregnant.

Phyllis always had the job of feeding our baby chicks and our young pullets that were on range near the cow pasture. To get to the pullets she daily had to cross over an electric fence made from barbed wire. One morning, as she was crossing the fence to feed the chicks, her maternity dress blew into the fence and got caught in the electric barbed wire, and she was totally entangled in the fence.

I heard some blood curdling screams coming from the pasture and saw her attempting to free herself from the fence but couldn't because of the electric shocks. I ran to the yard light pole where the main electricity disconnects and shut off the power from the entire farm.

That same fall my brother was picking corn with the picker and I usually hauled the corn loads home. The corncrib was nearly full so I asked Phyllis to run the rest of the load off the wagon into the elevator while I leveled the corn in the corncrib. I needed this help because the spout was getting plugged with corn as it slid down the spout.

She was starting and stopping the elevator for me so I could keep the corn pulled away from the spout. A gust of wind blew her maternity dress into the drive chain of the elevator motor and with one jerk the motor pulled her towards it. I heard her holler and she shut off the gas engine. When I stuck my head above the corncrib to see if we were finished I was shocked to see her standing there, naked as a college streaker. Her dress was in a ball around the bicycle chain and the pulley.

I shudder to think what could have happened. Phyllis could have been killed, lost an arm or leg, or had other impairments to herself and our expected child. When the dress ripped off of her she was freed from being entangled in the motor shaft. I realize how precious God was to protect her. How much differently the outcome could have been for both of those episodes--for Phyllis and our expected firstborn.

The doctor told Phyllis she would feel better during the latter part of her pregnancy. But she was feeling much worse and all night long she would crawl into a fetal position with cramps. At that time it was not considered safe to X Ray when you were expecting a baby. This was before ultra sound was operational so the doctors could not run the needed test until the baby was born.

Phyllis had swollen legs, so she went to the doctor's office for a check up and the doctor placed her directly into the hospital, not even permitting her to drive home. She was diagnosed with toxemia and her body was filling up with fluid. She was placed in isolation, without visitors except her parents and myself. After several weeks they decided to try shots to stimulate forced childbirth and after several days of shots and going in and out of labor the doctor gave up and decided to wait for the due date. Today, they would have performed C-section.

On the morning of March 14, 1956 when I was going to milk the cows, I heard the windmill making a squeaking sound. I decided after milking I needed to climb the windmill tower to drain the old oil, and add new oil. This was somewhat of a dirty dangerous job because the platform was small and the wind could turn the whole windmill head around and push me off the platform. I had just finished draining the little bit of oil that was left in the windmill. I was all covered with black grease and Mother shouted out of the house, "Richard, the hospital called and you must get there right away."

I climbed down that windmill three steps at a time, rushed in to clean up and get my clothes changed. I started for town as fast as I could chase the old 1952 Ford. All the way I was thinking, "Did something go wrong?" I rushed past the hospital reception desk. The clerk at the front desk was such a pain and always had to stop everybody to give them her permission to go upstairs. That morning all she saw was a streak going past her desk and before she could get off her chair to stop me, I already was up two flights of stairs headed for Phyllis's room. Phyllis wasn't in her room. My heart sank, and I quickly went to the nurse's station, "Where is Phyllis?" I asked.

The head nurse said, "Well, Richard, it looks like today you will become a father. You will find Phyllis in the labor room and you may join her there." Phyllis had gotten so weak and pale from being seriously sick for so long. Would she have the strength to give birth to our baby naturally or would she have to go into surgery in her already weakened condition. That afternoon she gave birth to a healthy baby boy whom we named Merlyn. It was several days before Phyllis and our newborn son came home. Even after the baby was born Phyllis continued to feel sick. No matter how hard she tried, she couldn't keep her food down. When Phyllis went to the doctor for her check up, he spotted her yellowed condition and hospitalized her.

One of my cousins took care of our newborn son, and neighbors and family helped in many different ways. She was diagnosed as having a gall bladder that was blocked with gravel. They called a specialist from Sioux City, who came to the Sioux Center Hospital. They found not only was the gall bladder totally filled with gravel, but also they found her tubes were damaged.

Phyllis had a very difficult time recovering from that whole episode. I remember one of the first nights after we had brought our son home. He was lying in a bassinet that my cousin's wife had finished covering with Phyllis's wedding veil. Phyllis had started that project before she was hospitalized.

Phyllis was sleeping so soundly, so I was going get out of bed to feed our son. I didn't want to put the lights on so I tiptoed in the dark to where I thought the bassinet was. I was totally disoriented. I ran into the piano and banged on the keys causing our baby son to become afraid and he started to cry. That was it. By this time Phyllis was awake and in a panic-stricken voice I called, "Help me Phyllis, I am lost." I was so afraid I would tip over the bassinet, baby and all. It took a mother's touch to put the whole situation back under control and the baby back to sleep.

Dad's Final Days

For the last ten years, Dad had been having various degrees of breathing difficulty. He was taken several times to the local hospital to be placed under oxygen. Then, for several days, he would perk up again. In May of 1957, Dad's breathing got so bad again he couldn't get the air in and out of his lungs. We called the ambulance and I rode in the back with him to town. When we were riding to the hospital, I was holding his hand, and he said to me, "Rich, this is the last trip, I won't leave the hospital this time." Those were some of the hardest words I have ever heard, he was giving up, after he had fought so hard all his life.

Dad never did anything half way. He always struggled and toiled until he accomplished what he started. Now for the first time in my life I heard him say that this time he was not going to win the battle. Dad's lungs were filling up with fluid and the doctor told us the next noon to call the family home-- there was nothing he could do to stop the lungs from filling up. The best he could do was to make him comfortable.

Dad had slipped in and out of a coma with most of the family standing around the bedside. We were talking to each other, concerned if our sister, who was coming home from California, would make it in time.

She was to arrive that night at the hospital around 11P.M. from California. Dad hung on, but didn't respond to anybody anymore. When my sister arrived in the room he acknowledged that she was there, and tried to talk for a short time. We couldn't understand how he subconsciously knew she was coming. After a short visit with her, he slipped back into a coma. May 30, 1957 Dad lost the battle with his physical body but his spirit entered into the presence of his Lord. His Savior, whom he confessed as his personal Lord, won all of Dad's battles.

When the news spread to our community about Dad's death, our family farmyard was filled with cars all day and into the evening. People streamed by, wanting to share in our grief and talk about what our father meant to them. My father was a man who could never speak or offer a prayer in public. When he would try, he would become nervous and would stammer and stutter in front of large groups.

Our father spoke volumes with his life. There is no doubt in my mind that his example to his family was far more important and beneficial to them than his inability to speak fluently. He never took advantage of anyone and always paid every debt promptly. Dad was generous and always gave everybody a full measure in all his dealings with others. I remember for years Dad would send checks monthly to help pay his mother's nursing home care, never complaining that he needed to help his mother. Dad also gave his children and his hired help the ability to learn from his farming expertise. He first helped his hired men, then he helped his children to get started in farming or in whatever occupation they chose.

The reason that I included this in my book is--I was a young man of 28 when he died, and my children and grandchildren never knew what a wonderful grandfather they had.

A New Daring Adventure

In 1958 Phyllis and I were living in a small house on the home farm and my mother lived in the large house. I wondered what the long-term effect of our situation would be. We had a few years of working Dad's farm in partnership with my brother. Phyllis and I were beginning to search and study what our future would be like with two families growing up and all working together on the same farm. We discovered that two individuals maybe could work together. On the long haul, when families grew up in that setting it would be better if each family struck out on their own.

More family partnerships ended up feuding rather than working in harmony. The relationship may go flawless until children are introduced as the working members. Then the problems might begin. We concluded it would be best if we both chose to operate our own farms independently.

I wrote to several companies about producing eggs exclusively as a business. According to our 1958 records of our 1000 layers on our farm, at that time, it would take at least 5000 laying hens to make a living.

I had worked for weeks to get financing for this project and at every banking institution I was turned down. I had all but given up the idea of having our own business. I was at the point of giving up and dejectedly walked into Wesselink's Insurance office to pay a bill. John walked up with a cheery, "Good morning Richard," and my response was, "I haven't been able to see any good in it." "Boy do you have it bad," John replied. "Why don't you come into my office and tell me about it." I had a person with a listening ear, so I poured out all the frustrations that I had bottled up.

John shared with me that morning about the experiences he had while on a battle ship during WWII, and how he felt the Lord spared him to help his fellow man. I talked to him about having many of the same feelings that he described. I then explained my proposal to him. John said, "Give me a day to study it. Also give me a list of people that you think might be willing to lend the money if I furnish the security."

I gave him a list that afternoon of people who might have money to invest in our farm. A day later he called and said, "I have all your money arranged."

The next morning when my brother came over, I approached him and proposed that we consider the separating of our partnership. The rest of the day we sat down and worked out the details. We would establish our poultry farm with the feeling in our hearts that the Lord had a hand in it. The Lord touched our Christian brother on a battle ship in World War II. In turn John touched my life with his kindness and understanding, as well as a host of other individuals.

I remember reading in the *Bible:*

> *"I have no need of a bull from your stall or of goats from your pens, for every animal of the forest is mine, and the cattle on a thousand hills. I know every bird in the mountains, and the creatures of the field are mine.*
>
> *"Psalm 50:9-11 KJV*

240

From that time on I considered the chickens in the coops were the same as the cattle on the hills; they were the Lord's. I had no doubt when we started the venture that the Lord gave us the chickens in the coops to be used to help others who were in need, spiritually and physically. I did not know exactly how he would use them, but I would soon learn.

Some friends and I started a prayer group in our poultry farm office every Monday morning. We would close our office for business for an hour and a half and open it for anyone who had prayer requests and needs. One morning John came to our office and said, "I am having a lot of physical difficulty in my life and I need the support of this prayer group." It was our privilege to be a support for John and to pray with him when he was struggling with his failing health.

Every week we asked the Lord to show what he wanted us to do or whom we needed to help. At times, by midweek, we felt we would want to pray, "Lord slow it down a little bit will you?" I am now a firm believer the Lord will use every part of our life that we are willing to surrender to him.

The Encounter With the Auditor

One Monday morning around 9 o'clock, the doorbell rang. There was a gentleman with an official looking brief case in his hand. He said, "I am with the tax division from the state of Iowa, and I am here to audit your records for five years." So I thought, "There go my plans for today." I was in a hurry because I had planned to accomplish a lot that day. In the evening I was going to take a person from our church to a David

Wilkerson crusade. Phyllis was going to stay with this person's wife. They were having marriage problems and we were going to discuss it one on one.

The tax auditor started five years back, and demanded to see every invoice of all the sales I made, and check them against my tax reports. It was a slow job and it was getting close to 4 PM but the state auditor only had approved one quarter of one year. By this time I was really getting bent out of shape because I had to get started with the chores or we couldn't get to the crusade.

I said to the tax auditor, "I am sorry, you are getting under my skin. I have a lot to do today and you only have finished one quarter of your five-year audit. I am going to have to ask you to leave before I get so angry that I say something I will be sorry for."

That night, while sitting on the bleachers in the Spencer, Iowa fair grounds, waiting for the speaker, I confessed to my friend that I had gotten quite angry with the tax auditor. I felt badly, realizing that perhaps the Lord maybe sent this person to us and that I blew it. I asked my friend to pray that somehow the Lord would forgive me and give me another chance. That night when I went to bed I prayed for the Lord to give me the right words.

When I went to bed that night, I fell into a deep sleep only to be awakened by some words placed in my mind. They weren't my words because I could not have thought them. I woke up Phyllis and said, "I believe the Lord has placed in my mind how to approach the tax auditor." "Why don't you go to sleep?" was her reply. But I continued, "When the auditor

242

comes tomorrow, I have to ask him, 'When you die and meet the great auditor in the sky, will your books balance?' Phyllis said, "Wait a minute, run that through again." "I have to ask him, 'When you meet the great auditor in the sky, will your books balance?' Then the next question that I have to ask him is, 'HOW will your books balance?' Phyllis' reply was a term that the young kids used in those days, "FAR OUT." My reply to that was, "That will give me a chance to share how my books balance through the finished work of Christ on the cross. Jesus carried my sins with him when he suffered for me and now my books balance because of Christ's work." Never in a hundred years would I have been clever enough to put together that statement or come up with those questions.

At 9 A.M., the auditor rang the doorbell. He walked into my office and started unfolding his books ready to begin the audit. I said to him, "Before you begin the audit, I have a confession to make." The auditor said, "That usually happens after I begin an audit." I replied by saying, "My confession has nothing to do with the audit. You see, I am a Christian and yesterday afternoon I became very angry and I told you to leave. I went with a friend to a Christian crusade, and while at that crusade last night I realized that the way I felt towards you yesterday was wrong. I prayed about it last night and asked God to forgive me.

During the night I was given a question that I must ask you and I believe the Lord placed it in my mind.

The question is this. **If you die and face the great auditor in the sky will your books balance, and, if the books**

balance, on what basis?" The auditor said, "That has nothing to do with the audit."

"No, you are right, but it must be important because I believe the Lord wanted me to ask you that question."

"Well, I go to church sometimes." he answered.

I replied, "You know, I believe that you have a lot of things bothering you and that you have a lot of anger inside of you." About that time Phyllis came in with fresh baked cookies and steaming coffee.

Then the discussion became especially good. The auditor shared his anger about his only daughter, who was dating a hippie and how he was not willing to forfeit his only daughter to this "no good." We shared with him about how his anger was hurting his situation between him and his daughter, and also shared some of our personal experiences with the Lord. It was already noon, and he hadn't started the audit for the day.

The auditor stood up and said, "I want to tell you, I knew already yesterday that your records are okay, so I'll ask one more question and then I will leave."

As he left, he thanked us over and over for our concern for him. As we watched him drive off, I thought, "It was no accident that this auditor came to our farm. The Lord wanted to teach us to wait on Him. He will always give us an opportunity to speak and the words to use." Every week that poultry farm prayer group became the launching pad to help us to be willing to hear and see what the Lord had already planned for our week.

I got ahead of my story. I am already telling you how the Lord was using our poultry farm. After getting the financing we took a brave move in 1959. We bought 5 acres of land on the edge of town and built our first 5000-layer house and a 1500 bird grower unit. But after the unit was built we felt we were under pressure from the city to close or move our poultry unit.

First we came under economical pressure when we were given a staggering commercial electric rate while other poultry and dairy farms in the city limits were placed on agriculture rate. For the size and electrical requirements that we needed for our operation, it was unrealistic. Then, when we applied for the next phase of our building plan we were denied building permits. We couldn't expand our operation to the west to build our grower unit so we were now boxed in. After a lot of thought we decided that we wanted to have our poultry operation located where our family would be happy and satisfied, and where we would not interfere with any of our neighbors' plans.

We took the plunge in 1962. We moved all our buildings to the country west of town. We bought 10 acres of corn ground and started three laying units of 3500 layers each and a pullet grower unit for 3500 chicks.

When we finished moving, and had the buildings re-established; we began to change our operation from producing table eggs to producing fertile hatching eggs. Producing hatching eggs on this size scale in the early 60's was a very daring venture and loaded with financial risks. The day old chicks had to be purchased from the Dekalb Research Company. The price we had to pay for day-old chicks was $3.45 per chick.

We grew into that phase until we purchased 30,000 day-old chicks and used various converted farm poultry houses to

245

accomplish this. The birds all had to be blood tested; and the eggs fumigated. Then we graded them all, packed them, and shipped them in a temperature-controlled truck. My life was one big whirl of activity. I was driven forward and onward, not paying any attention to personal health.

I had driven myself to the point that I would only sleep a few hours each night, and if I were on the road, I would only take short catnaps with my head on the steering wheel of the truck. Why did I do that? I believe I was too afraid to examine why I was driving myself. I was unwilling to look myself in the face and ask, "Why are you doing this to yourself? What are you trying to hide? Why are you working all the time so that you are walking around in a tired worn out stupor?"

Top: Unloading a truck and trailer load of hatching eggs delivered to Turlock California.

Bottom: The author and his wife standing by the "Van's Poultry Farm" sign on the farm that they established in Sioux Center, Iowa and managed for 31 years.

247

Chapter 16

Have Eggs, Will Travel

Meanwhile down at the poultry ranch, we were producing expensive hatching eggs without a guaranteed established market. We first started in a market region that covered the four states bordering Iowa. This soon was expanded to almost every state in the US, and also covered accounts in Manitoba, Canada. I would deliver the eggs, doing all the long distance hauling myself. I would force myself beyond limits no matter what the weather conditions. I kept pushing my time in the truck until the loads of hatching eggs were safely delivered. There were several years I made up to 123,000 miles a year to cover the accounts from New York to California and the northern and southern United States.

Once I headed for Canada in an ice storm. It was so bad- I took Phyllis with me to hold two propane torches on the windshield to keep a large enough hole thawed for me to be able to see to drive.

I traveled in snowstorms that were a complete white out and was shocked when I suddenly realized that I was traveling too close behind another truck. The truck windshield of my tilt cab was a few inches from the other trucks back end. That year we had 67 inches of snow through the area that I had to travel weekly.

The spring following all that snow, we had floodwaters so high the water was up to the truck door at the Sioux River crossing. I had a load of eggs that I had to get to the other side that day or lose my sale for the whole load of eggs. If I missed the delivery, it was possible that I would lose my account with Park Davis Drug Company. It was important because these eggs were used by Park Davis Drug Company to make human flu vaccine. The road crews had put up poles marking the road earlier and now were closing the road with a fence. I asked the crew if they thought I could make it across. They told me that with a truck you got about a 50/50 chance. Those were good enough odds for me. Remember, having just come from the military service I was driven to taking life-threatening chances.

I started through that water, and when I got to the approach of the bridge, the truck bounced badly a few times. I heard a loud noise as I got on the bridge. I had my seat belt loose and the door open, ready to jump out if I had to. Finally I made it to the other side. When I was on dry ground I discovered one of my rear tires had blown out. I waved to the work crew that I made it safely. I quickly changed my tire.

I still had to cross the Rock River, and my radio reported that the water already was going over the road there. Three days later I went back to the spot to look and discovered where the truck had bounced, the dirt had washed away under the approach to the bridge. The cement reinforcement rods were all that was holding up the road and truck. One reinforcement rod was bent upward and that evidently was what caused the tire to blow out. After I saw how close I was to losing my life in that floodwater I realized how foolish I was. I vowed never to ride in floodwater that is rushing over the roads again. I thought a lot about that incident later and realized, in my desire to please my best account, I foolishly crossed that river.

We, in our human nature, would say, "If that is all he cares about his life, let the fool go." Today, I believe what I did there was wrong, to risk my life under 50/50 odds of making it across the floodwater.

I am reminded in the *Bible*, how David took a chance in confronting Goliath, and was under God's protection because God had a plan for David. I couldn't justify why I took those foolish chances, and I knew that it was wrong. Even though I think it was wrong to take chances I still believe God in his mercy was with me. When you want to read about the providence of God, read the following *Psalm:*

> *"God is our refuge and strength, an ever-present help in trouble. Therefore we will not fear, though the earth give way and the mountains fall into the heart of the sea, though it's waters roar and foam and the mountains quake with their surging."*

> *Psalm 46:1 KJV*

As you can see, traveling daily with a very perishable product with a time deadline set by the hatchery caused me to take considerable risks; the roads were filled with high hazards and adventure. After what I experienced in the military service, nothing seemed dangerous anymore.

I learned that the Lord had his plan and a purpose for bringing me up and down the highways. While traveling the roads, the Lord wanted to use persons who would touch my life and I would touch theirs. Several of these individuals I met were on the 23 consecutive weekly trips I made to California hauling our hatching eggs. The need to make those trips all came about when all of Orange County, California chickens were destroyed by the federal government because the chickens caught exotic Newcastle disease from imported pet birds.

What Kind of Partnership do You Have?

On one of my first trips to a hatchery in Turlock, California, I asked to see the manager because the franchise was concerned about their share of the payments. They told me the manager would be available soon, so I went to the truck to rest. When he came to the truck, the manager noticed a sign on my glove compartment door that read, "One Way, Jesus Christ." The manager commented to me by asking me a question, "By the way, do you have a partnership with Christ?" I said, "Yes."

The next question he asked was, "What kind of a partnership do you have?" He waited a few seconds for my answer, and I didn't know how to answer him. To avoid embarrassing me he said, "Why don't you come into my office where it is cool, we can talk there." When I stepped into his large office I noticed that he had his walls and shelves covered with trophies, so I commented about the outstanding display of dairy cattle winnings.

He replied, "Those aren't mine, they are my partner's."

"Your partner sure must have done a good job raising them." I replied.

"Would you be interested in knowing more about how we started our partnership?" he asked. Since this was my first time meeting him and I would be seeing him for 23 weeks, it would seem proper to take the time to listen to him.

Please bear with me as I try to tell his story as he told it to me.

"This is my story." he said, "I was in grade school with Stanley who was my best friend.   Stanley and I both were in 4H club; we both were raising Holstein heifer calves. We also were both trumpet players. As kids will do, we always fooled around a lot together. So we came up with a plan, that when we got to our homes after school, which were several blocks apart, the first person home would play the taps on his trumpet. The second person would then play the reply or echo. We did this every night for weeks and weeks.   Everyone in our Turlock community knew when we arrived home from school."

Then the hatchery manager wiped the tears from his eyes and told about one night when he got home from school, played the taps, there was no response. When he called to his friend's house to ask why his friend Stanley didn't reply with the echo to his taps, they told him his friend Stanley had been taken to the hospital with appendicitis. His buddy Stanley, after surgery, developed an infection and the next day he died of complications. As he told the story he was choking back the tears.

He said, "You know Van, every night when I got home from school I would put my trumpet to my mouth but I couldn't play taps anymore." "Well," he sighed, "I took sick. My folks took me to a doctor. The doctor said it was appendicitis and sent me to the hospital. I was really afraid and said, "I don't want surgery."

My folks sent for the pastor, and when he came he said to me. "You know what happened to your friend Stanley? For you it most likely will be a clean case and nothing serious will happen to you." The pastor said, "I would be remiss if I didn't ask you, What is your relationship to Jesus Christ? And he asked again, 'What kind of relationship do you have with Christ?'

I thought for a while and said, "Well, I believe the Lord and I are buddies. If the Lord brings me through this I want to be partners with him, just like you preached about, Pastor."

The pastor prayed with me and I went into surgery praying that God would be my partner and bring me back to health. The surgery went well, and I soon recovered. The phone rang. It was Stanley's dad on the phone. Stanley's dad asked me if I wanted to show Stanley's calf as well as my own in the county fair. I wasn't sure until Stanley's dad said, "I believe Stanley would have wanted you to." I took the two calves to the fair and would you believe, my calf was the fair's grand champion and Stanley's calf took reserve champion.'

Some friends of my family said, "Don't sell those heifer calves but take them to Chicago to the *International Show*. These individuals, and Stanley's parents, together collected $3500 to pay the shipping of our cattle to the *International Show*. My calf won the International Show's over all grand champion. While at the show I got outstanding offers for my and Stanley's dairy heifers from all over the world. I sold my calf for an unbelievable price, took the money and brought 10% of the check to the church. When I got home, I felt miserable that I had given to my partner, the Lord, only 10%. I struggled, and asked myself, 'What kind of partner gives a partner only 10%.' Then I gave the other 40% to the Lord also. I then realized that whatever I did after that, 50% belongs to the Lord.

This was the beginning of our partnership. The amount of cattle that was shown and sold at fairs and all the other ventures has made me a very rich man. All the credit for the awards and the accomplishments goes to my partner. This is all because I had such a wonderful partner in everything I do. Since Stanley died, I never again had a close friend. But I never make any decision on anything now without consulting my partner first.

Again, Richard, I ask you, what kind of partnership do you have with Christ?" That question went through my mind as I unloaded my eggs and traveled from California back to Iowa to pick up another load. I also made up my mind that when I called the franchise, I would tell them that if the hatchery manager couldn't pay for the eggs, his partner could because He owns the cattle on a thousand hills.

The Run Away Returns Home

On my way home, I stopped to refuel at Las Vegas, Nevada. A very young girl, about sixteen years old, was at a small truck stop pumping fuel into trucks. She was pregnant and close to delivering her baby. I asked the girl, "Why is a pregnant girl your age pumping gas in the middle of the night?" She told me that she was seeing a boy friend that her folks didn't like. They didn't like him because he drank beer and liquor. "I kept dating him," she said, "and I soon discovered I was pregnant.

We didn't have any money but I took some from my folks and ran away with my boyfriend. Well, we got here in Las Vegas. He didn't care for me and one night he left me. Now the only job I can get is pumping gas at night. I need something to live on, and soon I will have a baby to care for."

That night I sat down on a grease barrel and told her the story of the prodigal son--how the son had lived a sinful life but the father was still willing to forgive and restore. Then I said to the girl, "Do you know that if you go to your parents and confess that you too have sinned against the Lord and against them, I don't know of any parent that would not take such a child back into their arms and forgive them."

She thanked me for our little visit. I went on my way and returned the next week with a load to gas up my truck there. I asked about the pregnant girl and was told she left there. When I asked, "Where did she go?" they told me, "She went home."

A Young Lady Without Friend or Family

On another trip, at an all night restaurant, I stopped for an advertised cheap steak supper at a gambling joint and took a booth across from the cashier. It was the middle of the night and a beautiful girl with dark complexion was looking so tired and sad. After a while I noticed she was rubbing tears from her eyes, so I asked her, "Can I help you, and why are you sad?"

She told me she was from the country of Columbia and was the oldest of 13 children. Her dad took all the money he could borrow so she could go to school, learn English and get a job in the United States. Then when she had a job, she could send money back home to help support her family. She said that she started out by working aboard ship to get to Los Angeles where she got a job as a maid. Then she went to Elko, Nevada where she now was a cashier all day at a gas station and at night was a cashier in the all night restaurant. She said, " I am so sad, I will never be able to marry because my husband would never let me work so much and send all the money home. If I don't send the money home, then my family back home will have to live on the street as beggars. That is why I am so sad, I have no friend."

I then shared my story how God spared my life in Korea and that I knew that Jesus would always be a friend to me.

She was wearing a crucifix around her neck. I went to her, lifted the necklace with the crucifix and said, "What is this?" She put her head down and said to me, "I forgot, I am so ashamed, God is always with me isn't He?" I said, "You know, Jesus never fails." She said, "I know it, thanks for reminding me."

She asked about my family. I showed her my family picture and told her we had three children by natural birth and two adopted children. She asked me, "Will you adopt me as your girl, and then I will have a father while I am in your country?" I again picked up her crucifix and said, "Put your trust in your Heavenly Father." She said, " I feel better now." I believe we both were uplifted by our little visit.

Help Me I Killed my Baby!

It was a hot balmy night.   I was traveling with the windows rolled down. The road was clear; the moon was bright that night, and I was traveling through a long stretch of desert sand. A car was slowly gaining on me, and soon we were riding side by side on the road. In the compact station wagon were a woman, and a little girl, who was standing in the back seat drinking a bottle of pop. The car slowly moved ahead of me and I watched the taillights in the distance.

After a few minutes the taillights suddenly disappeared. I thought they went over a little hill. I traveled a short distance and noticed the whole area was covered with a cloud of dust. Then suddenly, in the ditch, I saw the compact station wagon. The woman had the back door open and was screaming something. I stopped the truck and she was screaming, "I killed my baby, I killed my baby!" I ran over to the car and the little girl was wedged under the front seat so tight that the mother couldn't pull her out. I shone my light on the girl and her face was already turning blue.

I said, " We need to be quick, I will go through the other door and lift and pry the seat up while you try pulling her free." The seat bent up enough so that she could pull the girl out, but she wasn't breathing. I took the girl and blew air into her mouth a few times. She let out a couple gasps, then started breathing, and began to cry. I gave the child to her mother, and after a few minutes the girl said, "Mommy, why is the car in the sand?"

The mother told me she had reached back to take the bottle of pop from her daughter in the back seat. She thought

257

she must have turned the wheel in the process and lost control of the car. I surveyed the damage and found that the battery cable had come off and everything was full of sand. With a chain on my truck, I pulled her station wagon back on the road, put the air cleaner back on and brushed off the sand. I got the car running and bent the bumper somewhat straight. That was all that seemed to be wrong. The car seemed to drive okay, so I told her to take it easy for a few miles--and then if everything was okay, she could drive normally. She thanked me, left ahead of me and disappeared.

When morning came, I was driving through a small town that had a stop sign. By the sign was parked the woman and the little girl whom I helped. She asked if I would have breakfast with her.

She said, "I didn't thank you properly last night, and I wanted to also ask you a question—are you a Christian?"

I said, "Yes."

She jumped up and down like a child would at being surprised. When we were seated at the table she told me, like Paul Harvey says, " the rest of the story."

She and her husband were separated. She was on her way to see him and try to reconcile their differences. Her husband was working on a project in Denver. Early the night before, she was with her friends at Salt Lake City. They had a prayer gathering for her and begged her not to drive at night. She told them she wanted to drive at night because she didn't have air conditioning. So they prayed this prayer, "Lord, be with her on her trip and if there is any problem please send a

Christian to help. Lord, if there is a Christian who helps her, let that be a sign that you want the family to be re-united."

She looked at me teary eyed and said, "You were that Christian that the Lord sent to save my child." I shared with her how I believe that nothing happens by chance and that the Lord was the one who made all the arrangements. In that booth we prayed together and thanked the Lord for his revelation to us. We prayed for his continued protection for her and a successful reunion with her husband.

While driving back that day my heart was glad that I could be used in a small way. All I could think of was--isn't the Lord wonderful. Why would we underestimate God's timing and power when we know God numbers the hairs on our head and even cares for a small sparrow? So why not believe God had planned who would be able to help this child and mother in this time of need.

The Stalled Car by the Bridge

We had a mission emphasis weekend in our church and I had vowed earlier to the Lord that when and where the Lord showed me he wanted to use me as a witness, I would be open and available. I was willing, but I wasn't going to go poking into situations where I didn't feel the Lord was leading me. I always made it a practice to take my Bible along when I went anywhere.

I was taking a load of eggs to Lamar, Missouri. It was a heavy down pour all night long, with a lot of flooding all around the Midwest and I just heard about the flood at Rapid City, SD.

Before I left, I had tried to find the location of a hospital in Kansas City, MO. where a person from our church was very ill with cancer. I failed to get the hospital's location before I left and I felt badly about it since I was chairman of the sick visiting committee of our church.

Interstate 29 to Kansas City was still under construction and I had to take a detour over a road that was narrow and very dark. In the rain and the dark night shadows, I saw a car parked near a bridge on the side of the road. On the fender of the car were beer cans and three people huddled inside the car. I drove beyond the car about a half-mile and all of a sudden the Lord seemed to speak to my inner self, telling me to stop.

I stopped the truck and started arguing, thinking to myself that those people are drunk so why should I risk my life with some drunks. The Lord would not stop bothering me about that car so in the dark of the night I backed the truck up a half-mile and stayed about a block from them. I was afraid, so I took a big steel jack rod in my back pocket, holding one hand firmly on the rod behind my back.

As I walked closer, an old man came out of the car and said, "Please, please help us." He told me that he was helping his son move into a new house when they got a call that his wife had a severe heart attack and he should hurry home. His son's car was full of items to move so a neighbor of his son offered to take his car and bring him to Kansas City hospital. They were driving at a high speed when the car got hot and a frost plug jumped out. They lost all the water out of the car. The beer cans were being used to try to get some water out of the creek and into the radiator of the car.

The old man told me they had been there for four hours and no one stopped to help them. I loaded them all in the truck and brought the neighbor and his wife to a motel in the next town. Then the old man and I headed for Kansas City.

I asked the man the name of the hospital where he wanted to go. The one where he needed to go was the same hospital of which I needed to have the address. It was midnight when we got to the hospital and when I dropped him off at the hospital I gave him my card but forgot to ask the way back to the highway. I soon discovered that I was hopelessly lost in a very scary district. I didn't have the courage to ask the groups of guys, who looked like gangs, standing on the street corners. I could see one group looked like they were smoking pot and passing it around.

I prayed as I drove around saying, "Lord, you didn't take me here just to let me get hurt, help me find my way." Ahead of me about a block was a car with the hood up, and a person carrying a lunch bucket walking away from the car. I stopped and asked him the way to the highway entrance. He asked me which highway I was looking for and what direction I needed to go. When I told him, he said, "Wow! I live right at the entrance of that road. If I may ride along with you I will show you." He told me he was so afraid of being robbed and he wanted to get home quickly to call an all night wrecker service. He told me that he wouldn't have any wheels left on his car if he waited until morning to pull the car home.

The next morning I quickly unloaded my eggs at Lamar, MO, and hurried back to the hospital where I called on the member of our church. She was so surprised to see someone from her own church. I told the story about how I found the hospital and that I believed the Lord wanted me to give her a word of encouragement. We had such a meaningful time of sharing Bible passages with each other, and had a good visit.

A few days later I received a letter in scrawled handwriting from the old man I brought to the hospital.

It read, "Mamma is doing better--we are so thankful for men like you who would stop for people along the road, and thanks for bringing me to Mamma safely."

THE STONES THAT CRIED OUT

Witnessing to strangers has always been always been difficult for me. I was sometimes afraid of my own shadow. I was taking another load of eggs, part of the load to Lamar, Missouri and the other part to Springfield, Missouri. My plan was to arrive at Lamar around midnight, sleep in the truck and unload at 5 A.M. when the hatchery help would arrive. I was traveling down Highway 71. That night there was a storm with an awful tornado that ripped through Joplin, Missouri. I couldn't get through the road because of downed trees, and power lines hanging down, sparking across the pavement. I backtracked and got a motel to rest and wait for daylight. Before I started the day I read a passage from my *Bible*.

When he came near the place where the road goes down the Mount of Olives, the whole crowd of disciples began joyfully to praise God in loud voices for all the miracles they had seen:

"Blessed is the king who comes in the name of the Lord!" "Peace in heaven and glory in the highest!"

Some of the Pharisees in the crowd said to Jesus, "Teacher, rebuke your disciples!" "I tell you," he replied, "If they keep quiet, the stones will cry out."

As he approached Jerusalem and saw the city, he wept over it."

Luke 19:37-41 KJV

That morning, I first drove through the rubble of the tornado and saw the powerful hand of God in nature. Then while driving toward Springfield, MO, at a distance I could see writing on the sides of rocky cliffs. Everywhere I looked were signs saying, "Jesus Saves, Jesus is my Lord, is he yours? Jesus is the way truth and life." It suddenly struck me what I had read that morning, and I applied it to myself. If I refused to speak up for my Lord the rocks would cry out. I parked the truck right along the road and promised my Lord that I would try harder to speak up for him. If the Jesus people could risk their lives putting those paintings on the rocks, surely I should be willing to take risks for my Savior too. The rocks that day did not keep silent; they spoke to me and told me to be an active witness for my Lord.

I hope the Lord is patient with me because many times I have failed to be a witness. Almost always after the fact I say to myself, "Why didn't I say something, or man did I blow it there." Then at times, words will come out of my mouth that shock me because they weren't my thoughts or my words.

You Can Be a Sales General If You Try

I received a telephone call after a men's retreat in Omaha, Nebraska. There I had met the director of a mission of the Reformed Church in Annville, KY. They wanted me to fly down as a poultry consultant to their agriculture operation.

On the airplane flying down to Kentucky, a person seated next to me was bragging about his success as a salesman. He was selling a cosmetic and wanted to get me interested in signing up with his sales organization in a pyramid scheme. He was telling me how rapidly he advanced in the ranks of the company, and that presently he was earning $75,000 per year, after all expenses were taken off.

By now I was getting a little tired of his sales pitch. But after he had bragged about his financial status, he had the nerve to question me about my present earnings.

This person looked at me and said, "I bet you are not doing better than that."

"O yes I am," I replied.

"Do you net more than $75,000 a year?" he asked.

"Not that much in cash," I answered as I continued pretending to be looking at my magazine.

He asked, "Then do you have a big retirement plan?" My answer just rolled out, "You see sir, I am working for my Lord Jesus Christ. I am doing volunteer work for my Lord. Now the cash return isn't that great but my Lord has guaranteed me eternal life by trusting in Christ who died for me. So my answer is, yes, I do have a retirement plan. That is eternal life. I bet your plan has no offer like that."

Suddenly he became very quiet and finally said, "You know, I used to be a Baptist lay preacher. I preached in small churches and the pay was poor, so I left the ministry to go into this program."

I asked him, "Are you happy with your life?"

He said, "No, my life is in shambles, in fact my wife left me and my sons won't have anything to do with me. I am a man without friends and family so when I look at it that way I guess I have nothing."

The airplane taxied to the Lexington, Kentucky airport terminal. I wished him well in his search for success and he disappeared into the crowded airport.

When I ponder on what happened that week while I was in Kentucky I didn't seem to accomplish much, but I firmly believe the reason that I had to go down there was that the Lord wanted to have someone confront that salesman. It would cause him to examine his life, to question his own motives and goals and to have someone point him again to what has eternal value. It is so neat when you know the words you say to someone aren't your words, but it is the Lord guiding your thoughts.

The Hippies' Generation

Nowhere was the hippie generation more evident than on the highways of the USA in the 1970s and 1980s. It was a time in our history when a generation felt they were going to change the establishment. It also was a time when the extreme radical groups were standing against the war that was going on in

Vietnam. The slogan that was popular with that generation was, "Make Love, Not War."

The roads were full of hitchhikers who were floating from here to there, not having any goals. A lot of them migrated to California and the southern states to get out of the freezing cold. They were not necessarily from the poor families. The hippies were from every economic cross section of our country.

One spring day I was traveling home from a delivery in Illinois, and it began to rain and snow. Along the interstate were three girls dressed in very skimpy clothes, looking like they were freezing in the snow. I stopped to pick them up. Before hitchhikers were permitted in my truck I had them sign their name and address in a logbook I carried with me.

If they refused to do that, I would say, "Sorry," and drive on leaving them standing by the road. When the girls got in, I looked at their names, and was shocked to read the name of a very wealthy New York family. I asked her father's name and discovered that she and two of her friends were heading to Jackson Hole, Wyoming to the family's summer home. I knew it was true because I had seen a sign along the highway that said how many miles it was to their resort. I turned up the heater to warm them up and commented that their clothing was not proper traveling clothing for girls.

Their response was, "It sure gets us rides." They were not concerned about the risk. I gave them a choice, if they changed clothes at the truck stop while I ate my noon lunch, then I would take them to western Iowa. If they didn't dress properly they would have to find their own way. The weather was so lousy they went into the rest room and changed into jeans. When I was going to pay for my dinner I was told it was already paid for.

When we were back in the truck, one of the girls commented about my sign on my lunch box that said, "One Way, Jesus Christ."

She said, "You are one of these Sunday school boys." She then shared with us how she used to go to Sunday school. I asked if she remembered any of those songs. Then I asked her to sing them for us and when we traveled the roads we were all singing, "Jesus Loves me, and, "This Little Light of Mine." I asked them to sing with me, "What a Friend We Have in Jesus," and before we realized it, we had crossed the state of Iowa.

There was another interesting couple I picked up in Nebraska and took them all the way to Sacramento, California. The girl said she was the product of mixed race. She told me her mother was a maid in a high society southern home and when the lady of the house would leave, this girl's mother was expected to be available to have sex with the plantation owner whenever he desired.

She was born a child of this combination, and was raised in the home of the plantation owner. Now that she was a pretty young lady, her mother told her to leave and get out of the home before she also would become the sexual slave of the boss. This young girl persuaded a young man, who was the gardener of that plantation, to run off with her and they were heading to California.

The reason they chose California was that it was warmer and he would be able to work year around there in the nursery business. They already had spent some time in jail for vagrancy because they were hitchhiking. The judge who fined them asked if they had anything to say.

After he pronounced his sentence, she said, "Your honor, if you took your robe off I would call you a bigot. Today I witnessed you releasing other white hitchhiking vagrants but because we are of mixed race you make us do jail time. Your Honor, that is the work of a bigot." The Judge ordered when they finished their time in jail they were to be delivered outside the state and advised never to enter the state again.

As a matter of fact I thought they were a nice couple. She was educated and had a goal to become a lawyer. When I got near *Donner Pass*, I usually rested at a rest area before I went down into Sacramento. Since it was wet and cold outside I couldn't sleep on the seat with three of us in the cab so I fell sound asleep with my head on the girl's lap. When I got to Sacramento I left them off along the interstate highway. Before they got off the exit ramp they were picked up by the cops and again were jailed for a short time for hitchhiking on the interstate highway. When I got home Sunday I received a call from them thanking me for the ride and the help that I gave them.

During those years my family never knew whom I would be taking home with me. I would usually get home from my California runs on Saturday and if the weather were bad I would generally take a hippie hitchhiker home with me for the weekend. I would ask these drifters to go with the family to church to worship. One individual, who I believe, had never entered into a church before, went with us. The church was full and we were a little late so we sat in the balcony where we had folding theater seats.

This hitchhiker was looking so intently at all the girls that he didn't realize his seat was up and sat down, falling completely on the floor. This caused all the people in the balcony to rumble with laughter.

I don't know if any of our influence changed them but those times gave the family many interesting weekends as we heard about, and could discuss their confused lives. I soon discovered that in a high percentage of these drifters there was a divorce in the home. Of the kids that came from broken homes, a large majority of those were having a very difficult time accepting a new stepparent.

A School Boy In Search For Love

One day just outside of Council Bluffs, Iowa I picked up a schoolboy who was along the road. His mother and father had recently divorced, and his father, who had a drinking problem, was going on nightly drinking sprees. The boy got into trouble in school for sassing his teacher and displaying anger at other students and also for being in possession of a knife.

For punishment he was expelled from school for the rest of the week. Now we have a boy home all day without any supervision, angry with his dad for drinking and leaving him alone. He was bitter at his mother who went off to live with her lover in Grand Forks, North Dakota. Now added to it, he was angry at the school system that may not have understood the reason for his anger.

The school just added fuel to the fire by expelling him for a week. I picked the boy up and told him that I cared about him and would be able to take him as far as Sioux City, IA. When I got to Sioux City it was about 2 o'clock in the afternoon. I left him off on Interstate 29. The next morning I had a load of eggs to take to Watertown, South Dakota. The weather was cold with a mixture of rain and snow coming down, so I headed the truck back to Interstate 29. I was just on the highway when I noticed what I first thought was a dog or deer getting up out the ditch. To my surprise, there was the same boy that I dropped off the afternoon before. He had only traveled about 20 miles. He was wearing only a light jacket. He lay in that ditch all night and was soaking wet, near freezing and shivering from head to toe.

I turned the heater on as high as I could get it and gave him a blanket. When we got to Sioux Falls we stopped at a truck stop and I bought him a stack of pancakes and some hot chocolate. He was eating like a starved animal, and when I asked him when he last ate a meal he said, "Yesterday--all I had was a dry donut that I found in our house."

While driving to Watertown, I asked if he knew where his mother lived. "No," he said, "I don't know where my mother lives or even if she works. If I can find her, I hope that maybe she will let me stay with her, then maybe I can start school again." Before I left him at a truck stop I told him that I was a Christian and believed in the power of prayer. I held him tightly as I prayed for him. I prayed, "God, I believe you care for this boy because you have created him. Now give him success in finding his mother. When he finds her, may she have a mother's heart, and love and care for her son. Amen."

I instructed him to stay at the truck stop asking all the truckers if they were going to Grand Forks, ND. Then he should ask if they would give him a lift, but he should not try the highways, and should not take a ride unless they were going all the way to Grand Forks. I gave him some money for food for at least that day. When I headed to the hatchery, I drove away from that truck stop, heart sick about a boy who felt so rejected, unloved, misunderstood and filled with anger.

I thought, how selfish and reckless of parents to choose their present pleasure, then give little or no regard for the welfare of their family. This country is, and will continue to pay dearly for this negligence to family and family values. Many of the children from broken homes are children who personally feel responsible for their parent's problems, and the child feels they are unloved. These opinions, built up within them, produce depression. This condition leads to anger and far too often leads them into a learned response of lying, cheating, stealing and fighting all in progression to survive in this hostile home environment and in society.

What an abominable thing that a child should have to go through life feeling unloved by his/her own parent. What detestable implications it has on society in general that we are not more upset about the way these children are treated.

The Mountain That Disappeared

The springtime of the year, it seems to me, has a lot of beauty with the budding of the trees and the fresh flowing mountain streams. But this can cause some danger as the frost starts coming out. There are times that large rocks become dislodged and start rolling down the mountainside and onto the lane of traffic.

During this spring day I had traveled through part of Nebraska in wet, rainy weather and in Wyoming had stopped several times to put my head on the steering wheel to rest my eyes because they were getting tired of driving in the rainy glare. I was rushing to get through the section of Salt Lake City, Utah before the morning rush hour, because we had to drive through town, since highway 80 was not connected at that time.

The rain was coming down in torrents as I passed through Evanston, Wyoming and driving in the dark towards Salt Lake City, Utah. The water was gushing down the mountains taking with it small rocks which made driving very hazardous. I always went past a dam, which is east of Salt Lake near the junction of Highway 85. The water continued running onto the road making it hard to steer the truck. I wanted to see how high the lake was now after all this hard rain, but it was too dark.

I thought, on the return trip I will be able to enjoy the view because I usually came through this area during daylight. I guess it wasn't more than a short hour later they interrupted the radio broadcast to announce that Interstate 80 was closing because a large portion of the mountain had slid into the lake. This announcement also told everybody traveling on interstate

80 to keep clear of the area until the highway department could close the roads and reroute traffic. I had just traveled over that road less than an hour before. On my return trip, I went to look and there was about two-city blocks length of highway gone, it slid into the lake. Even today when I take the curve and see the beginning of the lake I seem to step on the gas when I think what could happen if the mountain gave way again.

Today it makes me very nervous taking long trips that require night travel. I would rather take lodging for the night than risk driving all night in the dark. In my travels I came across several accidents. One time in particular, I had to drive into a ditch to avoid hitting a small car filled with people. At another time a sports convertible was traveling along side a semi-truck in a very windy stretch of Wyoming, and while attempting to pass, the car was hit with a side gust of wind and was blown under the truck. The truck dual wheels caught it and dragged it into the ditch. The truck loaded with swinging beef rolled over on top of the car, killing all five passengers in that sports car.

There was also the incident of a motorcycle rider in Kansas City, MO. A small car passed me, and then decided to turn quickly onto an off ramp but a big Lincoln car was coming onto the highway from the on ramp. The two cars collided and piled up cross ways in front of me. I turned into the other lane, and then stopped quickly. But a guy in a motorcycle came around me and crashed into the side of the car while traveling at a high rate of speed.

When the dust settled, the driver of the cycle ended up crushed and lying under the car with every bone in his arms and legs broken in small pieces. With four guys, we lifted the side of the car enough that the driver of the Lincoln could pull the motorcycle driver under way. The driver of the Lincoln was a doctor going to work.

He felt the arms and legs and said, "If this man survives he will wish he hadn't."

I quickly hollered to an Afro-American across the interstate barrier, "Quickly, call for an ambulance and the police." His reply was, "Yes'sah Boss."

A motorcycle driver's chances of surviving in an accident, is not very good because of their lack of protection.

At the busiest time in making our hatching egg deliveries I personally would make 123,000 miles a year, plus keeping in touch with things that needed decisions on the farm.

God, Why Is There No One Here?

Phyllis and I often went on Lay Witness Mission weekends with a team of other Christians. We are invited by a church to share Christ's love with the members and their friends.

Every weekend experience was different and every weekend was an exciting time of sharing our faith.

On these weekends, the congregation, as well as the team members, had a lot of prayer for the power of the Holy Spirit to take control of the sessions. Our Saturday morning session was always a discussion on the power of prayer and how God answered prayer in our lives.

At this weekend another Christian and I were assigned to a Saturday morning coffee to lead and share in a home that was in an exclusive neighborhood of a major city. We had prayer at breakfast and asked that the Lord would bring to the coffee time the persons with whom he wanted us to share the good news.

We were brought to this home and it was almost time for our session and we noticed there were no cars there. So we prayed in the driveway saying, " Lord, bring to this coffee those whom you want us to share about your love."

The hostess, who had the table set with the finest silver and laden with goodies, greeted us warmly. The hostess apologized, wringing her hands saying, " I had six couples that were planning to come and they all canceled out the last minute. The worst part is, I had my daughter come home from college so she could serve us." I said, "Well, where two or three are gathered in His name, the Bible says that the Lord will be present, so let's have our session on the topic of prayer anyway."

As we were about to begin, she invited her daughter to join the three of us. We read some scripture concerning prayer and I asked the general question, "Have you ever had an answer to prayer in your life, and what did that do for your faith?" The college age daughter spoke up and said, "I don't believe in that bunk nor does my professor. He said he had performed thousands of surgeries and never yet seen the soul of man. I don't believe in that Christianity bunk. Prayer is only a mental exercise and it makes you feel good when you talk about it."

The mother spoke up and told how when she was a stewardess, an airplane was hit by lightening and they lost all power. The pilot told her to calm the passengers and ask them all to pray. They were dropping rapidly and she led the people in the cabin in the Lord's Prayer. When they got to the part that states, " For Thine is the Kingdom, the Power and the glory forever," the power came back on and the plane stabilized. She said, "It was like God had wrapped his arms around me and for days I walked around feeling God's presence." The daughter said, "Mom, why didn't you ever tell me that?" The mother said, "I didn't think it was important to you."

We shared for two hours that morning and the mother shared more about how God had guided her in the past. As we left that morning and got to the car we prayed this simple prayer. " Lord thank you for hearing our prayers and bringing to this coffee those whom you wanted there."

Sunday morning I was asked to pray with anyone who came forward to accept Christ. First, the daughter came down the aisle, then the mother came and a few minutes later the father came, with tears of joy running down his cheeks. seeing prayers answered in such a direct way.

Chapter 16

Life Is Like a Roller Coaster

Everything in our lives did not always go smoothly. Throughout our years of marriage we experienced the roller-coaster effect of highs and lows both financially and spiritually. Whenever we were on a high we would brace ourselves for the anticipated low.

The Crisis of Surgery

After 21 months of marriage we were extremely happy and thankful that God was going to give us the privilege of becoming parents. What we didn't plan for was that Phyllis would be hospitalized for 21 days with a seriously high albumen count and toxemia. She was placed in the intensive care unit in our local hospital. The story was told in detail in Chapter 14.

Within two weeks of having given birth to our son, Phyllis became very sick. Night after night we struggled to make her comfortable until she was so weak she would sleep a short time from complete exhaustion. Then we found out she needed major surgery to remove her gall bladder because her system was impacted with gravel. After my wife spent a week in the hospital I discovered they wouldn't dismiss her without cash for the hospital bills. This brought about our first financial crises because our hospital insurance was canceled a year earlier. In those days, as well as now, the hospital stays and doctor bills placed on an enormous financial load on individuals. I had a very difficult time getting Phyllis released from the hospital after her surgery, because I was unable to raise the funds. Not until I appealed and begged the bank president for help were we able to get the funds to get her released.

Our First Poultry Farm Brought New Independence

Then when we started out on our own, Phyllis and I were so happy that we had our buildings constructed, and our first batch of chicks was brought into the new building. We were so appreciative that we were blessed with this enterprise and looking foreword to a better life with our family. What a pretty sight to walk among all those chicks and hand feed them every morning.

The Chicks Began To Walk Strange

Along came the second trial when all of our 5400 young chicks, that were seven weeks old, were walking like ducks. They looked awful, and we started searching for answers. My cousin who was working in the feed mixing department at the local feed company, noticed that the feed company had received the wrong feed additive from their supplier. This mistake caused all our chickens to be poisoned and their kidneys ruined. It took months of work and many trips to research stations and several different laboratories analyzing the problem before we received an answer.

By this time the pullets should have been ready to lay eggs and there were still no eggs in sight. The laboratory told us the meat was okay but the liver and kidneys were ruined.

The chickens never would be profitable laying chickens and we should either butcher or destroy them.

We rented all kinds of small empty poultry buildings around town, and moved the pullets into these buildings. In order to put food on the table and also pay our interest payments we started daily butchering these young chickens. Without that income we would have had to close our newly established business. We got so efficient that we would butcher up to 10 chickens per hour from start to finish, that we sold for 75 cents per bird.

After months of hassling, we finally got our new replacement flock of baby chicks. They had a good start--they grew very fast, and matured properly. When they were 18 weeks old we were producing our first eggs from them. We were so thrilled that we could make some payment on our debt. While we lived on the poultry farm in town we were blessed with the birth of a second son, Bob and a daughter Donna.

The Kids Teased Me At School Today

Our joys were soon crushed when our son came home from school crying that some kids teased him that his dad had a stinky chicken farm and they all hated it. This pressure was made worse by the fact that the city was making it unfeasible for us to continue with our plans. This made us feel more unwanted instead of being delighted with our little enterprise and accomplishments.

I Marveled at How Everything Fit Together

While we were feeling trapped, a carpenter from town misunderstood, thinking that we were going to immediately shut down our place and was wondering if we wanted to sell our farm. He was willing to build us a new home in the country in exchange for our property if we moved all the buildings off.

This happened while Phyllis was gone for a week to a ladies spiritual retreat in Holland, Michigan. Then to my surprise, the same day, a person came that had country property he wanted to sell. He would be willing to sell part of his property that was nearby, but outside the city limits.

After talking to Phyllis by phone, we bought five acres of land, and placed an option on five acres more for future expansion. Now we were faced with the enormous task of trying to keep production, move the buildings and establish a farm where formerly a cornfield stood. So we moved the 210-foot building in three sections, 70 feet at a time.

Each time we would cut a section off and put up a temporary wall up so we could keep production until the next section was moved. When we had a section moved to the country, we would start chickens in that newly moved section so we could keep our egg customer base.

The Lord blessed our efforts and we had a place on which we again could produce eggs. We soon built a separate processing unit equipped with a new egg-processing machine. Now we could process 28 cases of eggs per hour. Again we had a place that was attractive, and a product that was in good demand. We were very pleased with the results of that move.

Phyllis Was Hospitalized Again

Phyllis's health again was deteriorating. She finally went to a specialist who performed corrective surgery. A year after she had corrective surgery she was scheduled for another corrective surgery. This time she was given a complete hysterectomy. The surgery took a long time and I can still see her face when the doctor told her it was a complete hysterectomy.

She voiced her disappointment very strongly because she wanted a larger family. I tried to encourage Phyllis and told her how happy I was that the Lord already had blessed us with two sons and a daughter but the next few days nothing I would say would comfort her. She was very discouraged.

The next evening when I went to see her in the hospital, she was visiting with some friends. Her hair was combed and there was a sparkle in her eyes that I hadn't seen for some time.

She said, "I have something to tell you later tonight."

When our friends left the hospital room she said to me, "How would you like a baby?"

You're Lying in the Hospital and You Want a Baby?

My reaction was, "You are lying in the hospital and you want a baby?" As I jumped out of my chair I continued; "We have three children, what do you want with another baby?" Phyllis said, "My doctor called from Sioux City and he has a young girl patient who will soon have baby. We can adopt the baby if we pay the mother's and the baby's expenses."

My reply was, "How can we first get this bill paid for and then pay that bill as well? I doubt it."

That night I prayed to the Lord that He would show us what His will was for that baby.

I wrestled with God and every time I said, "No," God pointed out to me that each time I said no, it was for a selfish reason. By the time the sun started to break in the sky that morning I was on the lawn of my banker asking him for money to adopt a baby. I said, "I need to borrow money, we want to adopt a baby." He said, "In the many years that I have been a banker I have never had a request for money to adopt a baby. I don't know how I will word the loan but I will give you the money."

I left and went to the hospital to see Phyllis. She asked me, "What are you going to do today? You are here so early." My answer was, "I am going to our attorney because there is a baby the Lord wants us to have." Then I told Phyllis about my wrestling with the Lord, and how the Lord managed to point out to me that if I said no it was only because I had selfish reasons.

We shared together that we had no doubt from that moment on that it was the Lord's plan that we would be the parents of that child. Then two weeks after her hysterectomy on April 17, 1968 we were informed that our baby girl was born and we could pick up our daughter on Sunday afternoon. We named her Susan.

Would You Like to Adopt Another Child?

When Phyllis went back to the Sioux City, Iowa Clinic to get a check-up she was asked if we wished to adopt again. Then on November 16, 1970 we were informed that our son was born two months prematurely. A few days later when we asked when our son would be released, they told us that he was on oxygen and couldn't breathe on his own. They also told us that they thought he would need a lot of oxygen and they weren't sure the baby would ever be well. If we didn't want the baby the State would then take care of him.

The next weekend I went to a Men's Brotherhood Convention in Minneapolis. There some friends gathered in my room for prayer that God would give us a clear answer. The next morning I knew that baby was our child. It came very clear to me that if Phyllis and I were expecting a child by natural birth we wouldn't say, "This child isn't perfect, turn it over to the State." That would be unthinkable, so now why would this child chosen by God to come into our home be any different.

We called our attorney, and then called to the hospital that we were going to assume the responsibility of the care of our adopted child whom we named Evan. When our son got home he was so tiny that we often said he was the size that could fit in a cigar box. We later discovered that our adopted son's mother was very careless with her health while pregnant with her baby. This reckless life style had a permanent effect on our son's health and size later in his life.

Our Extended Cruise Vacation

Back at the farm we had very loyal and skilled employees who were like family to us. At this time we also had a person who helped take care of the house and children while Phyllis supervised our egg processing plant.

We realized that both Phyllis and I had been under a constant stress for a long period of time and that it would be important for the two of us take a much-needed vacation. After looking at all the options we decided to take a vacation on a cruise ship. The cruise we chose was more expensive than we wanted, but we reasoned that our job required us to work 365 days a year. We only took short business trips, many of them with the truck loaded with eggs. So this time we would go on a nice 14 day cruise and extend the time longer both at the beginning In Los Angeles, California and at the end in Puerto Rico.

We started at Los Angeles and went to Cabo San Lucas, where we lay on the beach for several hours listening to the waves breaking against the rocks. At dinner we were assigned a table for the trip. At our table we met a Jewish couple. The wife was recovering from a stroke and had lost all her self-confidence. He took her on the cruise to help her gain emotional strength. Another couple sitting at our table, worked for an electrical company that built transmission lines all over the world. He was the company's advanced engineer who did the "on site" studies. This friend was going to be our guide when we arrived at Acapulco. He quickly hired a taxi to take us around. We first watched the cliff divers dive. Then we went to an old castle that had a mote around it with a drawbridge that could be lowered to permit entrance to the castle.

We noticed some school children coming, so he stopped the cab and after they lowered the bridge, we went in behind the school children. We couldn't understand the Spanish as he was speaking to the students, so we explored the castle on our own. We must have spent more time looking through the rooms then we thought. The students were already gone and the drawbridge was up again.

We were trapped inside. We ran around looking for a way out but couldn't find a way to scale the wall because of the water all around the castle. We heard the ship's whistle, which was the signal that the ship was leaving in a half hour. Finally in a tunnel we spotted a man who was painting a scene of the castle, that understood our problem. He had a key, so he went to the tower and lowered the bridge for us. Our taxi had left us, so we ran for the boat. As we got there they were untying the ropes and lifting the gangplank. We were all winded, but very thankful we didn't miss that ship.

Later we went through the Panama Canal. It took us a whole day to traverse the entire canal. There is always a long line of ships and boats waiting to go through. We had to wait in the hot sun until our ship had its turn to go through the locks. What a neat experience!

In the Atlantic we went to ports in the Virgin Island chain that included St. Thomas, Willemstad, and Curacao. We also spent a day in Caracas, Venezuela. Our last stop was at Puerto Rico where we spent several days seeing the sights and enjoying the white sand beaches. Phyllis and I spent some valuable time together on that vacation, talking, planning and having fun together. It was truly a mountain peak on our roller-coaster ride. When we got home, we were pleased to be home again; the Lord had lifted our spirits and refreshed us.

An Unexpected Tragedy

While I was gone some of the eggs had not all been sold so I put on an egg sale in a large group of stores. We had just finished unloading a semi load of new foam egg cartons. These were placed in a storage area in the back of our processing room. We had just filled a storage semi with eggs that were already processed. It was parked in the building and the eggs were ready for me to load on our delivery truck to take to the stores. That morning the wind was blowing in such strong gusts, like only it can do in Iowa, and I knew that driving the truck would be difficult at best. I walked through the processing room to greet the workers and one of the help informed me that the lights were flickering a bit and the back cooler was feeling somewhat warm.

I called to my maintenance man to check why the lights were flickering. I was walking to the house to get my invoices from the office, and as I was going to step in the house I glanced over towards the processing unit and saw that the whole back end was in flames. I ran in the house and shouted to Phyllis, "Fire, Fire, call the fire Department!" I ran outside to get the workers out, shut down the machine and hollered, "Every body out, we are on fire!" The fire hit the semi load of oil base foam cartons and it was like it hit gas.

The hired man tried to get the diesel truck started but it wouldn't start in the building because it already did not have enough oxygen to start. I motioned him to get out of the cab before it exploded. I crawled under the truck and put a log chain on the axle. A neighbor happened to come by with a tractor and I said, "Quick pull our truck out of the fire." With a quick jerk on the chain, his tractor managed to pull the burning truck out of the building. The fire department had just arrived, quickly put out the fire on the truck but the wires were already burned off and the aluminum box was already soft from the heat. I ran in the building to pull out some eggs and retrieve my records.

I was delayed by a TV reporter who shoved a microphone in front of me and asked, "What did you all lose in this fire?"

"It isn't what I lost," was my answer, "it is what the Lord permitted me to save. All the employees got out safely so I saved everything important to me. They all got out of the burning building with out anyone getting hurt and I am thankful for that." That statement was never aired on TV even though they did a whole story about the fire.

Friends Came To Our Rescue

That night our maintenance man and another employee's husband worked all that day and night and rewired the burned out truck. We fought the fire all that day and that night we were totally exhausted, dirty and depressed. Phyllis came out to me by the rubble and said that a group of friends were getting together to have prayer for us being that we lost so much. In a short time we had lost the entire heart of our operation, all our egg cartons, our egg cases, and thousands of dozens of eggs. Every supply we needed to run our poultry farm, including our two tractors was destroyed. What remained was now only a clump of twisted steel with very little insurance to cover what it would take to replace supplies, equipment and the cost of rebuilding the buildings.

We discovered that the fire was caused by the wind jerking on the electric wires. Then an anchor bolt broke that held the electric entrance cable. When the entrance cable bent and broke, it cut the wire going into the building. The wire was forced against the bent pipe causing the pipe to become red hot like a welder. The pipe must have shot sparks over the foam egg cartons, which started the blaze immediately.

We went to our friend's home for the prayer meeting for us. When we left to join them, the fire was about out. While at our friend's house we sang praises to our God and others read encouraging passages of Scripture for our reassurance. We were totally fatigued but much encouraged by the support of our friends.

When we got home the fire had reached cases of egg oil in pressurized cans that were buried in the rubble. When the oilcans got hot they were exploding under the pressure. These cans were going up in the air like rockets, shooting burning oil into the air and the fire was spreading very fast. I remember I was holding a pitchfork and trying to move those cases of oil out of the fire, but it was impossible to move them.

The Lord Was There All The Time.

I remember praying, "Lord I am tired, and I have been fighting this fire all day. I have told you before that this farm is yours and that I am only managing it for you. I have done all that I can do; I'm tired and can't go on any more. I am going to bed. It is in your hands--I know you will take care of it."

I went to the house and Phyllis asked. "Aren't you going to call the fire department back to put out the fire of those exploding cans?"

"No," I said, "it is in good hands, I am going to bed."

I went to bed with complete trust that the Lord was in charge. I slept like a baby because everything we had left was surrendered to the Lord. It was up to him to care for it, I couldn't any more.

The next morning the fire was completely out, not even a hot spot anywhere. A friend and prayer partner brought a tractor over because my tractors had all burned as well as all my supplies. The tractor was given to us to use so we could start the massive clean up job.

How were we going to process our eggs that I had on sale in the stores and where would we get the supplies? The stores needed eggs today. Every time some one would ask for something, we would soon discover it had burned up in the fire. Everywhere I turned, employees had many questions that needed answers. The whole family came home so together we struggled with examining our decision, "Where do we go from here?" We knew that we couldn't continue without a massive input of capital and then our production units wouldn't justify the expenditure.

The family, after spending long hours in discussion, came to a conclusion that we had only one choice, and that was to expand our laying houses and increase our volume to the point that the rebuilding could be a reality. To continue, we needed to have nearly a million dollars of borrowed money. That was a scary thought, and not something that we accepted lightly. The family said, "Dad, you love your work, you are good at it, go for it."

The very next day the first thing we had to do was pour cement for a new processing plant. We installed new equipment on the cement floor and built the building around it while the workers processed eggs. Next we built a 15,000 pullet-growing unit and then a 30,000 laying hen house.

The Big Question

As you can see, throughout the years, we experienced highs and lows financially and spiritually. It seemed to me that right after a spiritual high it was immediately followed by a low with a time of persuasive testing. These trials and testing were either within our family, our business or our personal lives. I often questioned what was happening because the trials always seemed to come after experiencing an exceptional spiritual high. My question was this, "After a high encounter, were we then placed on the agenda by the devil for a trip into the wilderness, or was God in his love and mercy preparing us for the upcoming trial that was about to happen?" I will not attempt to explain how the devil operates and much less try to explain the actions of the Almighty God. I have come to weigh the two thoughts carefully and came to a conclusion by examining very important principles from Scripture.

"Blessed is the man who perseveres under trial, because when he has stood the test, he will receive the crown of life that God has promised to those who love him. When tempted, no one should say, "God is tempting me, for God cannot be tempted by evil, nor does he tempt anyone." James 1:12-13 KJV

The first conclusion is that the devil is evil, and has a strong desire to see us stumble and fall and miss the joy of our personal walk with God. He will do all in his power to mar that relationship.

The second conclusion is that God only wants what is best for his children. I lean on the knowledge that God gives us our spiritual highs that we might be able to reflect back upon them when we are going through problems. We notice in Scripture that the children of Israel always were told to reflect back how God led them through the Red Sea with his mighty arm and out stretched hand. When the children of Israel were in difficult times, the prophets would tell them to look back at what the Lord did for them at that point in their journey. I believe that God gave us those high spiritual adventures to reflect back and be encouraged to go foreword from there.

How Can We Pay Our Bills With Double Digit Inflation?

After the fire of 1978, we had to work night and day to bring and keep the operation out of red ink. In the early 1980s we experienced a high interest rate of 18% connected with everything we bought at inflated prices. It was impossible for us to make a profit above such a large debt load and the extreme interest rate. This was coupled with ads that appeared in the magazines, telling people to cut back on eating eggs because of high cholesterol.

Through a lot of effort and God's providence we were always able to face our commitments and meet the financial challenges. We at times denied ourselves buying anything but the very basic things the family needed to survive.

Keeping My Promise

Then five years after the last vacation, we took the three oldest children to Japan to see World Exposition 1970 and tour Japan. One of the reasons we went to Japan was that we had a Japanese trainee in our home in 1962. When he left, the children asked if we would ever go to Japan. I said to the children, "Sure we will, the day we get 50 cents a dozen for our eggs, we will all go to Japan," thinking that would be an impossible goal to reach. In 1970 the children reminded me of the promise I had made because the price had reached 50 cents per dozen eggs.

I decided it was important for me to keep my promise so we took the three oldest children with us to Japan. We left Sue, who was just a toddler, with Phyllis' sister. We also spent a few days in Hawaii. The World's Fair was also in Japan that year. The day we spent at the world's fair was interesting but very taxing. We had an opportunity to visit the Russian pavilion. This was at the height of the cold war and the Russians were trying to impress the world that Communism was superior to any system in the world.

We were just looking at a large display showing what the women were wearing in one of the other countries. The display showed fine mink coats, expensive diamonds and fancy fur lined boots. It showed how much more the children were advanced in their education and in their abilities than what the children were in the rest of the world. Finally Phyllis couldn't stand it any more and she said to me quietly, "What a bunch of bologna."

Just like that a person from that country came out of nowhere and confronted her with a clenched hand up in the air to give her an understanding that if you say one more word you'll get it. We took a roll of film in that pavilion and all the pictures turned a strange yellow color, with nothing visible in the picture. Then in the USA pavilion the children were pleased to be able to sit in the first space capsule and see the moon rock.

A Side Trip To Taiwan

On part of the trip we went to Hong Kong and then to Taiwan where we visited the Mackey Memorial Hospital where our church was supporting a missionary doctor. Later when we returned home we were asked to go out, tell the story and solicit funds for the hospital. We raised over $25,000 for the rebuilding of that hospital.

Phyllis and I had an opportunity to make return visits to Japan, one time to help our former Japanese trainee with a problem he was having trimming the beaks of small chickens. Fortunately I was easily able to solve that problem. His work crews were working off a very long electrical cord on a reel. It was so long that they lost most of their electrical power.

We were very impressed how fast the country developed in those few years between our first visit and this one.

After that trip Phyllis and I were ready to get back to our every day routines. But our lives were to be anything but routine.

One Saturday evening our family was finishing supper and a pickup came speeding onto our yard. The driver jumped out of the pickup, rushed to the house and hammered on our door. When I opened it he said, "Quick, go over to our farm, my wife is going to commit suicide." And he drove off. Phyllis and I got right up without finishing the meal and rushed to the farm. When we got there, the wife was crying and putting away the dishes. She had a suicide note written out with instructions lying on the table. We gave her a hug, and told her she was loved and asked her if she was willing to share what led her to feel that life was not worth living.

She shared how she had gone out with some friends to a tavern when she was supposed to be at a church meeting. After being encouraged to have a few drinks she went out to a park with a person at the bar and had an affair. Then her husband found out about it and she said, "Now my life isn't worth living." Phyllis and I spent a big part of the night with her. Then we began working with this couple to try to resolve this mess and work towards healing.

I had an appointment to visit with her to talk about how she could untangle the mess she was in. I was searching the Scripture for passages that pointed to God's forgiveness and that God would restore a person who repents. I felt tired so I went outside to get some air. I came back inside and told Phyllis that I was having trouble controlling my mind.

"You're too tired," Phyllis replied, and told me to take a nap. I lay down and fell into a deep sleep. During my sleep the Lord revealed that this woman's husband was unfaithful.
He was having an affair with her best friend, and her best friend helped set up this affair so that this person could divorce his wife and blame his wife for her adulteress affair. The reason they arranged to have his wife get involved with this affair was so he could get a "clean" divorce. I was told in my dream to warn the husband by reading to him Proverbs 7:7-23. When I woke up I told Phyllis all about the dream. Phyllis said, "Do you know what that passage says?" I told her I didn't know so she looked it up and read it to me.

> " I saw among the simple, I noticed among the young men, a youth who lacked judgment. He was going down the street near her corner, walking along in the direction of her house at twilight, as the day was fading, as the dark of night set in. Then out came a woman to meet him, dressed like a prostitute and with crafty intent. She is loud and defiant; her feet never stay at home; (now in the street, now in the squares, at every corner she lurks.)
>
> She took hold of him and kissed him and with a brazen face she said, "I have fellowship offerings at home; today I fulfilled my vows. So I came out to meet you; I looked for you and have

found you! I have covered my bed with colored linens from Egypt .I have perfumed my bed with myrrh, aloes and cinnamon. Come, let's drink deep of love till morning; let's enjoy ourselves with love! My husband is not at home; he has gone on a long journey .He took his purse filled with money and will not be home till full moon. "With persuasive words she led him astray; she seduced him with her smooth talk. All at once he followed her like an ox going to the slaughter, like a deer stepping into a noose till an arrow pierces his liver, like a bird darting into a snare, little knowing it will cost him his life" Proverbs 7:7-23 KJV

I was shocked at what Phyllis read to me. I was now sure I had received a message from the Lord in a dream; there was no doubt in my mind about it. Because I had no knowledge of the content of Proverbs seven, how could I have picked that Proverb? I again told Phyllis all of what was revealed to me while I was asleep. I canceled the wife's appointment and called the husband to come because I had an important message to give to him.

When he came, I confessed to him that I had something very scary to share with him. I told him about how I felt before and while I was asleep; that I thought the Lord had revealed to me the secrets of his heart and the Lord gave me a message to give to him. He listened when I shared with him what I discovered while I was sleeping. He started to squirm. Then I told him I was asked in the dream to give him a message from

Scripture. I took and opened my Bible and slowly read from the Scriptures, *Proverbs 7:7-23*

Every verse in the passage of Scripture was applicable to the situation of this man.

As I closed the Bible I looked at my friend and said, "I have one question for you and I want an honest answer. "If what God told me is truth then this isn't from me, but it is God's warning to you. Now, is what I shared with you truth or not?"

He put his head down and said, "This is for real." Then I said to him, "Then I have delivered the message that God gave to me. You go and straighten up your life."

Their marriage was not strong enough to survive all that deception, and trust could not be reconstructed.

I discovered that when we were praying each day, "Lord use me, I will try to be available," I had better be prepared for some very heavy assignments.

A New Open Door

The poultry business gave me additional opportunities to travel. One day I was working on some broken equipment on the farm.

Phyllis came to me and said, "I just received a call from a person who wanted to talk to you. He says he is with the State Department."

My answer was, "You bet." thinking there was some joke she was going to pull off on me again.

She said, "No, I am serious, this is the number that you have to call, and you must ask for this person."

297

Now I was the one who was worried--my mind went all over the place. I had sold some hatching eggs to Canada and overseas to Hungary; what could have gone wrong? It took me a couple days before I had enough courage to call that number.

When I finally called, they informed me that they were looking for a person in the poultry business, that was knowledgeable in all the fields of the industry, and would be willing to be a consultant. He said, "I was told by a professor from *Iowa State College* whom you worked with, that you were president of the *Iowa Egg and Poultry Association.*

This professor has recommended you, and has submitted your name as the qualified person to fill the assignment."

The State Department and the Feed Grain Counsel wanted to send me to North Africa, to the province of *Tunisia;* on the *Food For Peace* program to try help them untangle Tunisia's egg quality problems. They were sending a three-man team.

I was to work on the production problems and discover what was causing them to have such poor quality eggs in the market place.

After spending one day going through their poultry farms and the processing sheds, I discovered that they had an abundance of problems that needed attention. I then was to give presentations by slides and lectures, all around the country, conducting meetings where the egg producers would gather.

The US Embassy made a big deal out of all the meetings. They had two translators in booths with every person attending having been given headgear on which they could dial one of three languages. Each meeting was covered by TV, radio and news reporters and every day they were making a big publicity deal out of the United States being there to help their agriculture industry.

There were a lot of national political undertones in regard to my consulting work there.

My meetings went so well that large groups would stay after the seminars for question and answer time. This time would go through afternoons and into the evenings. I received one of the nicest complements from the State industry leader. He said, "Mr. Van, you are truly a walking poultry encyclopedia."

One of the interesting and solemn parts of that trip was a stop at a coliseum where, hundreds of years before, the Roman soldiers would come for rest and relaxation. There, sitting high above the arena the soldiers would come to watch the lions murder the political and spiritual prisoners. They showed me where the lions were kept and where the prisoners were held until the so-called games would begin. It gave me goose bumps all over my body because I could visualize how the Christians were cruelly held in those coliseums, and then made sport of as the lions were brought in.

There was another thing that I thought was remarkable on that trip. There were five of us riding in the car, one American consultant was from a Jewish background, two of us were Christians and two Tunisian men in front were from Arabian background. We were traveling from northern to southern Tunisia and I noticed that all through the countryside the farmers were leading sheep to the towns and villages. The sheep were soon sold, and then the buyers led them away one by one.

I asked what was going on with all the sheep going to the cities. The Arabian driver said, "Today is a feast day--we are all fasting, for tonight we will get together with our families and have a feast to celebrate what happened to our forefather years ago.

"Will you explain what your feast is about?" I asked.

" Yes, you see, our forefather was asked by God to sacrifice his son and just before he was going to kill his son, God stopped him. There, caught in the bushes, was a sheep that God told him to sacrifice instead of his son."

The Jew whispered to me in the back seat, "That wasn't THEIR father, it was OUR Father Abraham." I thought it was neat that all three who were in the same car claimed Abraham as their father. The Arabians were offspring of Ishmael; the Jews, descendants through Isaac, and the two of us Christians are spiritual children of Abraham. We should all have been fasting that day, and we also should have been invited to the feast that night. What a small world when we reduce it down to the fact that Abraham was the father of us all. The Jew was personally very offended to have an Arab call Abraham "his father."

My next assignment was to go to Taiwan and set up egg quality standards for the industry. I was appalled how up to date they were in production techniques, yet how far behind they were in the care of the eggs after they were produced.

They had purchased equipment from the US and Japan but it appeared like no one had instructed them in proper sanitation methods in order to maintain quality.

That trip put me in contact with the industry leaders and with the *National Health Department* and *Agriculture Department* as well as the US attaché who was acting ambassador.

The hours that I had to keep, along with jet lag, were so hard for me. I had to be up at 4 a.m. and they always insisted that I go out with them for our evening dinner.

They would question me until late hours, about how poultry farmers did things on our farms, and what methods we used to process eggs. Every night it was a different city with a different group and always-different type foods. Every morning I had to have a report ready of the previous days activities for the Feed Grain Council representative in Taiwan. He was not an easy person to work with, and writing those reports daily was no little task for a tired body because of the time constraints.

Many times I wondered how God could so wonderfully lead our lives--yet our lives seemed to always be so complicated. Was it because we were always trying to limit God to what our small human minds could comprehend? When will I understand that I cannot ever begin to comprehend God's plan and purpose for our future? Why don't I just sit back and enjoy the trip that God had already all planned out for my life?

Chapter 17

Those Golden Years

For years, we had gone on short camping vacations with three and sometimes four families. We never ventured very far, but we went to the mountains near Denver, and the Black Hills in South Dakota. We went several times to Minneapolis to the Morris T. Baker Park. We always had great food and great times on these little outings. With these same friends we also sat out the old year and brought in the new year. We often talked about the three couples going together to Europe for an extended vacation.

One year we received shocking news. One of the couples of our group went to California for a winter vacation and the husband came home with a severe back pain. The doctor diagnosed it as bone cancer. That changed everything. We decided that our group should go with our pastor's tour group to Israel and then before coming home we would tour part of Europe. While we were on that trip the Lord gave our friend reasonably good health and it turned out to be our last outing that we enjoyed together. We missed our friend deeply after the Lord called him to come to his eternal home. It was very difficult to understand. He was young in age and in spirit. We lost a great friend and his family lost a wonderful husband and father quite early in their lives.

We now were experiencing the empty nest syndrome in our home; it was so quiet in the evenings. Our youngest son enlisted in the Marines for training to be an MP (Military Police) We, in this stage of our lives, were beginning to be able to take the time for, and have the privilege of enjoying our grandchildren. As we reflect on our lives, we wish we could have taken the same amount of time to spend with our children.

Van's Poultry Farm, as we entered into the late 1980s, had expanded to two farms under our ownership. Besides that we managed one contract pullet growing house, plus five contract layer houses located within 30 miles of our egg processing plant. We had a total of 250,000 chickens under our management. The city council of Sioux Center (which is the town where our main plant was located) hired a new city manager that worked to bring a new shopping mall to our small city. We soon became aware that these plans would include an attempt to again annex a large area into the city in order to increase the tax base. This in turn, would also increase the city's borrowing capability, which was needed to complete the city mall concept. The plans included incorporating our main poultry operation and our west unit. This meant we would soon be back to square one, where we started from in 1959, under control of the city.

We discovered a law in the state of Iowa that stated that a farm protective zone could be established if there were enough acres of land that were connected together. All the owners, residents and non-residents of the land had to agree and sign intent into the protective zone. This zone then had to be approved by the County Board of Supervisors. So we launched a two-pronged attack, one was to establish the protective agriculture zone, the second to try and defeat the annexing vote to cancel out the plan. For several months we worked on establishing the agriculture zone and finally had all the required signatures.

The next step was to get the Board of Supervisors to approve it. When we took the documents from all the farmers of the required acres, which adjoined each other, to the Board of Supervisors it was the first time we could tell that the Board was receiving pressure to delay taking action. They did so by finding a small technicality and also called for a hearing.

At that hearing I made an appeal for the farmers. During the hearing I received shortness of breath and severe chest pain. A friend helped me out of the room by opening a door in the hallway to get me some air, which slowly gave me some relief.

The Board of Supervisors finally accepted the agriculture district but the city took it to the state attorney general to ask that he rule whether or not the agriculture district could be established after an annexation was developing. He ruled in the city's favor stating that the city's action to attempt to annex was prior to the approval of the agriculture district. Then the annexing went to a vote for approval or disapproval, where every eligible person in the city and those in the annexed area had a right to vote.

We lost by a very narrow margin. This meant we now were back under the city's jurisdiction, that we spent so much time and money moving away from in 1962. I was discouraged and depressed. Along with the defeat, my health was getting worse and I was continuing to have shortness of breath. What should we do next?   Here I am, 60 years old, too weary to take on any major move or new venture.

I went back to the hospital to get more physical examinations and underwent massive tests. The doctor spotted what they thought was a bulge on the side of my heart muscle. They told me it looked like an aneurysm developing and might not be operable. My doctor said if an aneurysm breaks, you only have a few minutes to live. I had already lost two brothers with massive heart attacks at relatively early ages.

My doctor said to me, "I would advise you to reduce all possible stress that you can from your life, and if I were you I would get my house in order."

We had learned that our daughter Donna was planning to get married, and that she would have her wedding in her home church in Arizona May 19, 1990. We had planned to take the car so our daughter Sue and her son Beau, who were both in the wedding party, could ride with us. None of us had seen the Grand Canyon, so a friend of mine suggested we take the route through scenic Red Mountain and through Durango, Colorado.

Since this was in the month of May, our friend said it would be such a fine scenic trip. The weather was great all day with only a few scattered clouds in the sky. At 4:30 that afternoon we stopped at a gas station to fuel up and I asked how long it would take to cross Red Mountain. The gas attendant said about 2 to 3 hours. An older person stuck his head from under a car and said, "Buddy I think you would be wise on figuring 4-5 hours to get across." We called ahead and took a motel on the other side of the mountain in the town of

Durango. When we got to the car I said, "Sue will you drive? Mother drove far enough, it's your turn to take the wheel." Sue started driving but when we got to the base of the mountain the sky became overcast. Soon after, as we started up the mountain it began to sprinkle big raindrops.

When we looked down the edges of the road we soon discovered that the edge of the road was unprotected by guardrails. It looked beautiful traveling up this two lane-winding road, but it was rather scary. Sue was driving and I could see fright in her eyes when she would look down, and her fingers on the wheel started turning white.

We pulled over to let Phyllis drive. I couldn't do any driving at all because of my condition. When we got back on the road it began snowing, not flakes, but they were more like little snowballs. It snowed so hard that soon everything was white and visibility through the windshield was near zero. There were no turnouts anywhere and warning signs were posted everywhere not to park because of dangerous avalanches.

Sue was scared (as were the rest of us) and held on to Beau, not wanting to look out of the window. Phyllis reduced her speed to a scant five miles per hour because the windshield wipers couldn't push the snow off if she drove faster. I had to stick my head out of the car window and look for the edge of the mountain. I would look out the window and tell Phyllis, "Turn right--now straight--turn left--right a little--left."

This is how we were inching up Red Mountain with the roads quickly getting a heavy snow cover. I was trying hard to guide the car that way but suddenly I didn't see the road anymore. I hollered, "Stop, stop." Phyllis stopped.

I stepped out to see, and discovered I was standing on the edge of the cliff, looking straight down. All of a sudden I couldn't see any edge of the road because the road had curved back and our car bumper was hanging over the edge of the cliff. The edge had a drop off of hundreds of feet. Straight down below we could see the tops of trees.

My heart was pounding and my knees started to shake. I sat on the car seat with my head in my hands.

Phyllis recognized it for what it was. God sent his angels and stopped the car on the edge of the cliff to spare our lives. Our prayers that we offered for the Lord's traveling mercies were answered in a spectacular way. It was a freak early spring-snow storm that didn't give anyone a warning.

We arrived at Purgatory One o'clock in the morning, a three-hour trip that took us nine hours. When we finally got checked in at the town of Durango, the owner marveled that we made it across in that snowstorm. He told us that every year families lose their lives crossing that mountain pass. That night when we got in bed we couldn't pile enough blankets on our beds to warm up. We were made warm by our thoughts of gratitude to a merciful God who gave us protection and that we were spared to be alive to celebrate our daughter's beautiful wedding.

Service To God and Fellow man
Is An Important Facet Of Life

All my life I was a member of the *Reformed Church In America*. I worked in many positions in the local church, and also was appointed several times to represent our local church at area classis. Then I was appointed to work with the Regional Synod of the West, and while serving there, I helped establish the Synod of the Heartland, and was appointed to represent them on the General Synod Executive Committee for five years.

While I was working in the Finance Committee of the Regional Synod, I became familiar with the "Charitable Remainder Uni-trust." This uni-trust is an instrument whereby you can give your assets to the church tax free, and live on the interest for the remainder of your life and the life of your spouse.

When we were together as a family in Arizona for the wedding, Phyllis and I called a meeting with the children. We introduced a plan where we would give our farm, which was our total assets, except our home, to the church in an irrevocable Charitable Remainder Uni-trust. The family decided if that was what Phyllis and I desired to do, all the children would give their 5 % stock into the trust as well. When they all decided to go along with our plan and gave their equity, it made me so proud of their generosity.

November 1990 the transaction was made with the family transferring ownership of the farm to the Trust. The Trust then sold the farm to some of the employees along with two other individuals familiar with the egg business. Phyllis and I immediately made plans to build a new house in town with a goal to move into it by April 1991.

I was asked to come to Sioux Falls Veterans Hospital somewhere around Thanksgiving of 1990 to receive the results of my latest tests. It appeared like I was developing an aneurysm. The doctor strongly suggested that I should go to

Minneapolis Veterans Hospital to have the doctors do tests on my heart and arteries. They decided to do it in Minneapolis Veterans Hospital because they had a surgical team that could be present in case of an immediate need for open-heart surgery.

When they started running preoperative testing, the surgical doctor came into the ward along with my attending physician and said, "We have scrapped your surgery because we found a mass on your lymph nodes and it looks like it is cancer. I will not do heart surgery on anyone with cancer. My hands are too important for me to operate on a person with cancer."

A few minutes later my attending physician came back into the room and said, "I am so sorry, first about your report, and also the way the surgeon told you. He is a great surgeon but he also has the world's worst bedside manners."

The same hour the nurse came in with a stack of get well cards from people from my home church and the first card had this promise from Scripture that really struck me as I read the verse over and over again.

"For I know the plans I have for you," declares the LORD, "plans to prosper you and not to harm you, plans to give you hope and a future."

Jeremiah 29:11-13

That was the message I received and I accepted it as coming from the Lord who touched that wonderful person to send the encouraging card.

God still had a plan for my life. His plan was that I would call upon the Lord and he would hear, no matter how bad the situation looked. The next three weeks involved test after test to determine what type of mass they had discovered.

The latest MRI showed that it wasn't what they had previously thought--a developing aneurysm, but it appeared to be a mass that had taken over a part of the lungs. After several biopsies and three weeks in the hospital they found that the mass was *Sarcoidosis*. The mass was on the lymph nodes of the lungs and was against the heart, that is why it looked like an aneurysm. *Sarcoidosis* is a chronic disease.

I was told that the mass might be arrested with large doses of a drug called Prednizone, but the scar tissue would remain on my lungs. During my hospital stay, which lasted three weeks, our country was involved in the Gulf War. The scenes were on TV in my ward on CNN. Hour after hour we would see the tanks staging for battle. I couldn't get away from the sight of those tanks.

I got flash backs from the Korean War when I had to walk along side of a tank. I could hear and see the tank tracks as they went, crushing the bodies of wounded and dead soldiers who were lying on the road up to Old Baldy. This was the only passable route for the tanks to take to Old Baldy.

For seven hours I wept and wept trying to get away from that awful scene and dreadful sound. An older nurse shook me and asked if I was ever in battle since I was sobbing and unable to control it. She said, "You have bottled your feelings up for all these years, now you couldn't bury them any longer by your long hard work."

I was forced to watch those tanks repeatedly on TV in the ward. Finally there was more pain than I could hide or bury, "Go ahead have a good cry, " the nurse said, "you still have a lot of pain bottled up. Don't be afraid to talk about it and cry if you want. I'll get a private room even if I have to trade beds around--you need to be by yourself."

The next day along with more testing and treatments, I was put under psychological testing and the doctor determined that I was suffering from severe PTS (Post Traumatic Stress).

Then I knew why I was having so much trouble with hives all those the years after my military discharge. It was why I had to take all kinds of downers, to keep from going crazy because of the rash. When they released me from the hospital I was placed in the care of a resident doctor in Sioux Falls, SD. VA Hospital. I was also placed in a group for therapy with other veterans who were suffering with the same problem.

It was then that I discovered that almost all the veterans who suffered PTS went through their life trying to find ways of escaping their past military experience.

I, like many others became a workaholic and buried myself in work. Others sought their escape through drinking beer, whiskey and wine or anything that would dull the deep pain from which they were trying to escape. Others are constantly in trouble because of fighting with everybody, trying to be and remain macho. Others went from job to job, partner to partner, never being able to find inner peace.

These are some of the many ways that individuals will use to try to cope with their PTS. Most of the ways veterans use to bury the after effects in themselves all seem to become self-destructive.

When the veterans choose to use alcohol to hide their pain, it becomes a continual cycle of highs and lows, then when they come off a drink they try to bury each low with more and more binge drinking.

There are some who are contrary to everything, they fight and argue about anything. They eventually find themselves friendless, lonely and hopelessly depressed before they finally seek help. For me, my drive was for more and more work. The more elevated and extended the use of my adrenaline, the better I felt. But finally my body couldn't keep up that pace because I had sacrificed my health.

I was very fortunate that I went into the military service knowing Christ as my Savior and Lord. This helped me, because I could experience God in such a personal way during the times that I was totally unable to carry on. I could count on my God being with me and I always knew that loved ones were there upholding me in prayer.

I have not escaped the nightmares. Many of my nights are still filled with terror. I still go through the terrible experience of the feeling of fighting rats running all over my body while lying in my Korean bunker--seeing them poke their heads in the sand bags and the ceilings hunting for food. I find myself hitting at them. My wife knows when it starts, because I swing my hands and scream, and then she wakes me up to bring me back to realty.

I find it so hard to rest when I sleep. I relive the emotion and tension of an enemy sneaking up to our trenches at night. I find myself giving a mighty yell and kick with my feet to clear off all my blankets so I can fight the enemy. The sounds of war endure in my ears and the sight of a comrade mortally wounded reaching out for help when none is available. It is difficult when at night the war becomes a reality again. I still haven't shed the feeling of helplessness and the feeling of guilt that I should have done more to protect my buddies. I know that I have to put aside some of the deep emotional feelings and believe my God who carried me this far will carry me the rest of the journey.

Writing these thoughts give me pain. But it is refreshing to be able to lift them out of the deep inner parts. I want to try to release them from the inner self where they have been bottled up far too long. For I know that they have been choking me off from the joy that I should be experiencing in my daily walk with the Lord and my family and friends.

We thought that after we had retired life would be much easier. Phyllis and I would be traveling to our families who live on both the east and west coast and in between. As we neared retirement we helped establish, along with some friends, a poultry complex in a very primitive part of the Dominican Republic for the Haitian refugees who were slaves to the cane industry. It was called, Huevos Para Todos, (Eggs For Everyone). We made five trips to the Dominican, each trip lasting 2-3 weeks. We lived with them in their villages and along with teaching and training, built a poultry complex for nine village churches. Our daughter and I wrote a poultry manual with the help of a translator, so the Haitians could follow it in their poultry management.

The Day The Curtain Came Down

In June of 1993 Phyllis and I drove to Vancouver, Canada to attend my last executive committee meeting at the Reformed Church General Synod

While we were there, it seemed that everything what we achieved and were striving for fell completely in shambles. My first message that day was that the Dominican government was shutting down the Haitian refugee poultry project because they wanted us to build a sewage storage pit for the chicken house. This would defeat part of the purpose for the use of the manure for fertilization of their fields and gardens to enable the Haitians to grow fruits and vegetables for their families. The second reason for building the farm was that the eggs were being used to feed expectant mothers and small children in nine small village churches.

The next call that morning was from the former employees who bought our poultry operation. They told me that they were totally insolvent. No firm was willing to feed their million plus laying hens because of their cash flow problems. This new firm had bought another farm, which more than tripled their operation in a few years time without the proper capital to do it.

When we called our banker, he told us that it appeared to him that our Trust was improperly secured and it looked like the church's funds were gone. This meant that Phyllis and I no longer had trust interest income and our only source of income was our government Social Security check.

Those two messages were too much for one morning, so I asked to be excused from the next General Synod meeting and

314

Phyllis and I went for a walk along the ocean. We sat on some driftwood just staring into the distance at the waves were crashing against the shore. That was what our lives seemed like--everything was crashing down. Where do we start? What good could come from this mess? What is God trying to tell us?

Phyllis and I just sat there all morning looking way out at the water, drinking in what God had done through his wonderful gift to us humans, and the gift and beauty of His creation. While walking back to the meeting, a Spanish friend from New York met us in the middle of a busy street intersection. When we met, I said, "Good morning," He replied, "Rich, what's wrong" and he and his friends took Phyllis and me back to the sidewalk. There on the busy street corner we talked, and we formed a circle of prayer.

My Spanish friend from Synod was a Latin American chaplain in a New York prison. He said, "These are our people, the Haitians are hurting." We will take care of that problem for you because they are our Christian brothers. You have enough things to take care of. We shared with them the details and they said, "We will take care of the problem at the Dominican Poultry Farm."

There in Vancouver, Canada, on that busy street corner, we unloaded our burdens and our Spanish brothers in Christ started carrying half of our load. They also in turn lifted our spirits and helped us focus away from our problem so we could concentrate on Christ, the work of the church and on our meetings.

What followed those phone calls that one day in Vancouver, were years of legal maneuvering. To make matters worse, the trust officer, who was an attorney, failed to fill out the papers for the Trust so everything was invalid. We started to get some action when we finally got an attorney from Des Moines, Iowa to represent the Trust and us. After many phone calls, letters and trips to Des Moines and more and more depositions, we hired a retired judge to arbitrate the case. After a long hard day of negotiating we accepted a settlement, but we had to pay a very substantial sum to our attorney. The family lost three years of interest and retained for the church only a bit more than one third of the trust funds.

We found, through that experience, God's provision in so many ways. He provided for all our daily physical needs. We also discovered that He gave us wisdom far beyond our capabilities. We found that what was stated in *Proverbs* was true. We were always amazed at how the Lord guided our thoughts. The Lord truly did turn our ear to wisdom and applied our heart to understanding,

> *"If you call out for insight and cry aloud for understanding, and if you look for it as for silver and search for it as for hidden treasure, then you will understand the fear of the LORD and find the knowledge of God. For the LORD gives wisdom, and from his mouth come knowledge and understanding. He holds victory in store for the upright, he is a shield to those whose walk is blameless, for he guards the course of the just and protects the way of his faithful ones. Then you will understand what is right and just and fair- for every good path. For wisdom will enter your heart, and*

316

knowledge will be pleasant to your soul. Discretion will protect you, and understanding will guard you. Wisdom will save you from the ways of wicked men, from men whose words are perverse."

Proverbs 2:3-11 KJV

At this time Phyllis applied for and received the job as Volunteer Coordinator for First Reformed Church and was responsible for developing the program of volunteers. I now had discontinued my overseas work projects because of health reasons. Most of the areas we worked in were very primitive and had very little, if any, medical help if it was needed. I continued to concentrate on my work of helping others. There are volunteer programs, which are designed to help those who find themselves in need.

I also found that my ability to help those who had financial problems could be helped by reason of my experience in that area. We gained knowledge from our personal experience. I too could help them with new understanding of their usual questions such as, "How are we going to pay our bills?"

Through these programs of helping others we developed lasting friendships that I will hold and cherish for the rest of my life.

I have discovered the reality of the truths of the Scripture and from my experiences in life. When you reach out to others you are not only giving, but also you will also be receiving.

"Cast your bread upon the waters, for after many days you will find it again".

Ecclesiastes 11:1 (KJV)

This is one of the Bible principles, which I have witnessed repeatedly in my life, things that we have done in a small way for others always came back in an abundant harvest in the most unexpected ways.

This year the Lord willing I will be celebrating my 71st birthday, and we have enjoyed spending part of our winters in northern California. This also is the year in which we have started a new millennium and wonder what changes will arise in this millennium. Will it be the golden age for our country or will our nation continue to experience more spiritual decay? When I see how Christian principles have eroded in my lifetime, I compare them to the Scriptural principles being watered down.

The Lord will judge those who have no regard for life of both the unborn and the aged. The Lord will also deal with those who translate the Scripture for their own personal selfish interest. This is the way they can feel religious but stray further and further from his commandments.

I do have concerns for those who will have the responsibility of leading their families and this nation in the new millennium. I am pleased to see large groups of parents and young people rise to the challenge. Many of our young people are sick and tired of this permissive society and want to raise their families with a solid set of principles based on God's commandments. God will always care for His children as he has promised.

Retirement and New Areas of Service

The last few years we have been spending our winters in California. Here we are enjoying the ocean and scenery at Pebble Beach.

319

Chapter 18

Synopsis

This book had its beginning because of the encouragement and support I received from family and Christian friends. As was stated in the foreword, when I reflected on my life's experiences it is very evident that all the praise must be given to God for the way God guided me through the events of my life.

It also became apparent when I started examining my life. I realized that the emotional experiences I had while serving in Korea left results that stressed me for at least 50 years. One of the propelling forces that kept driving me foreword was to never take time for an idle moment and only slept when my body dropped from fatigue. I didn't want any time to ponder on the past because I wanted my mind to eradicate or hide from the past.

During those 50 years, I did not feel free to express my inner feelings about my experiences, so as a result I suffered with unimaginable skin disorders, which gave a lot of discomfort. Along with skin disorders I also walked the floor night after night with facial pain and immobilized face muscles.

The only way that these conditions would subside was when I took sedatives. When one sedative became ineffective, then hopefully there would be a new one that would be helpful. Throughout the first 50 years of my post military life, I used most of the sedatives that were available by prescription.

The first break came when I broke emotionally during the Gulf war during my stay in the Minneapolis VA Hospital. It was then that the condition was recognized for what it was, Post Traumatic Stress Syndrome. When I started to receive professional counseling, it was then my skin disorder disappeared along with the horrible weeping sores.

The facial problems did not disappear because I suffered facial nerve damage when a shell blew up in his bunker in Korea. The nightmares continue because it appears that the subconscious mind will not let me forget the past.

For any person who has been in trauma, my recommendation is to allow yourself to feel your pain, don't bury it, because in any form it will be harmful. Always be in touch with your humanity; it is normal to have deep feelings after suffering trauma.

When I returned I acknowledged the fact that in my basic training and my Korean tour of duty, the tendency was to take risks and chances that the average person would consider to be foolish. The daring and fearless actions required by a combat soldier, were then carried over into my civilian life. I admit to taking absolute foolish chances to try and please the customer. No matter what the risk, floods, snowstorms, or personal exhaustion and discomfort, I kept driving myself until I obtained my objective.

This was what I was trained to do as a combat soldier and felt that was required of me as a person who was directing a business. I was born into a basic humble country home, a child who was raised during and after the depression, educated in a one-room country schoolhouse with one teacher who had to teach 26 pupils in all eight grades, and teach every subject.

Very early in life I experienced two major life-threatening illnesses, scarlet fever and a ruptured appendix. While in the hospital with the latter, I came to know *Christ* as Healer. The knowledge of a loving personal Lord came about through the book, "In His Steps," by Charles Sheldon.

The next major encounter with *Christ* was an Easter sunrise service, which led me to see Christ as Savior and a friend who walks and talks with you along the way. This discovery led me to make a public stand in the church. It does not take a rocket scientist to figure out that I experienced God's providential protection throughout my entire life, but it became especially very evident during my military career. There I experienced first hand the literal translation unfolding in front of my eyes.

> *"He who dwells in the shelter of the Most High will rest in the shadow of the Almighty.*
>
> *I will say of the LORD, "He is my refuge and my fortress, my God, in whom I trust."*
>
> *Surely he will save you from the fowler's snare and from the deadly pestilence.*
>
> *He will cover you with his feathers, and under his wings you will find refuge; his faithfulness will be your shield and rampart. You will not fear the terror of night, nor the arrow that flies by day, nor the pestilence that stalks in the darkness, nor the plague that destroys at midday.*

A thousand may fall at your side, ten thousand at your right hand, but it will not come near you.

You will only observe with your eyes and see the punishment of the wicked.

If you make the Most High your dwelling—even the LORD, who is my refuge—

Then no harm will befall you, no disaster will come near your tent.

For he will command his angels concerning you to guard you in all your ways;

They will lift you up in their hands, so that you will not strike your foot against a stone.

You will tread upon the lion and the cobra; you will trample the great lion and the serpent.

***"Because he loves me,"** says the LORD, "I will rescue him; I will protect him, for he acknowledges my name. He will call upon me, and I will answer him; I will be with him in trouble, I will deliver him and honor him. With long life will I satisfy him and show him my salvation." Psalm 91 (KJV)*

The Lord is more than a protector. The Lord also asks his children to carry out his work on earth. Even though I was unwilling and hesitant, I finally realized God would not let me refuse. The Lord wanted me do what I thought was unthinkable and impossible, but I believe because of the Lord's deep love for the church he expects us to do his work no matter how unpopular or difficult it is.

The way that the I knew it was from the Lord was because it was made clear through Scripture in such a way that it would be impossible for me not to see God's hand in all of the circumstances of my life.

I believe that God wants his children to occasionally look back just like the children of Israel were instructed to look back at their past. We also should have these markers in our lives where God met our needs, to remember how the Lord led us through those situations here, and what the Lord did for us at that place in our lives.

We are to reflect on those times, then gain strength from those identification points by remembering how God dealt with us at that time. The knowledge of God's dealing with us in former times will help our faith become stronger. When our faith is strengthened, we will have no doubt, that no matter what happens in our life, God will be waiting for us and will lead us in the future.

There is another area that I wish to share from my observations of life. It has also been my perception that there is a relationship that exists between the percentage of my life that I am willing to surrender to Christ, to the amount of peace and joy I will have in my Christian walk. This may sound like a contradiction but it is not.

I believe when I first committed my life to Christ, I took small steps of surrendering portions of my life to Christ. It became very apparent when I said in regard to different areas of my life, "Lord, you may have control of that area,"(although it wasn't in such a direct way) that the Lord gave me peace and joy.

When I said, 'Lord, I will read Scripture and lead Bible study in front of my youth group, it was then that I experienced the Holy Spirit helping me prepare and deliver the message. This helped me continue into greater submission that produced more peace and inner joy.

It is now my belief, if I want to experience all the joy and peace that Christ has to offer, I must be willing to surrender all. I will not forget the night that I was concerned about the safety of some of our church's young people when we saw them disappear into a motel room with some sailors. All that night I prayed to the Lord for their safety. The next morning because of my tired weary body I came late for the morning prayer breakfast and sat at the table alone with Phyllis. When we were seated, the doors came open and through the doors came the same girls with the sailors behind them.

When we had our circle of prayer the first prayer was from one sailor as he prayed, "Lord thank you for these girls who took us into the room with this group of Christian kids so that we could sing and read the Bible, and more importantly that I found you last night." The second sailor repeated this prayer. When it was my turn to pray, through tear filled eyes, all I could say was, "Thank you for answering my prayers last night."

Notice, all I prayed for was the protection of the girls. God had a bigger plan; he was interested in the souls of two sailor boys. All the way home from that conference did I remember what the speakers said? No, but I sure remembered what the Lord did in that motel room that night. The Lord taught me that he had far greater plans than I had prayed for. The Lord taught me to never underestimate what God can and will do. That night I set a marker to remember that when God answers prayer his answers are far better and greater than we even dare expect.

I will also not forget the night that 16 Bethel Bible students with our pastor were in a basement room, studying about God telling Abraham that he was, "Blessed to be a Blessing."

The pastor was emphasizing that point to us when the door opened and a shaggy stranger walked in and asked, "Can I sleep in the church tonight?" "Well, no. We don't allow anybody to sleep in the church," no doubt thinking about the rash of stealing happening in the churches. The man turned around and walked out.

Then suddenly some of use realized what we just did. A person in need of help, the Lord blessed us, we were studying about being a blessing, and we failed to follow the teaching. Two of us ran after the man. One of us searched the church, and I went out on the street and could not find the man. I drove around the small town and the stranger was nowhere to be found.

What happened that night was that we were being tested and we miserably failed the test. Who was the stranger? Where did he go? Was it an angel sent to test us? I can't answer any of those questions.

One thing I CAN tell you. That night I learned that what God told Abraham; he also meant for you and me.

> *"I will make you into a great nation and I will bless you; I will make your name great, and you will be a blessing.* Genesis 12:2 (KJV)

This concept was taught to us in the Bethel Bible Series, "Blessed To Be A Blessing." From that time on, I realized that I should never bypass an opportunity to be a blessing to others.

It is my prayer that after reading this book, the reader will have no doubt that God still leads and guides his children with His heavenly providential care. That without a shadow of doubt, the reader can acknowledge, with me that we serve a living God who is concerned with the smallest details of our lives. We see that Job, in his suffering, acknowledged God's care over him.

> "You gave me life and showed me kindness, and in
> your providence watched over my spirit."
>
> Job 10:12 (KJV)

We also know from Scripture that our God is an unchangeable God.

> "Don't be deceived, my dear brothers. Every good
> and perfect gift is from above, coming down from the
> Father of the heavenly lights, who does not change
> like shifting shadows."
>
> James 1:16-17 (KJV)

We also read that God would enter into the literal battle for his children.

> On that day I will strike every horse with panic and
> its rider with madness," declares the LORD. "I will
> keep a watchful eye over the house of Judah, but I
> will blind all the horses of the nations.

Then the leaders of Judah will say in their hearts,
'the people of Jerusalem are strong, because the
LORD Almighty is their God." Zechariah 12:4-5 (KJV)

I firmly believe that the triune God had a hand in my choice of a life long partner. I purposely have not enclosed in this book any of the highs, lows, challenges, joys, and all the experiences we encountered in the raising of a family of 5 children. These are individual stories left for them to tell as they write their stories about their lives.

To all those who read this book and especially to my children and grandchildren, and if the Lord wills, my great grandchildren, it is my prayer that you may *Experience God* in every aspect of your lives and that you may live in obedience to His will. There are two reasons for a Christian not growing; it is either being disobedient, or spiritually dead. Serve the Lord as you determine where He is leading you. Then I know your lives will be filled with that inner peace and joy that only Christ can and will give you.

Mature Christians are not spectators; they are servants.

The Author

Richard Van Regenmorter

Additional copies of this book can be
purchased from:

P&R PUBLISHERS

1440 1st Ave SE

Sioux Center, Iowa 51250

Email: April through October

vanrrich@mtcnet.net

Email: November through March

vanrrich@aol.com